100
HIKES in™

NEW
MEXICO

100
HIKES in™

NEW
MEXICO

Third Edition

CRAIG MARTIN

THE MOUNTAINEERS BOOKS

THE MOUNTAINEERS BOOKS
is the nonprofit publishing arm of The Mountaineers Club,
an organization founded in 1906 and dedicated to the exploration,
preservation, and enjoyment of outdoor and wilderness areas.

1001 SW Klickitat Way, Suite 201, Seattle, WA 98134

© 2010 by Craig Martin

First edition, 1995. Second edition, 2001. Third edition, 2010.

Manufactured in the United States of America

Copy Editor: Joan Gregory
Cover and Book Design: The Mountaineers Books
Layout: Peggy Egerdahl
Cartographer: Craig Martin and Pease Press Cartography
Photographer: All photographs by the author unless otherwise noted

Cover photograph: *Pueblo Bonito from the Pueblo Alto Loop*
Frontispiece: *Box Canyon from the top of the trail at El Morro*

Library of Congress Cataloging-in-Publication Data
Martin, Craig, 1952–
 100 hikes in New Mexico / Craig Martin.
  p. cm.
 Includes index.
 ISBN 978-1-59485-078-3 (ppb)
 1. Hiking—New Mexico—Guidebooks. 2. New Mexico—Guidebooks. I. Title. II.
Title: One hundred hikes in New Mexico.
 GV199.42.N6M37 2010
 796.5109789—dc22

                    2009045530

ISBN (paperback): 978-1-59485-078-3
ISBN (ebook): 978-1-59485-407-1

CONTENTS

Trails at a Glance • 10
Introduction • 15

SOUTHERN SANGRE DE CRISTO MOUNTAINS
1. Atalaya Mountain • 36
2. Big Tesuque/Bear Wallow Loop • 39
3. Nambe Lake • 42
4. La Vega Loop • 44
5. Spirit Lake • 47
6. Deception Peak • 49
7. Glorieta Baldy • 52
8. Cave Creek and Horsethief Meadow • 54
9. Stewart Lake • 57
10. Beattys and Mora Flats • 59
11. Pecos Baldy Lake • 61

NORTHERN SANGRE DE CRISTO MOUNTAINS
12. Trampas Lakes • 64
13. South Boundary Trail • 66
14. Cebolla Mesa/Big Arsenic Trails • 68
15. Lobo Peak • 70
16. Williams Lake • 73
17. Gold Hill • 75
18. Wheeler Peak • 78
19. Columbine Canyon to Hondo Canyon • 80
20. Heart Lake and Latir Mesa • 83
21. Sawmill Park • 86
22. Horseshoe Lake • 88
23. Comanche Creek • 90
24. McCrystal Place • 93
25. North Ponil Creek • 95
26. Little Horse Mesa Loop • 97
27. Capulin Volcano Rim Trail • 100

JEMEZ MOUNTAINS AND BANDELIER NATIONAL MONUMENT
28. Ojitos Wilderness • 104
29. Tent Rocks Canyon Trails • 106
30. Cerro Picacho • 108
31. Red Dot and Blue Dot Trails • 110
32. Falls Trail • 113
33. Frijoles Canyon • 115

34. Yapashi Pueblo • 118
35. Cerro Grande • 121
36. Guaje Ridge • 123
37. Caballo Mountain • 126
38. Cerros del Abrigo Trail • 128
39. Valle Grande Trail • 131
40. East Fork of the Jemez River • 133
41. Jemez Falls and McCauley Hot Springs • 135
42. San Pedro Peaks • 137
43. Window Rock • 139
44. Rim Vista Trail • 141
45. Ojitos Canyon Trail • 143

NORTHWEST PLATEAU AND ZUNI MOUNTAINS

46. Chavez Canyon • 146
47. Kitchen Mesa • 148
48. Box Canyon and Mesa Montosa • 150
49. Cruces Basin • 153
50. Continental Divide Trail, San Luis Mesa • 156
51. Bisti Section, Bisti–De-Na-Zin Wilderness • 159
52. De-Na-Zin Section, Bisti–De-Na-Zin Wilderness • 161
53. Pueblo Alto Loop • 163
54. South Mesa Loop • 166
55. Peñasco Blanco • 168
56. Gooseberry Springs Trail • 170
57. Big Tubes • 172
58. Zuni-Acoma Trail • 175
59. Chain of Craters Wilderness • 177
60. Narrows Rim Trail • 179
61. El Morro Rim Trail • 181

CENTRAL MOUNTAINS

62. Cerrillos Hills Historic Park • 184
63. Petroglyph National Monument Trails • 186
64. La Luz/Tramway Loop • 188
65. North and South Sandia Crest/10K Trail • 191
66. Pino Canyon • 193
67. Rio Grande Bosque • 195
68. Manzano Peak • 197
69. Manzano Crest Trail • 200
70. Fourth of July/Albuquerque Loop • 202
71. Copper Canyon/South Baldy Loop • 204
72. Potato Canyon • 207
73. San Lorenzo Canyon • 208
74. Chupadera Peak • 210

75. Vicks Peak • 212
76. El Camino Real • 215
77. Broad and Valles Canyons • 217
78. Indian Hollow • 219
79. Baylor Pass • 221
80. Dripping Springs Natural Area • 223

SOUTHEASTERN MOUNTAINS

81. Alkali Flat Trail • 228
82. Dog Canyon • 230
83. Three Rivers Petroglyph Site • 232
84. Big Bonito Loop • 234
85. Argentina Peak • 236
86. Last Chance Canyon • 239
87. Sitting Bull Falls • 241
88. Devils Den Canyon • 244
89. Yucca Canyon • 247
90. Rattlesnake Canyon • 250

GILA RIVER REGION

91. Datil Well • 254
92. Pueblo Creek • 256
93. Whitewater Baldy • 258
94. The Catwalk and Beyond • 260
95. Frisco Box • 263
96. Turkey Creek Hot Springs • 265
97. Middle Fork/Little Bear Loop • 268
98. West Fork of the Gila River • 271
99. Hillsboro Peak • 273
100. Percha Box • 276

Sources of Additional Information • 279
Index • 283

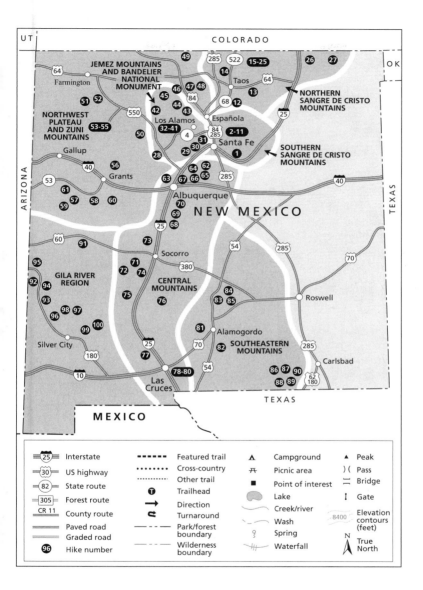

Opposite: Middle Fork of the Gila River

TRAILS AT A GLANCE

NUMBER/NAME	DISTANCE (ROUND-TRIP)	DIFFICULTY	BEST TIME	HIGHLIGHTS
1 Atalaya Mountain	7	difficult	Apr–Nov	views, wildflowers
2 Big Tesuque/Bear Wallow Loop	8	moderate	Apr–Nov	views, water, wildflowers
3 Nambe Lake	6	strenuous	June–Oct	quiet lake, wildflowers, aspens
4 La Vega Loop	7	strenuous	May–Oct	views, water, wildflowers
5 Spirit Lake	10.8	strenuous	June–Oct	quiet lake, aspens
6 Deception Peak	6	strenuous	June–Oct	views
7 Glorieta Baldy	12	strenuous	May–Oct	views, solitude
8 Cave Creek and Horsethief Meadow	5 or 10	difficult	June–Oct	unusual stream, wildflowers
9 Stewart Lake	13	strenuous	June–Oct	high lake, fishing
10 Beattys and Mora Flats	12.5	strenuous	May–Oct	wildflowers, water, history
11 Pecos Baldy Lake	12.5	strenuous	June–Oct	views, lake, wildflowers
12 Trampas Lakes	10	difficult	June–Oct	high lakes, water
13 South Boundary Trail	11	moderate	May–Oct	views, history, solitude
14 Cebolla Mesa/Big Arsenic Trails	7.4	moderate	Mar–Nov	views, river, fishing
15 Lobo Peak	11	strenuous	June–Oct	views, solitude
16 Williams Lake	4	moderate	June–Oct	high lake, views of high peaks
17 Gold Hill	10	strenuous	June–Oct	views, wildlife
18 Wheeler Peak	14	strenuous	June–Oct	views, state high point
19 Columbine Canyon to Hondo Canyon	8 or 12	easy/strenuous	June–Oct	views, water, wildflowers
20 Heart Lake and Latir Mesa	12.4	strenuous	June–Sept	views, lake, water
21 Sawmill Park	11	moderate	May–Oct	wildflowers, water, history
22 Horseshoe Lake	13.5	strenuous	June–Oct	views, lakes, wildlife
23 Comanche Creek	7	easy	May–Oct	views, history, solitude
24 McCrystal Place	6	easy	May–Oct	views, history, solitude
25 North Ponil Creek	7	easy	May–Oct	history, water, wildflowers
26 Little Horse Mesa Loop	6	moderate	May–Oct	water, history
27 Capulin Volcano Rim Trail	1	easy	Year-round	volcanic features, views

NUMBER/NAME	DISTANCE (ROUND-TRIP)	DIFFICULTY	BEST TIME	HIGHLIGHTS
28 Ojitos Wilderness	4.5	easy	Year–round	unusual geology
29 Tent Rocks Canyon Trails	3	easy	Mar–Nov	slot canyon, views
30 Cerro Picacho	8	difficult	May–Nov	views, water
31 Red Dot and Blue Dot Trails	7.5	moderate	Year-round	views, river, history
32 Falls Trail	4.8	moderate	Mar–Dec	waterfalls, river
33 Frijoles Canyon	7.5 (w/shuttle)	easy	Mar–Nov	views, water, history
34 Yapashi Pueblo	12 (w/shuttle)	difficult	Apr–Oct	views, history
35 Cerro Grande	4	moderate	May–Nov	views, wildlife
36 Guaje Ridge	9.5	difficult	May–Nov	wildfire recovery, views
37 Caballo Mountain	14	strenuous	May–Nov	views, solitude, wildlife
38 Cerros del Abrigo Trail	6.5 (w/shuttle)	moderate	May–Sept	views, solitude
39 Valle Grande Trail	2	easy	May–Sept	views, wildlife
40 East Fork of the Jemez River	4.6 (w/shuttle)	moderate	Apr–Nov	wildflowers, water, wildlife
41 Jemez Falls and McCauley Hot Springs	5.6 (w/shuttle)	moderate	Apr–Nov	waterfall, water, hot springs
42 San Pedro Peaks	16.5	difficult	June–Sept	views, wildlife, water
43 Window Rock	9	moderate	Year-round	natural arch, views
44 Rim Vista Trail	4.6	moderate	Mar–Dec	views
45 Ojitos Canyon Trail	12	difficult	Mar–Nov	views, solitude
46 Chavez Canyon	3	easy	Mar–Nov	slot canyon, views
47 Kitchen Mesa	4.6	easy	Apr–Nov	views
48 Box Canyon and Mesa Montosa	10	moderate	Mar–Nov	views, fossils, frozen seep
49 Cruces Basin	8	moderate	May–Nov	mountain meadows, solitude
50 Continental Divide Trail, San Luis Mesa	10	easy	Mar–May, Sept–Nov	geology, solitude
51 Bisti Section, Bisti–De-Na-Zin Wilderness	3 to 10	easy	Mar–Nov	badland views

NUMBER/NAME	DISTANCE (ROUND-TRIP)	DIFFICULTY	BEST TIME	HIGHLIGHTS
52 De-Na-Zin Section, Bisti–De-Na-Zin Wilderness	4 to 5	easy	Mar–Nov	badland views, solitude
53 Pueblo Alto Loop	5.3	moderate	Year-round	views, history
54 South Mesa Loop	4.5	moderate	Year-round	views, history
55 Peñasco Blanco	8	easy	Year-round	views, history
56 Gooseberry Springs Trail	6	difficult	May–Nov	views, wildflowers
57 Big Tubes	2	easy	May–July, Sept–Nov	volcanic features, lava tubes
58 Zuni-Acoma Trail	7.8 (w/shuttle)	difficult	Mar–Nov	volcanic features, history
59 Chain of Craters Wilderness	8 or 20 (w/shuttle)	easy or moderate	Mar–May Sept–Nov	volcanic features, solitude
60 Narrows Rim Trail	7.5	moderate	Mar–Nov	views, natural arch
61 El Morro Rim Trail	2	easy	Year-round	history
62 Cerrillos Hills Historic Park	5	easy	Year-round	views, history
63 Petroglyph National Monument Trails	7	easy	May–Nov	history
64 La Luz/Tramway Loop	9.5 (w/tram)	strenuous	May–Nov	views
65 North and South Sandia Crest/10K Trail	9.5	moderate	May–Oct	views
66 Pino Canyon	9	difficult	Apr–May, Sept–Nov	views, solitude
67 Rio Grande Bosque	8.5	easy	Year-round	unique environment, river
68 Manzano Peak	11	difficult	Apr–Nov	views, solitude
69 Manzano Crest Trail	12 (w/shuttle)	moderate	Apr–Nov	views, solitude
70 Fourth of July/ Albuquerque Loop	4.3	easy	Sept–Nov	fall colors
71 Copper Canyon/ South Baldy Loop	10.4	strenuous	Apr–Nov	views, solitude
72 Potato Canyon	6	easy	Apr–Nov	waterfall, water
73 San Lorenzo Canyon	1 to 8	easy	Year-round	geology, narrow canyons
74 Chupadera Peak	9.5	moderate	Sept–May	views, winter hike
75 Vicks Peak	12	strenuous	Apr–Nov	views, solitude

NUMBER/NAME	DISTANCE (ROUND-TRIP)	DIFFICULTY	BEST TIME	HIGHLIGHTS
76 El Camino Real	3	easy	Sept–May	history
77 Broad and Valles Canyons	9	easy	Sept–May	geology, history
78 Indian Hollow	4.5	moderate	Year-round	geology, unique vegetation
79 Baylor Pass	5 (w/shuttle)	moderate	Year-round	views, history
80 Dripping Springs Natural Area	5	easy	Year-round	views, history
81 Alkali Flat Trail	5	moderate	Year-round	unique landscape
82 Dog Canyon	9.5	strenuous	Sept–May	views, water, history
83 Three Rivers Petroglyph Site	3	easy	Year-round	history
84 Big Bonito Loop	9.25	difficult	Apr–Nov	views, solitude
85 Argentina Peak	6.5	moderate	Apr–Nov	views, water, solitude
86 Last Chance Canyon	8	moderate	Sept–May	views, water, vegetation
87 Sitting Bull Falls	7.5	moderate	Year-round	waterfall, views
88 Devils Den Canyon	5	moderate	Mar–May, Sept–Dec	views
89 Yucca Canyon	5	moderate	Sept–May	views, fossils
90 Rattlesnake Canyon	6	moderate	Sept–May	unusual environment, vegetation
91 Datil Well	3.5	easy	Mar–Nov	views, history
92 Pueblo Creek	8	easy	Mar–Nov	unusual environment, water
93 Whitewater Baldy	11	difficult	May–Nov	views
94 The Catwalk and Beyond	5.2	moderate	Mar–Nov	unique trail, history
95 Frisco Box	9	difficult	Year-round	narrow box canyon, hot springs
96 Turkey Creek Hot Springs	10	moderate	Apr–Oct	desert canyon, hot springs
97 Middle Fork/Little Bear Loop	12	moderate	Apr–Oct	desert canyon, water, hot springs
98 West Fork of the Gila River	14	moderate	Apr–Oct	desert canyon, water
99 Hillsboro Peak	10	moderate	Apr–Oct	views, solitude
100 Percha Box	4.2	easy	Sept–May	narrow canyon, water

The narrows of Broad Canyon are sliced through red volcanic rocks.

INTRODUCTION

Like a richly colorful Navajo rug, New Mexico is a blend of vibrant, dissimilar peoples woven into a unique cultural fabric. Native Americans have lived in large, permanent villages in the high desert for 1,200 years and continue to live in traditional pueblos. The Spanish were the first Europeans to settle the high deserts along the Rio Grande, and Spanish and Mexican cultures still play a dominant role in the state. Anglo-Americans arrived in the mid-nineteenth century, and in many places in the state, they remain the minority.

New Mexico's landscape is similarly diverse and contrasting in geology and biogeography. The southern half of the state meets most tourists' expectations of the Southwest: broad desert valleys separating rock-pile mountains. Many are surprised to find that the Rocky Mountains extend into New Mexico, such that the north-central region is dominated by snow-covered peaks. Strangely eroded badlands, recent lava flows, shimmering dune fields, and rugged river gorges are all part of the natural tapestry of the state.

The rolling hills of the Great Plains extend into the eastern third of New Mexico. Covered with a sea of grass, this part of the state is home to extensive, private ranches. Little public land and thus few hiking opportunities are afforded by this pattern of land ownership. Public lands—national forests, Bureau of Land Management holdings, national parks, and national monuments—are concentrated in the mountainous central and western thirds of the state. This book focuses on the wide diversity of trails found on public lands within New Mexico's mountains.

Alpenglow—sunset's pink wash over the snowcapped peaks of the high mountains—has given a morbid but appropriately spiritual name to the southernmost range of the Rocky Mountains, the Sangre de Cristo. The flanks of the range were settled by Spaniards around the start of the seventeenth century, years before the better-known colonies on the shores of the Atlantic Ocean at Jamestown and Plymouth. Driven by religious zealotry—and not a small dose of gold lust—the Spaniards came to the foothills of the Rockies and settled Santa Fe as their capital. On crisp, sparkling winter evenings, the setting sun turned the nearby mountains a pastel red, a regular phenomenon that over the years influenced a switch in the name of the range from the generic Sierra Madre to Sangre de Cristo—the Blood of Christ.

The highest peaks of the Sangre de Cristo Mountains in New Mexico dominate the north-central part of the state. Alpine scenery surrounds Wheeler and the Truchas (trout) peaks, both above 13,000 feet. The high country extends from the Colorado border to just south of Santa Fe. Much of the range is within the Carson and Santa Fe national forests, and the high peaks are protected by the Wheeler Peak, Pecos, and Latir wilderness

Looking down Sanchez Canyon toward the Rio Grande from the St. Peters Dome Trail

areas. Scattered high lakes and tumbling mountain streams are an added attraction, and fishing is excellent in most waters. The scenery may not be as dramatic as the more popular outdoor playgrounds in neighboring Colorado, but New Mexico's alpine terrain is far less crowded.

To the south, the Sandia Mountains leap from the eastern edge of Albuquerque, rising to over 10,000 feet within only 2 horizontal miles from the foothills. The rugged granite cliffs of the Sandia Wilderness create challenging hiking opportunities on the doorstep of the state's largest city.

West of the main chain of the Rockies lie the Jemez Mountains, the remains of a huge volcano that blew out 50 cubic miles of ash in a Mount St. Helens–style explosion. Here one can have the unique experience of hiking for miles inside a long-dormant volcano at the Valles Caldera National Preserve. The western flank of the Jemez range is broken by deep canyons carved into soft rock. About 700 years ago, the well-watered canyons attracted farmers from the Ancestral Pueblo culture. On the canyon floors and in the juniper woodlands on the mesas, the Ancestral Pueblos built thousands of living quarters, ranging from summer farming huts to five-hundred-room pueblos. Bandelier National Monument protects a large number of these ancient pueblos.

The northwest corner of New Mexico sits atop the Colorado Plateau, home of horizontal sedimentary rocks, striped mesas and buttes, and long vistas. The rock layers here are the same as in better-known localities such as Canyonlands, Arches, and Mesa Verde national parks. This colorful landscape was also home to the Ancestral Pueblo people, and their abandoned homes are scattered throughout the region, reaching a glorious pinnacle in the huge pueblos at Chaco Canyon. On the southern edge of the plateau, recent volcanic activity has created El Malpais—the Badlands—where hikers can roam lava flows, explore lava tubes, and climb small volcanoes.

Below Interstate 40, which cuts east to west across the upper third of the state, the character of New Mexico changes to island mountains surrounded by seas of grasslands and desert plains. In the central region, the Manzano, Magdalena, and San Mateo mountains rise over 10,000 feet, providing a haven for cool-weather tree species, such as alpine fir, amid the desert. The scattered units of the Lincoln and Cibola national forests offer miles of hiking within these ranges.

Southern New Mexico is a land of lonesome mountain ranges separated by more than neighborly distances. Between the ranges lie dry desert plains, long fingers of the Chihuahuan Desert reaching up from Mexico. Tough-leaved creosote bush characterizes the monotonous basins, and the foothills of each mountain are adorned with desert rock gardens. Here plants take on strange and wonderful shapes, such as Mickey Mouse–eared prickly pears, dagger agaves, grass-skirted yucca, and spider-legged ocotillo.

Each of the wrinkled mountains rising from the basins has its own unique characteristics. The high peaks of the Sierra Blanca in the southeast part of the state are northern in character, with summits clothed in fir and spruce forest. Indeed, the name Sierra Blanca—White Mountains—comes from the range's annual snowcap, a rare sight in desert latitudes. Along the Rio Grande, the Organ Mountains barely reach 8,000 feet, but their jagged ramparts of granite lend an attractive backdrop to the desert near Las Cruces. To the east, the massive limestone pile of the Guadalupe Mountains is best known for its plentiful and extensive caverns, but on the outside the range is no less interesting. Pygmy forests—stunted by severe and frequent wildfires—cover the range; canyon walls and mountain fronts are composed of repeating layers of gray limestone, thick with the fossil remains of ancient sea life.

In the southwest quarter of New Mexico, high desert mountain ranges are drained by the Gila River, a major tributary of the Colorado River. These dry mountains are part of the state's largest concentration of wilderness. Best known is the Gila Wilderness, the first area in the country to receive such a designation. Nearby, the long Black Range is protected in the Aldo Leopold Wilderness, named in honor of the man who originated the wilderness concept in the Southwest. Good-sized streams flow through the region, and their canyons are ideal for hikers.

HIKING SAFETY IN THE LAND OF ENCHANTMENT

Hiking in New Mexico is eminently enjoyable if you are well prepared and ready for the unexpected.

Hike Preparation

Before venturing into the backcountry of New Mexico, consider the possible hazards that may be encountered on the trip. Using a map, become familiar with the terrain. Carefully study the main route and determine quick escape routes for use in an emergency. Obtain a weather forecast for the time of the hike and adjust plans to avoid potentially dangerous storms; always pack adequate foul-weather gear and warm clothing. In spring and summer, check for burning wildfires and know the fire danger rating in the area. Before heading out, leave a detailed itinerary with a trusted friend. It is best not to hike alone, but experienced hikers, who plan carefully, do and can enjoy complete solitude in the wilderness.

The Rio Grande is a constant part of the landscape along the trails through the bosque in Albuquerque.

Keeping an Eye on the Weather

New Mexico's diversity of landscape and range of elevation creates a climate noted for its extreme variations. Temperatures range from summer highs of over 100 degrees Fahrenheit in the southern desert to winter lows of minus 40 degrees Fahrenheit in the northern mountains. Even within a single day, hikers often find temperature swings exceeding 35 degrees. These conditions make it important for hikers to enter the backcountry prepared for extremes, always carrying an extra layer of warm clothing and raingear.

In general, spring is characterized by a mixed assortment of weather conditions throughout the state, with the one constant being high winds. Mornings are cold and afternoons warm to hot, such that dressing in easily removed layers is advised to ensure a comfortable trip. Cold fronts frequently sweep across the state, dumping wet snow to push spring back into winter. Before starting out on springtime mountain hikes, plan carefully and keep an eye on the weather forecast. In the southern half of the state, spring hiking conditions are usually delightful, but winds and even snow are possible through late April.

In the summer, high temperatures in southern New Mexico preclude comfortable hiking at low elevations, but the southern mountains are pleasant to hike in during the warm months. Summer conditions are often ideal in the northern part of the state, with warm days and cool nights through June. Early to mid-July brings a change as moisture moves in from the south, generating almost daily thunderstorms. The storms are often violent, with high winds, hail, and frequent lightning.

September and October can bring ideal hiking conditions. Blue skies and windless days prevail along with cool days and chilly nights. In the south, these conditions can last until early November. Fall hikers should always ascertain the current weather forecast before starting on a trip. Blustery, fast-moving cold fronts can bring heavy snow to the northern mountains as early as mid-September, although these storms usually wait until mid-October. Each fall, search-and-rescue teams are kept busy by hikers who head unprepared into the backcountry regardless of the forecast.

Mountain trails in the north are closed by snow by late October or mid-November. In the south, mountain trails are often open until December but desert hikes are possible throughout the winter, except when surprisingly cold storms bring wind and snowy conditions for a day or two at a time. Always know the latest weather forecast before any winter trip.

Lightning, Flash Floods, and Wildfire

Open spaces are no place in which to be caught during a summer thunderstorm: New Mexico ranks second in the nation in number of lightning-caused deaths per year. Plan to be off ridges and peaks before noon. Storms build rapidly, and hikers need to be constantly vigilant of the weather. When caught by an unexpected storm, stay off ridgelines and open mesa tops, and keep out of meadows and away from lone trees or rocks. Seek safety in low ground, in extensive forested areas, or in large caves. When no shelter is available, avoid small caves and shallow depressions. Stow backpacks and other metal objects at least thirty feet away, and use clothing to insulate yourself from the ground. Squat on two feet and keep as low a profile as possible.

A great paradox of hiking in the dry Southwest is the serious threat posed by running water. Precipitation may be rare in the desert, but summer storms can nonetheless produce inordinate amounts of rain in a short time. Water quickly collects in drainages, turning a dry streambed into a raging torrent within minutes. Stay out of dry washes and arroyos during storms, and never set up camp in a dry watercourse. Be aware that a storm in the upper portion of a drainage can send a wall of water down to a sunny, lower portion, so keep an eye on the surrounding weather. Do not try to ford streams filled with floodwater. Be patient—high flow rates usually subside in a few hours.

An increasing threat to the landscape and to hikers is wildfire. Records indicate that the Southwest is in the midst of the drought portion of its climatic cycle. In addition, grazing, fire suppression, and other factors have created unnaturally dense forests. The result is conditions ripe for uncontrollable fires that jump into the crowns of trees and burn thousands of acres of pine and mixed conifer forest. Thus, hikers need to be extremely careful with fire. Always use a stove to heat water or cook food. Except in emergencies, don't build campfires.

For their own safety, hikers should be aware of prevailing fire conditions during the fire season, which extends from mid-April to at least the onset of the summer rainy season in July. Keep abreast of existing fires that may be near the area of an intended hike by checking fire agency sites on the Internet. When hiking, be aware of smoke and the prevailing wind direction and speed. Fires can spread 10 or more miles in a day under hot, dry, and windy conditions.

On a practical level, high fire danger frequently results in closure orders from April through July on New Mexico national forest lands. Fire danger closures have shut down the Lincoln National Forest in April and May in several recent years. Also, the Cibola and Santa Fe national forests have been closed for one or two months a year. Areas burned in recent wildfires may also have to shut down to public access for up to two years. It is always a good idea to check on current closure before setting out on a trip.

Drought, along with wildfire, creates another potential safety concern on trails. Dry conditions frequently allow insects to infest trees in forest and woodland areas. Insect-killed ponderosa pine and Douglas fir stand as snags in forested areas for up to ten years on average. Eventually, the snags fall or wind snaps them off at weak sections of the trunk. Any standing snag should be considered a hazard tree, particularly on windy days. Avoid hiking in most forested areas on windy days. If caught in an area with plentiful snags when the wind comes up, watch the trail ahead and identify hazard trees before you pass them.

The Dome Fire scorched 17,000 acres of the Jemez Mountains in 1996.

Importance of Water

Along with sunny skies comes a dry climate where water is precious to all living things. Hikers will lose water to temperature regulation, increased respiration, and increased metabolic rates. By the time a hiker feels thirsty, he or she is already a quart low on fluids. Maintaining body fluid balance is a critical part of hiking in New Mexico.

Excessive fluid loss can lead to heat exhaustion, a potentially serious condition; symptoms include reduced perspiration, rapid pulse, dizziness, and general weakness. Hikers with any of these signs should immediately get out of the sun and drink large quantities of water. Without careful attention, heat exhaustion can lead to heat stroke, a much more dangerous condition characterized by no perspiration, hot skin, and a high body temperature. These signs indicate a medical emergency requiring urgent attention. First aid is an immediate reduction of body temperature by moving to a cool location, increasing fluid intake, and applying cool compresses to the skin.

Heat-related medical problems can be avoided by drinking plenty of water before starting out on a hike and then drinking regularly during the trip. Plan on at least a half gallon of fluid per person per day for day hikes and a gallon per person per day for overnight trips. For day trips, a hydration system with a 100-ounce bladder is ideal.

Shooting stars along Sawmill Creek

Protection from the Sun

The near-constant blue skies of the high desert are no myth, but there is a price to pay. Skin cancer rates are high in the Southwest, and visitors and natives alike must take precautions against too much of a good thing. Summer and winter, hikers must protect themselves from the sun.

The best protection is a long-sleeved shirt and long pants, even in summer. Light colors will help reflect the intense summer sun, and a loose fit will help keep hikers cool. Wide-brimmed hats are standard equipment all year long. Additional protection for the eyes is provided by high-quality sunglasses that screen at least 95 percent of the ultraviolet radiation.

In addition to protective clothing, hikers should use copious sunscreen. Apply an SPF 15 or higher formula at least every four hours. Sweatproof types of sunscreen stay on well during exercise. For full protection, coat hands, neck, face, and ears.

Elevation Factors

Many mountain trails in New Mexico lead to elevations above 8,000 feet. Out-of-state hikers unaccustomed to altitude can often avoid problems with high elevations by allowing at least two days to acclimate at a mid-range elevation before attempting a hike above 9,000 feet. Thin air increases exertion and visitors should slow down to a comfortable pace, which may be considerably slower than their normal hiking speed. Quick ascents above 10,000 feet can lead to a variety of medical problems, such as mountain sickness. Symptoms include headache, nausea, weakness, and general achiness. Problems usually disappear with a return to lower elevations, but if symptoms persist, medical attention is required.

Critter Complications

Eight species of rattlesnake reside within the borders of New Mexico, and at least one type is found in all habitats ranging from lowland deserts to conifer forest. In the north, most rattlesnakes are found below 7,000 feet, but they are occasionally spotted up to 9,000 feet. In the southern part of the state, rattlesnakes are common at all elevations up to 10,000 feet.

Rattlers hibernate during the winter months and into May in the north. In summer, they avoid hot sunshine and are generally encountered at night. Use caution and a flashlight when hiking at dusk or at night. Rattlers are most active in the daytime during spring and fall. Snakes will be found sunning on ledges or in the partial shade of trees. Hikers can avoid rattlesnakes by staying on the trail and always watching their footing. Most bites occur below the knee, and high-top boots and long pants afford some protection from snakes. Off the trail, never place your hand on a ledge above your head. The buzzing rattle of the snakes is an effective warning of their presence, although many a hiker has unknowingly stepped directly over rattlers, hidden behind rocks or logs in the trail.

In the fall, bugling bull elk can be heard in the northern mountains.

Although the once-common grizzly bear is no longer found here, black bears inhabit all forested mountain ranges in New Mexico. Bear encounters are infrequent but increase during dry summers. A bear spotted along a trail will usually turn tail and be quickly gone. Hikers who encounter a bear should make the bear aware of their presence by talking in conversational tones, and make certain not to get between a mother and her cubs. In camp, it is good practice to tie food or items that smell like food such as toothpaste in a tree at least ten feet off the ground and four feet from the trunk. This will also protect your camp from other wild critters. If a bear does get food or equipment, do not attempt to take it away.

Scorpions range throughout New Mexico and are most common in the southern half of the state. New Mexican species are not deadly and have stings similar to that of bees. Scorpions hide under rocks and tree bark during the day, coming out at night to prey on insects. Their secretive habits make them easy to avoid; most hikers will never see one. Because scorpions seek damp, dark places, it is, however, a good idea for backpackers to shake out clothing and check shoes and boots before putting them on in the morning.

Bothersome insects are pleasantly absent from most parts of New Mexico, but two kinds of arthropods found here carry serious diseases and should be avoided. Tall grasses are home to ticks, which are most abundant in spring and early summer. Although Lyme disease has not yet been found to originate in New Mexico, it may arrive soon. Ticks do carry Rocky Mountain spotted fever and Colorado tick fever. Symptoms for both are flu-like. Check for ticks after each trip. Check your animals, too. If any are found, remove them with tweezers, and for several weeks, watch for signs of illness.

More serious in nature is the presence of bubonic plague. This life-threatening disease is carried by fleas living on host animals. Thus, it is important to avoid contact with wild animals, particularly members of the rodent family, dead or alive. Camp away from animal burrows. After an outdoor trip in New Mexico, anyone with high fever and swelling in the armpits and groin—particularly visitors who have returned home where plague is not known to occur—should alert physicians to the possibility of plague.

Hantavirus is another life-threatening disease found not only in New Mexico but also throughout the world. Carried by the deer mouse, hantavirus is a serious respiratory illness. Humans primarily contract this disease by inhaling dried mouse urine or saliva that is carried on particles in the air when the rodent's habitat is disturbed; but it can also be transmitted through

Elk tooth marks on aspen

ingestion of contaminated food or water. Flu-like symptoms—fever, headache, rapid breathing, and cough—are followed by a rapid increase of fluid in the lungs. Half of all cases end in death. Avoid hantavirus by avoiding rodent-infested areas and by taking a few simple precautions. Backpackers should use a tent with a floor and pitch it on a campsite away from rodent burrows. Store food in sealed containers and off the ground. Be particularly vigilant during years following a large piñon nut crop, because rodent populations will also be high at this time.

What to Bring Along

Preparation is often the difference between an enjoyable outdoor excursion and a disaster. Careful planning for all hikes, no matter what distance, is important for the safety of all hikers. An excellent starting place for loading a pack is the list of the Ten Essentials from The Mountaineers:

1. Extra clothing
2. Extra food
3. Sun protection, including sunglasses
4. Pocketknife
5. Firestarter candle or chemical fuel
6. First-aid kit and snakebite kit
7. Matches in a waterproof container
8. Flashlight
9. Map
10. Compass

Ocotillos leaves appear only when there is adequate moisture.

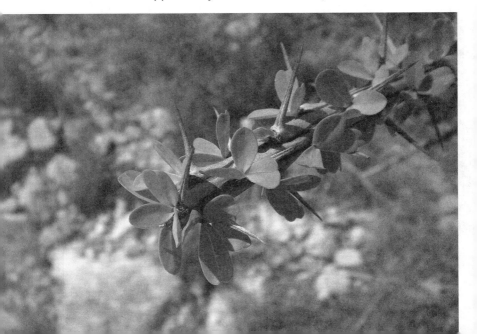

Clothing

Hikers in New Mexico are likely to encounter a wide range of temperatures during the course of a day. To meet the challenges of weather, always dress in layers. In cool seasons—spring and fall—begin with a zipper-neck shirt made from a moisture-wicking synthetic material. Synthetic-material tights or nylon pants are also suitable for this time of year. For an insulating layer, a light- or mid-weight fleece jacket or pullover is an excellent choice. When it is colder, fleece pants are warm and offer good protection even when wet.

Proper dress is important in summer, too, when low temperatures and rain or even snow are always possible at high elevations. Wear a long-sleeved shirt and long pants made of light synthetic. For an overnight trip, add a light fleece jacket and pants. Carry extra, warm clothing, even in July and August.

In all seasons, carry raingear. Getting wet is the most serious threat to backcountry hikers, because a drenching from a storm can quickly lead to hypothermia. Anticipate summer showers every afternoon by carrying a rain jacket and pants. Waterproof outer layers are even more important in spring and fall when temperatures can quickly drop to dangerous levels. Breathable, waterproof materials are best, allowing hikers to stay cool even in summer.

Footgear is an important part of hiking equipment. Sturdy, lightweight boots are best for comfort and help reduce erosion to the trail. Because of the dry climate, light-duty boots with fabric and leather uppers are adequate for much of the hiking in New Mexico. These are generally a few ounces lighter and are cooler than other boots, but they often lack good waterproofing. For mountain hiking, especially during the summer rainy season, waterproof boots with full leather or synthetic uppers are recommended. Heavy boots also offer additional protection on rough, rocky trails. Proper socks can also add to comfort. A combination of thin liner socks with thicker synthetic or wool padded outer socks works best.

Maps and Navigation

A good state map will lead you to the vicinity of the trailhead. Pick one up at one of the tourist information centers around the state, or call the New Mexico Tourism Division (see "Sources of Additional Information" in the back of this book). Maps of the state's five national forests will be helpful in locating most trailheads and are available for a moderate fee from the Forest Supervisor offices, also listed at the end of this book.

The outline maps included with each hike in this book are meant as general guides and, particularly for longer hikes into the backcountry, should not take the place of large-scale maps. Nothing can substitute for the most recent United States Geological Survey (USGS) 7.5-minute quadrangle maps. The maps required for each hike are listed in the summary block at the start of each hike. Topographic maps are available at many retail outdoor outfitters around the state. Digital maps allow for detailed trip planning. They permit accurate determination of distances; the selection of predetermined, low-impact campsites; and an estimate of exertion level based on elevation gain and grade. Mapping software will also allow creation of customized maps for any trip. For cross-country explorations, digital maps are used to feed data to GPS receivers to keep hikers on course. Excellent digital coverage of New Mexico is available from several manufacturers.

The latest generation of GPS receivers offers another dimension of safety for hiking in the backcountry. In conjunction with topographic maps, GPS units help hikers accurately determine their location within a few tens of feet.

Water

The importance of water to hikers in New Mexico cannot be overstated. Low humidity, high temperatures, and high elevation combine to create conditions that require hikers to carry at least a half gallon of water per person for a day hike and at least a gallon per person per day for an overnight trip. Always keep an emergency supply of water in the support vehicle.

Hikers should bring all the water they need on day trips, but carrying sufficient water for an extended stay in the mountains is difficult. Plan to camp near water. All water taken from backcountry sources must be treated before use. Cattle often graze in the backcountry and share water sources with hikers. Giardia, a protozoan parasite that causes an unpleasant and potentially serious intestinal disorder, is present throughout the state.

The safest method of treating water is to boil it vigorously for ten minutes. Because water boils at a lower temperature at high altitude, boiling time must be increased above 7,000 feet. Chemical treatment with chlorine or hyperiodide tablets is an easy method of water treatment. Mechanical filters can treat large volumes of water in a short time, but they vary in efficiency. For the safest results, use a filter with a 0.02-micron screen.

RESPONSIBLE HIKING

As in most states, visiting New Mexico's backcountry comes with certain responsibilities that, when carried out, assure continued protection of and access to the state's wild areas.

Private Land

Complicated land ownership laws dating back to the days of Spanish rule and the abundance of mining claims have left New Mexico checkered with pockets of private land within public use areas. As a result, eight of the hikes in this book pass through private land and many other trips pass close to private property. To avoid problems with landowners, note the boundaries of public land on the hike maps and obey all No Trespassing signs.

Three hikes cross private land on public easements negotiated by the Forest Service or the Bureau of Land Management: Atalaya Mountain (Hike 1), Copper Canyon/South Baldy Loop (Hike 71), and Broad and

Chihuahuan desert vegetation, with ocotillo, agave, and sotol, covers the lower reaches of Dog Canyon. (Photo by Jessica Martin)

Valles Canyons (Hike 77). In addition, three hikes require crossing private land to access the trailhead: Glorieta Baldy (Hike 7), Williams Lake (Hike 16), and Petroglyph National Monument Trails (Hike 63). In each case, hikers are permitted to cross private land on the trail or road. Do not stray from the designated pathway, though, and leave all gates as they are found. These easements are the result of the landowners' generosity, and their continuance is dependent upon courteous and respectful use by hikers. Landowners can close access through their property at any time. Before starting out on one of these hikes, check with the managing agency on the current status of the easement.

For the Kitchen Mesa (Hike 47), and Box Canyon and Mesa Montosa (Hike 48) trips, permission to hike must be obtained at the Ghost Ranch Office, as detailed in the hike descriptions.

Minimum Impact Use

Before the explosion of wilderness use over the last thirty years, hikers gave little thought to what they did or left behind in the backcountry. But with increasing numbers of wilderness users, it has become necessary for each hiker to consider the impact that his or her trip has on the trail, the environment, and other trail users. Current thinking is best expressed by the phrase, "leave no trace." All hikers should carefully plan how they can minimize their impact on the outdoors while still enjoying the wilderness experience.

Minimum impact use goes far beyond common sense. All hikers should carefully study the ways they can become clean users of the backcountry and develop an attitude that every user shares responsibility to leave the wilderness in its pristine condition. The following suggestions are based on Leave No Trace materials developed by the National Outdoor Leadership School, the Bureau of Land Management, the National Park Service, and the U.S. Forest Service:

At home. Minimum impact hiking begins at home with careful planning. A well-thought-out trip reduces the potential for a damaging and costly search-and-rescue operation. Carry a map and compass, and know how to use them to stay on the planned route as well as to determine location when lost. Before starting a trip, hikers should leave a detailed itinerary of their trip with a knowledgeable friend. Also, reduce waste before hiking by repacking food in reusable containers that will not be inadvertently left behind.

On the trail. When hiking, be considerate of other trail users. Hike quietly, and rest off the trail on rocks or other durable surfaces that will not show signs of trampling.

Trails and the surrounding terrain can be easily damaged. On established trails, hike single file to avoid widening the tread. On muddy stretches of trail, hike in the established tread to avoid creating new tracks. Do not shortcut switchbacks, a practice that leads quickly to severe trail erosion. When hiking on routes with no established trail, hike abreast to avoid repetitive trampling of vegetation, and step on rock or sand whenever possible.

Wild irises in the meadow below Sawmill Park

In camp. Select a campsite that already has distinct signs of use or one in an area that will not be damaged. Locate sites at least 200 feet from water and trails, with the distance increased to a minimum of 300 feet in deserts. In river canyons, camp on sandy beaches or gravel bars below the high-water line. The best campsites are also away from and out of view of other campers.

Most packaging material will not burn completely, so pack out all trash and all uneaten food. Buried food will soon be discovered and excavated by animals, increasing their dependence on unnatural food sources.

Minimize the impact of campfires by cooking with a backpacking stove. When building a campfire, use existing fire rings or a metal firepan and burn only small-diameter dead and down wood. Before leaving, make certain the fire is out, then remove the cold ashes from the ring and scatter them away from camp. Dry washes and sand or gravel stream banks below the high-water line make good locations for pit fires. To remove signs of a pit fire, scatter the remains, then fill in the hole. In desert areas, the small amounts of dead wood available are important to the ecosystem and should not be used for fires. Carry in all firewood or go without.

Human waste is best disposed in a "cat" hole at least six inches deep, placed at least 200 feet from camp and the nearest water. After use, cover

Petroglyphs on a horizontal surface are unusual.

the hole with natural materials. Do not bury toilet paper with the waste; pack it out. When cleaning cooking utensils, use only a small amount of biodegradable soap. Remove and pack out food particles. Dishwater should be broadcast over a wide area away from camp and water sources. In desert areas, hikers should increase the distance of all waste from water sources to 300 feet.

In narrow river canyons, special precautions must be taken. In silty rivers with large flow volumes, urine and wastewater can be dumped into the flow; the large volume will dilute the waste. In mountain canyons with low flows, urinate on the banks below the high-water line to allow some filtration before the waste reaches the clear stream. Human waste should be packed out of narrow canyons or left in holes well away from the main or side streams.

For more detailed information on how to reduce user impacts on the wilderness, contact Leave No Trace (see "Sources of Additional Information" in the back of this book).

Selecting a Hike

This book holds an eclectic collection of hikes. Trips in several categories were selected. Hikes judged to be New Mexico classics—ones that most resident hikers as well as hikers who visit the state will want take—are of course included. The climb to the summit of Wheeler Peak is one such classic; hikes through the blazing reds of autumn in Fourth of July Canyon and across the shimmering dunes at White Sands are other examples. Also included are a large number of hikes in out-of-the-way places that see few visitors. Trips to Valle Vidal, Sawmill Park, Devils Den, Vicks Peak, and many others fall into this category. Other locations are little known and deserve recognition, such as the Three Rivers Petroglyph Site, the Rim Vista Trail, and the Cruces Basin Wilderness. Personal favorites of mine are hikes with a special historic or natural history focus. Hikers on the Cerrillos Hills, in Chaco Canyon, on the Catwalk, and on El Malpais will find a wealth of historic or geologic features that make these true explorations rather than simple hikes.

In most instances, hikers will find clusters of three or more hikes listed for a given mountain range or canyon. The clusters were designed to provide a full weekend of hiking opportunities with a minimal amount of driving.

Throughout this book, five abbreviations are used in connection with roads. Interstate highways are designated with I, U.S. highways with US, New Mexico state highways with NM, county roads with CR, and Forest Service roads with FR.

Use the summary table at the beginning of each hike description to select a hike honestly suited to your skills. Hikers unaccustomed to walking at elevation should look carefully at the hike distance and elevation range and gain. Visitors should wait several days before tackling trips over 8 miles long or with more than 2,000 feet of elevation gain.

The summary block for each hike provides the following information:

Distance. Unless otherwise noted, the distances given are for round-trips. Hike distances were measured with a GPS unit or with mapping software.

Difficulty. A subjective evaluation of exertion level required for each hike, biased toward casual hikers and those unaccustomed to elevation. Ratings used are easy, moderate, difficult, and strenuous.

Easy hikes have little elevation gain (usually less than 500 feet) on easy-to-follow trails that traverse relatively flat terrain. These trips are suitable for visitors coming from lower elevations, for novice hikers, and for families. Moderate hikes are typically between 4 and 10 miles long, involve climbing between 500 and 1,500 feet and exhibit some steep sections. Difficult trails include those with long, steep sections that gain more than 1,500 feet and usually cover more than 10 miles; however, shorter trails that traverse rough surfaces may be rated as difficult. Trips that require sustained climbing to gain more than 2,000 feet of elevation, or those that cover long distances above 9,000 feet, are rated as strenuous and should be attempted by strong and experienced hikers only.

Elevation range. The highest and lowest points of the hike.

Elevation gain. The cumulative elevation gain for the route as described, including all ascents, as determined with a recording altimeter or with topographic mapping software.

Best time of year. The best months to take each hike, based on an average year, which rarely occurs. The weather in New Mexico is notoriously variable, and hikers should always consult the latest weather forecast before starting out on a trip.

Water. The location of potential drinking water along the route. When possible, hikers should carry enough water for the entire hike and not depend on nature to provide a safe and adequate supply. Remember that all water should be treated before use.

Maps. The best available maps for the hike; all USGS maps listed are 7.5-minute quadrangles.

Managed by. The landowner or managing agency for each hike: who to contact for more or up-to-date information. A list of addresses, telephone numbers, and websites is provided in "Sources of Additional Information" at the end of this book.

Features. The attractions that make each hike worthy of the reader's attention.

A NOTE ABOUT SAFETY

Safety is an important concern in all outdoor activities. No guidebook can alert you to every hazard or anticipate the limitations of every reader. Therefore, the descriptions of roads, trails, routes, and natural features in this book are not representations that a particular place or excursion will be safe for your party. When you follow any of the routes described in this book, you assume responsibility for your own safety. Under normal conditions, such excursions require the usual attention to traffic, road and trail conditions, weather, terrain, the capabilities of your party, and other factors. Keeping informed on current conditions and exercising common sense are the keys to a safe, enjoyable outing.

The Mountaineers Books

Opposite: *Falls on the Rio Nambe on the way to Nambe Lake*

SOUTHERN SANGRE DE CRISTO MOUNTAINS

1 | ATALAYA MOUNTAIN

Distance: 7 miles, day hike
Difficulty: difficult
Elevation range: 7,330 to 9,121 feet
Elevation gain: 1,800 feet
Best time of year: April to November
Water: carry water
Map: USGS Santa Fe
Managed by: Santa Fe National Forest,
    Española Ranger District
Features: views of Santa Fe and the Sangre de Cristo Range

A climb to the top of Atalaya Mountain on the outskirts of Santa Fe provides hikers with a unique view of the old city. The steep but pleasant trail leads through shady piñon and conifer forests to the summit. Santa Fe, with its historic plaza and sprawling new growth, spreads out below. A couple hours on this trail can be a welcome relief from the usual tourist fare in Santa Fe. Be aware that summer weekend mornings can bring a lot of hikers to the trail.

To reach the trailhead from the intersection of Cerrillos Road and St. Francis Drive in Santa Fe, go south on St. Francis 0.2 mile and turn left onto Cordova Road. Following the signs to Museum Hill, continue 1.3 miles, passing Old Pecos Trail, where the name of Cordova Road changes to Armenta Street. At a T intersection, turn left onto Camino Corrales. In 0.2 mile, turn right at a four-way stop onto Old Santa Fe Trail. Just beyond the entrance to Museum Hill, turn left onto Camino del Monte Sol. Following signs for St. Johns College, turn right onto Camino de Cruz Blanca. In 0.5 mile, at the entrance to St. Johns, turn right (south) and park in the lot near the entrance at the signs marking the Atalaya Mountain Trailhead.

Walk east past the information kiosk as Trail 174 winds through junipers along the edge of the Arroyo de los Chamisos. Bear right at the intersection with the Dorothy Stewart Trail. After dropping into the arroyo, watch for signs marking the trail, which soon exits the east (left) side of the streambed to enter a narrow side canyon. The winding path leads along an easement

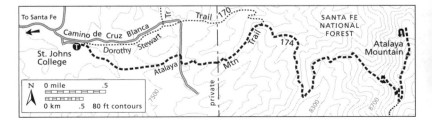

Hikers on the ridgeline segment of the Atalaya Mountain Trail

Hikers on the summit of Atalaya Mountain enjoy the view of Santa Fe.

through private land; stay on the trail in this section. At mile 0.8, cross a road, climb stairs, and head right around a small ridge. Pass through a fence at mile 1.1 and gain a ridge that offers the first views of Atalaya Mountain. In another quarter mile, intersect Trail 170. Bear right onto a wider trail as it contours around the southwest slope of a ridge through tall ponderosa pines.

At the nose of a spur ridge at mile 1.75, a sign offers hikers the choice of an easier or a steeper route. No matter which choice you make, the grade is steep from here to the summit of Atalaya Mountain. The easier route to the right is a better-designed trail and using it will help reduce erosion problems that have long plagued the upper trail. Swing around the nose of a ridge, then head north again through pink granite hills. At mile 2.6, begin a half-mile long series of switchbacks that lead to the ridge above. Turn left and continue 0.4 mile to the summit, where a reward of fine views of the city of Santa Fe and the Jemez Mountains awaits. After enjoying the view, turn around and descend by the same route.

2 ┆ BIG TESUQUE/BEAR WALLOW LOOP

Distance: 8 miles, day hike
Difficulty: moderate
Elevation range: 8,225 to 9,675 feet
Elevation gain: 2,000 feet
Best time of year: April to early November
Water: Tesuque Creek
Map: USGS Aspen Vista
Managed by: Santa Fe National Forest,
   Española Ranger District
Features: shady conifer forest, aspen stands,
   flowing water, wildflowers in summer

The Big Tesuque Trail is the forgotten link in the extensive trail system on the west face of the Sangre de Cristo Mountains near Santa Fe. Hikers flock to nearby trails, but Big Tesuque is usually an excellent choice for a walk in solitude. This loop, which is a variation of the popular Bear Wallow Triangle

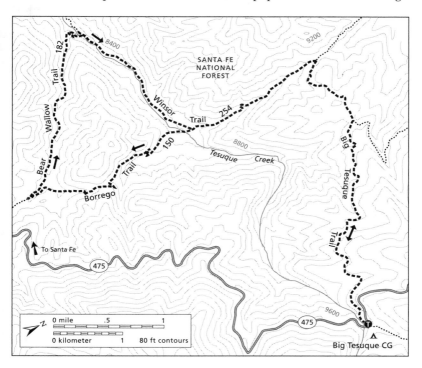

Big Tesuque Creek near the trailhead

hike, is delightful in midsummer, when wildflowers dot the meadows, or in fall, when the canyon slopes become golden with turning aspen leaves. The aspens, colonizers of the forest following fire, are evidence of the crucial role wildfires play in maintaining the forest mosaic in the Sangre de Cristo

Mountains. The huge aspens along the trail date from fires in the early decades of the twentieth century.

The trail starts directly across NM 475 from Big Tesuque Campground on the north side of Tesuque Creek. Reach the trailhead from the Santa Fe Plaza by taking Washington Avenue north 0.5 mile to Artist Road, also identified as NM 475. Turn right onto NM 475 and head toward the Santa Fe Ski Area, noting your mileage. Big Tesuque Campground is on the right (east) side of the road in 11.7 miles.

From the parking area, carefully walk across NM 475 and pick up the well-worn path that dives from the road and heads toward Big Tesuque Creek. At the creek, angle downstream. Two hundred yards from the trailhead, bear right and climb above the stream as it cuts across an aspen-dotted meadow. The trail is soon out of earshot of the stream and swings along a minor drainage. Pass through a hikers gate and into a second meadow, which reaches a colorful maximum of wildflowers in early July. For the next mile, the trail contours in and out of side canyons under stately Douglas fir and shimmering aspen. The thick canopy occasionally opens to offer views down into the surprisingly deep canyon of Tesuque Creek.

About 1.5 miles from the trail's start, intersect the Winsor Trail 254. Turn left and follow the trail along a saddle, then follow the tread as it descends steeply to the left (south). In a minute, take the left fork that climbs slightly then contours around a hill. When the trail reaches the next major drainage, it heads left and descends toward Tesuque Creek. The trail drops through a second-growth mixed forest with Douglas fir, ponderosa and limber pine, and broad-leafed maple and Gambel oak, with a liberal dash of aspen.

Shortly before reaching Tesuque Creek, angle left onto the Borrego Trail 150. After 100 yards, cross the stream using a log for a bridge. Continue the easy climb over a low ridge, first along a small drainage, then up two gentle switchbacks. About 3.1 miles from the start, reach the top of a saddle and drop steeply for about two hundred yards. At the next intersection, angle sharply right and descend the Bear Wallow Trail 182 toward Tesuque Creek. The trail crosses the drainage several times before climbing up the north wall of the deepening canyon. After 0.75 mile on Trail 182, the route goes over a rocky slope. The sound of tumbling water rushes up as the trail turns sharply around the nose of a ridge and descends two switchbacks to meet Tesuque Creek.

Cross the small stream on a log bridge and again intersect the Winsor Trail. Turn right and begin the ascent along the creek. Over the next mile, an abundance of delightful lunch spots can be found between the trail and the stream.

The Winsor Trail climbs continually with a few steep, rocky sections. After about a mile of climbing, arrive again at the junction with the Borrego Trail. Turn left to retrace the route up the Winsor Trail to the Big Tesuque Trail, and from there back to the trailhead.

3 NAMBE LAKE

Distance: 6 miles, day hike
Difficulty: strenuous
Elevation range: 10,250 to 11,385 feet
Elevation gain: 2,100 feet
Best time of year: mid-June to mid-October
Water: Rio Nambe
Maps: USGS Aspen Basin; USFS Pecos Wilderness
Managed by: Santa Fe National Forest,
    Pecos Wilderness, Española Ranger District
Features: high-country scenery, fall aspens, picturesque
    stream, alpine lake

Nambe Lake is a crystal-clear gem tucked in a glacial valley between Lake Peak and Santa Fe Baldy. It lies barely a half mile from the lifts at the Santa Fe Ski Area, but the rock bowl that holds the lake is like another world. That such spectacular scenery can be found so close to Santa Fe surprises more than a few hikers who venture up the mountain to gaze into the waters.

From Santa Fe, take Washington Avenue north from Paseo de Peralta 0.1 mile to Artist Road, NM 475. Turn right and head toward the Santa Fe Ski Area. Continue about 14 miles to the parking area at the ski basin. Park at the Winsor Trailhead at the northwest corner of the lot near an information kiosk.

The Winsor Trail 254 begins behind the information board and immediately passes over a footbridge. Turn right, following the arrows on the signs pointing to Lake Katherine. Several switchbacks lead up the slopes of Aspen

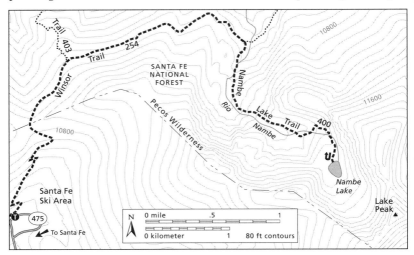

Shallow Nambe Lake is surrounded by rocky cliffs.

Peak and to a saddle at the Pecos Wilderness boundary, 0.75 mile from the start. Pass through the fence and walk downhill on a north slope shaded by alternating groves of spruce and aspen. At mile 1.1, continue straight at the intersection with Trail 403 to the left. After a mile of gentle descent, listen for the cascades of the Rio Nambe in the steep canyon to the north. In a few minutes, just before reaching a narrow meadow that holds the stream, angle right (south) on a distinct trail (Trail 400) marked for Nambe Lake.

Although the beginning of the trail is distinct, the rest of Trail 400 is difficult to follow. However, hikers can simply head up the drainage on any one of several routes that climb steeply parallel to the Rio Nambe. Each of the interwoven trails leads upcanyon, but when in doubt, stay close to the stream. The rocky main trail parallels the stream on a steady climb. Just below a bowl-shaped meadow that offers wonderful views up the canyon, the trail crosses to the left side of the stream. The bowl breaks up the ascent and makes an acceptable turnaround point for weary hikers. Another steep segment leads to a boggy valley at mile 2.5. As the trail passes the bog, watch for displays of purple monkshood, tall arrowleaf groundsel, and fuzzy American bistort.

Beyond the bog, cross to the right side of the stream and make the final pitch to the lake. Pass towering granite cliffs and deep talus fields where pikas squeal their alarm call. In a few minutes, reach the basin where Lake Peak looms directly above. Calm, fishless Nambe Lake reflects like a mirror the surrounding rugged circle of rock, and it is worth the effort to walk around the lake. After enjoying the views, return to the trailhead via the same route.

4 | LA VEGA LOOP

Distance: 7 miles, day hike or backpack
Difficulty: strenuous
Elevation range: 8,890 to 10,850 feet
Elevation gain: 2,600 feet
Best time of year: late May to mid-October
Water: Rio Nambe
Maps: USGS Aspen Basin; USFS Pecos Wilderness
Managed by: Santa Fe National Forest,
   Pecos Wilderness, Española Ranger District
Features: high-country scenery, fall aspens,
   picturesque streams

New Mexico's mountains offer high-country wildflower displays from mid-June through the end of August. Any trail can put hikers in the thick of the

La Vega is one of the largest meadows in the high country of the Sangre de Cristos.

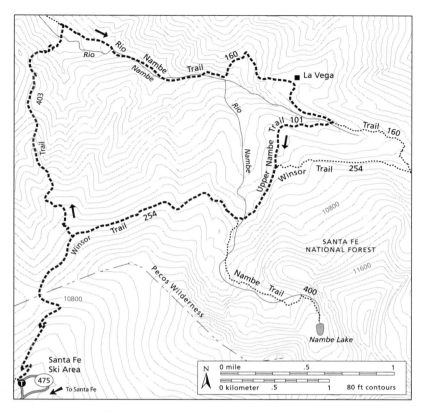

show, but the La Vega Loop has an advantage over others because it offers a wide variety of habitats, some spectacular scenery, and a pretty good workout. The destination, La Vega, is one of the loveliest meadows on the west flanks of the southern Sangre de Cristo Mountains (*vega* means "fertile plain" in Spanish). The meadow's lush grasses and colorful flowers are rimmed with forested peaks. Along the way is the humid canyon of the Rio Nambe, which in July turns lavender with mountain bluebells.

This loop uses Trail 403, nicknamed "The Elevator Shaft" by locals. The very steep drop on Trail 403 suggests that this loop be walked in the direction described. This trail is a downhill workout and not always easy to find or follow. Only experienced hikers should attempt this descent.

Like other hikes leading into the eastern Pecos Wilderness, the La Vega Loop begins at the northwest corner of the parking area at the Santa Fe Ski Area. Follow the directions to the trailhead for Hike 3, Nambe Lake.

Begin hiking behind the information kiosk on the Winsor Trail 254. In a few steps, turn right (north) to follow the signs for Lake Katherine. Climb the flanks of Aspen Peak on switchbacks to reach a saddle at the boundary

Swirling lines of minerals in banded gneiss in the Sangre de Cristos

of the Pecos Wilderness, 0.75 mile from the start. In 0.3 mile from the saddle, turn left onto Trail 403 and begin a steep drop into the canyon of the Rio Nambe. The route doesn't provide any niceties like switchbacks, it simply barrels downhill for 1.5 miles. The trail is faint at times, so hikers must watch carefully for the route.

At the bottom of the south wall of the canyon, cross the Rio Nambe on a log bridge and continue north for a minute to intersect the Rio Nambe Trail 160. Turn right and begin a climb along the cascading stream, fording the little river twice in the next mile. The trail grade increases when the trail swings away from the Rio Nambe, up a side drainage and into an aspen meadow. At the head of the meadow, the trail doubles back to the right and climbs along a ridge. Once over the top, drop to a small stream, then make another short climb to reach La Vega.

Rock cairns mark the way along the southern edge of the forest-rimmed meadow to a trail sign identifying La Vega. From the trail sign, you can pick out a lunch spot, explore the meadow, or head to the far side of La Vega to find a secluded campsite.

To continue on the loop, return to the trail sign and pick up the well-defined trail heading south and downhill into the forest. After descending 0.25 mile, turn right onto the Upper Nambe Trail 101, heading toward the Winsor Trail. In a few steps, cross a stream, then swing right to parallel the stream for a few hundred yards before making the short climb to the Winsor Trail. At the intersection, turn right and follow the trail across the Rio Nambe. The route climbs gradually along the north slope of Ravens Ridge, which is shady and often chilly. Pass the junction with Trail 403, continuing on the Winsor Trail back to the saddle at the wilderness boundary and then down the steep hill to the trailhead.

5 SPIRIT LAKE

Distance: 10.8 miles, day hike or backpack
Difficulty: strenuous
Elevation range: 10,250 to 11,050 feet
Elevation gain: 2,600 feet
Best time of year: late June to early October
Water: Rio Nambe, Spirit Lake
Maps: USGS Aspen Basin and Cowles;
   USFS Pecos Wilderness
Managed by: Santa Fe National Forest,
   Pecos Wilderness, Española Ranger District
Features: high-country lake, mountain scenery, fall aspens

The climb to Spirit Lake is a summer getaway from the tourist crowds in Santa Fe, but on weekends the Winsor Trail receives heavy use by hikers. The views from the trail are among the best in the southern Sangre de Cristos and encompass the Jemez Mountains, the Rio Grande Valley, and a close-up look at Santa Fe Baldy. Fall colors are spectacular in this part of the range, making this a popular hike in late September. Spirit Lake itself holds rainbow and cutthroat trout, so take along a fishing rod. A few campsites are in the woods surrounding the lake, but regulations require campsites to be more than 200 feet from the water.

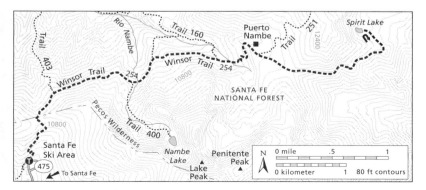

Santa Fe Baldy along the way to Spirit Lake

From Santa Fe, take Washington Avenue north from Paseo de Peralta 0.1 mile to Artist Road, NM 475. Turn right and head toward the Santa Fe Ski Area. Continue about 14 miles to the parking area at the ski basin. Park at the Winsor Trailhead at the northwest corner of the lot near an information kiosk.

Begin hiking on the Winsor Trail 254, immediately crossing a bridge and turning right. The first 0.75 mile of trail is the steepest of the trip, climbing 600 feet on several graded switchbacks. At the top of the ridge, pass through a gate in a fence and enter the Pecos Wilderness. A stop here for a breather may attract a flock of gray jays tame enough to eat peanuts from an outstretched hand.

A long, pleasant stretch of trail drops gradually on a steep slope high above the Rio Nambe through a deep fir forest dotted with aspen. The deeply shaded north slope can hold snow into late June. At mile 1.1, pass Trail 403 dropping steeply to the left. Cross the headwaters of the Rio Nambe at mile 2.2 and follow the trail as it contours to the northeast. As Santa Fe Baldy comes into view, the trail swings east, passing through small meadows of summer wildflowers. Cross another small stream at mile 3.3, then climb the next ridge on gentle switchbacks to reach Puerto Nambe, a broad saddle between Santa Fe Baldy and Penitente Peak, at mile 4.2.

Again heading east, walk through the splendid meadows atop the broad saddle, with Santa Fe Baldy to the left and Penitente Peak to the right. Pass the junction with the Skyline Trail 251 to the left and continue straight on the Winsor Trail. Hike single file to prevent further development of parallel tracks across the meadow. The trail drops slowly from the east side of the saddle, traversing a forested south-facing slope. A little more than a mile from the saddle, cross a short spur ridge, then drop more sharply to the lake basin. Enjoy the shade of the huge firs surrounding Spirit Lake. The trail's gentle grades make the return trip easier than expected.

6 | DECEPTION PEAK

Distance: 6 miles, day hike
Difficulty: strenuous
Elevation range: 10,000 to 12,200 feet
Elevation gain: 2,200 feet
Best time of year: late June to mid-October
Water: carry water
Maps: USGS Aspen Basin; USFS Pecos Wilderness
Managed by: Santa Fe National Forest,
    Española Ranger District
Features: spectacular summit views

The unmaintained trail to the summit of Deception Peak offers a chance to climb above tree line only a short distance from the Santa Fe Plaza. The weariness brought on by the steep grades of the trail easily melts away amid the grand scenery along the entire second half of the route. From the summit, all of northern New Mexico seems to flow around the base of the mountains. The higher summit of Lake Peak is less than a half mile away, and confident hikers who can safely scramble on loose rock can extend this trip to include the adjacent peak. In any case, hikers will want to linger on the ridgeline and drink up the sights. Be mindful of the weather—particularly in summer—and be prepared to hustle down from the summit if a storm is brewing.

From Santa Fe, take Washington Avenue north from Paseo de Peralta 0.1 mile to Artist Road, NM 475. Turn right and head toward the Santa Fe Ski Area. Continue about 14 miles to the parking area at the ski basin. Park at the Winsor Trailhead at the northwest corner of the lot near an information kiosk.

Begin hiking at the information kiosk for the Winsor Trail 254. In a few steps, cross a footbridge and turn right (north), following the sign that points toward Lake Katherine. Immediately begin climbing several switchbacks to reach a saddle at the Pecos Wilderness boundary about 0.75 mile from the start. The Winsor Trail continues straight ahead, but for this hike take the unmarked but easy-to-follow trail that heads right (east), parallel to a fence. This social (unofficial, well-trodden) trail follows the crest of Ravens Ridge through the conifer forest along the boundary of the Pecos Wilderness. After walking about 1.5 miles from the start, cross a meadow and come to a spectacular viewpoint looking down into the meadows below Nambe Lake and at the humpbacked summit of Santa Fe Baldy to the north. Backtrack a few yards from the viewpoint and pick one of several routes heading south and climbing steeply. Pass two rocky outcrops on the south flank of Ravens Ridge that make for a scenic snack stop.

The ridgeline soon narrows and the branches of the trail are squeezed together. A small boulder field confuses the route for a few yards: If you lose the trail, stay to the left of the boulders but don't descend from the ridgeline.

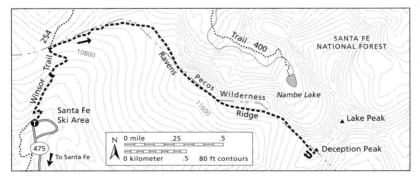

Mushrooms growing in the lush forests of the Sangre de Cristos

In a few minutes, gain a summit and follow the northern edge of the ridge-line to another rounded summit before dropping 100 feet and crossing a saddle. After the crest of Lake Peak comes into view through the trees, reach a third summit and drop across another saddle.

Climbing from the second saddle, suddenly break out above tree line. Angle up to the top of the ridge on a faint trail, then turn left to reach the summit of Deception Peak, which is about 0.2 mile to the north. The view from the summit stretches from Colorado to central New Mexico. The ridge-line connects to the north with the 200-foot-higher Lake Peak. Many hikers choose to enjoy the view from Deception rather than risk the rugged and exposed trail to the sister summit.

To return, retrace your steps or follow the ridgeline down in the direction of the electronics towers on Tesuque Peak to the south. A well-worn trail starts at the edge of the forest at tree line. A half mile of walking leads to the top of the Tesuque Lift at the Santa Fe Ski Basin. It's a knee-stressing descent under the lift to the old Sierra Lodge. From the lodge, pick up a service road to the right or the left to return to the trailhead.

7 | GLORIETA BALDY

Distance: 12 miles, day hike
Difficulty: strenuous
Elevation range: 7,800 to 10,199 feet
Elevation gain: 3,500 feet
Best time of year: late May to mid-October
Water: carry water
Maps: USGS McClure Reservoir and Glorieta
Managed by: Santa Fe National Forest, Pecos Ranger District
Features: outstanding views, solitude

Apache Canyon at the foot of Glorieta Baldy is a seemingly remote area just a few miles from Santa Fe. A series of old trails and logging roads create a nice loop through just the canyon, or the trip can be extended up steep ridges to the peak itself. While the Apache Canyon loop route is 6 miles and an ideal midwinter walk, the full trip up Glorieta Baldy is a strenuous climb for spring or fall. The summit view stretches from the level plains to the south to the heart of the Sangre de Cristo Mountains to the north. Note that none of these trails are shown accurately on the USGS 7.5-minute quadrangle map.

Reach the trailhead from Santa Fe by taking the Old Pecos Trail south to the Old Las Vegas Highway. Turn left and go 3 miles, then turn left onto CR 67C. At a T intersection in 1 mile, turn right onto CR 67. Immediately after the pavement ends in 2.2 miles, bear left onto CR 67A. Drive slowly through the

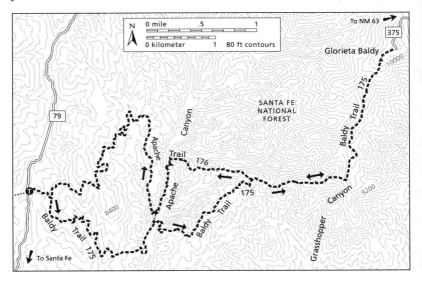

The rounded dome of Glorieta Baldy forms a portion of the eastern skyline from the Jemez Mountains across the Rio Grande.

village of Cañada de Los Alamos. Climb steeply out of a small valley, and at the top of the hill, cross a cattle guard and bear left. In 0.7 mile, enter Santa Fe National Forest and again bear left. Now on FR 79, continue 2.8 miles to a four-way intersection and park your vehicle.

Begin walking on the signed "Dead End Road" to the east. In 0.25 mile, pass around a gate, and in 100 yards, turn right onto the Baldy Trail 175. The trail follows a ridgeline, then dives off to the left (east). Several switchbacks lead to a double-track road. Turn left onto the logging road and continue eastward as it winds through a cluster of drainages and ridges, with the aptly named Shaggy Peak to the east. After almost 1 mile on the double-track, another sign points the way to the trail that leads steeply down into Apache Canyon.

Under the tall Douglas firs of the canyon bottom, turn left onto the trail heading upstream. Enjoy the running water and open meadows in the canyon for about a half mile. Just after the second stream crossing, near a tall, dead cottonwood, stay to the left side of the meadow to the junction with the Apache Trail 176. Bear right to continue on the Baldy Trail 175, which soon begins the rigorous ascent of the ridge between Apache and Grasshopper canyons on sharp-angled switchbacks. The grade eases once the trail reaches the top of the ridge, but the ridge itself is a steep ramp leading east. Views of Shaggy Peak to the right enliven this stretch of trail.

About 5 miles from the start, the trail is marked with two posts. At this point the trail swings left (north) onto the ridge that culminates in Glorieta Baldy. Enter a meadow where the trail disappears, following the signs to the forest on the other side where the trail is again easy to follow. Several more meadows follow in the last mile to the summit, all offering outstanding views. Reach the summit, with a lookout tower and accompanying road, about 6 miles from the start.

When it's time to return, retrace your steps down the ridges to the floor of Apache Canyon and the junction with the Apache Trail 176. Turn right and ascend steeply on the Apache Trail, traveling a ridgeline that offers fine views of Glorieta Baldy and Thompson Peak. After 1 mile on the ridge, intersect a graded road. Turn left and follow the winding road across drainages and ridges for 2.5 miles back to the trailhead.

8 | CAVE CREEK AND HORSETHIEF MEADOW

Distance: 5-mile day hike or 10-mile backpack
Difficulty: difficult
Elevation range: 8,400 to 10,150 feet
Elevation gain: 2,100 feet
Best time of year: late June to mid-October
Water: Panchuela, Cave, and Horsethief creeks
Maps: USGS Cowles and Truchas Peaks;
    USFS Pecos Wilderness
Managed by: Santa Fe National Forest,
    Pecos Wilderness, Pecos Ranger District
Features: stream flowing through a cliff,
    colorful meadows, fall aspen display

It's a curious twist on the old disappearing stream trick. At The Sinks in Wyoming, the Lost River in Idaho, and a score of other spots, visitors can watch a river suddenly disappear into the gravels of its bed. At Cave Creek in the Sangre de Cristo Mountains, the stream in question makes a detour into a cave to flow a hundred yards inside the bordering mountain, then trickles out into the sunlight again. Limestone is the key here, and water seeping into fractures in the rock gradually formed the surprisingly deep caves. Some of the stream water is perhaps diverted within the caves to travel a system of fissures and contribute flow to springs farther down the creek.

The short, easy stroll to the caves is suitable for all hikers, including families. Those wanting a longer hike can continue up Cave Creek and over a divide to enter Horsethief Meadow, an extensive grassland with plenty of campsites. A fault determines the trend of the picturesque valley, which reputedly served as a secluded hideaway for holding horses stolen from ranches on the plains to the east of the Sangre de Cristos.

Reach the trailhead by taking I-25 east from Santa Fe to the Glorieta/ Pecos exit 299. Turn left, pass over the interstate, then immediately turn right onto NM 50. Drive 6 miles to the village of Pecos. At a T intersection, turn left

The flow of Cave Creek disappears into two caves along the way to Horsethief Meadow.

Wild iris bloom in early summer in the high meadows of the Sangre de Cristos.

onto NM 63 and continue about 20 miles to the site of Cowles. Turn left (west) onto FR 121 and, just across the Pecos River, make a sharp right onto the single-lane FR 305, which leads in 1 mile to Panchuela Campground and the trailhead. A small day-use parking fee is required.

Begin walking at the west end of Panchuela Campground, heading upstream along Panchuela Creek on Trail 288. Cross a bridge and follow the trail as it continues a gentle climb along the slopes above the valley floor. Pass the intersection with the Dockwiller Trail 259. In 1.5 miles, the trail crosses Panchuela Creek and begins to follow the smaller Cave Creek. In about ten minutes, watch and listen carefully. When the sound of the stream suddenly quiets, look for the caves on the opposite side of the creek.

About half of Cave Creek's flow is diverted into the tunnels. The stream itself widened the fractures in the limestone wall, dissolving away the rock and creating dark passages. Enter the caves with caution due to the slippery rocks and the dark passage.

Hikers going only as far as the caves should turn around and return by the same route. To continue to Horsethief Meadow, resume the climb up Trail 288. The trail climbs high above the creek for the next mile. Bear slightly right at the junction with Trail 251 to continue on the trail now identified as Trail 251. About 4.3 miles from the start, the trail angles away from Cave Creek and begins to climb a side drainage on steep switchbacks. Almost at the divide, pass through a small meadow that is loaded with wildflowers in

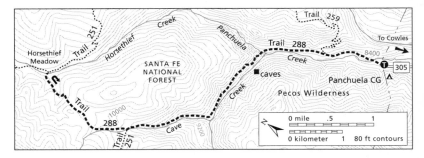

July. Once over the low saddle, drop quickly down into Horsethief Meadow, which stretches north and east. After enjoying the peaceful meadow, return by the same route.

9 | STEWART LAKE

Distance: 13-mile loop, day hike or backpack
Difficulty: strenuous
Elevation range: 8,200 to 10,300 feet
Elevation gain: 2,800 feet
Best time of year: mid-June to early October
Water: Stewart Lake
Maps: USGS Cowles; USFS Pecos Wilderness
Managed by: Santa Fe National Forest,
    Pecos Wilderness, Pecos Ranger District
Features: high lake, fishing, good base camp

The ramble to Stewart Lake is an exhilarating trip along canyons and ridges of the main crest of the Sangre de Cristo Mountains. The destination is a high lake held gingerly in the cupped hands of the surrounding forest. The trail leading to this picturesque spot offers one of the gentlest climbs to a glacial lake in the range. The emerald green pool of Stewart Lake invites a

Violet wood sorrel

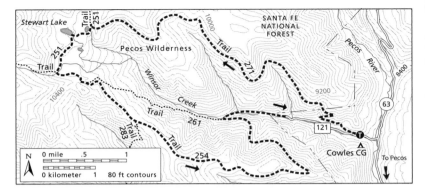

quiet respite, and the local trout may tempt hikers into a bit of angling, so take a fishing pole. The timber stands surrounding the lake provide many inviting campsites and make this an excellent base camp for exploring the surrounding high country.

The trailhead is located near Cowles Campground. From Santa Fe, take I-25 east to the Glorieta/Pecos exit 299. Turn left, pass over the interstate, then immediately turn right onto NM 50. Drive 6 miles to the village of Pecos. At a T intersection, turn left onto NM 63 and continue about 20 miles to the site of Cowles. Turn left (west) onto FR 121 and in a few yards park at the Cowles Campground.

Look for a sign on the north side of the road pointing to Trail 271. Begin walking on the trail, then in a few yards turn left, away from Cowles Campground, and begin climbing on the flanks of a long ridge. A series of switchbacks ease the steady grade as the trail continues to travel high above Winsor Creek through conifer stands and aspen groves. Around 3.5 miles from the start, cross over a saddle and enjoy views to the south and west. At mile 4.6, drop down a hill to intersect Trail 251. Bear left and complete the trip to the lake in 0.5 mile.

Enjoy the lake, then continue south on Trail 251 for 0.5 mile to the intersection with Trail 254. Turn left and follow Trail 254 as it descends a long ridge. At mile 5.6, pass the junction with Trail 261 on the left. Continue down the ridge on Trail 254. Near mile 7, the trail enters a meadow and is joined by Trail 283 from the south. On a faint trail, swing around the left side of the meadow and stay on the ridgeline trail (don't drop into the head of Holy Ghost Canyon). After reentering the forest, the trail is again easy to follow as it continues the descent.

About 2.5 miles past Trail 283, watch carefully for a poorly marked, sharp left turn. Drop on the north slope of the ridge to mile 11 and the intersection with Trail 261 near the bottom of Winsor Canyon. Turn right and walk 1 mile to the end of the trail, then walk FR 121 another mile back to the trailhead.

10   Beattys and Mora Flats

Distance: 12.5 miles, day hike or backpack
Difficulty: strenuous
Elevation range: 9,250 to 10,400 feet
Elevation gain: 3,000 feet
Best time of year: late May through late October
Water: Pecos River, Rio Valdez, Rio Mora
Maps: USGS Elk Mountain and Pecos Falls; USFS Pecos
    Wilderness
Managed by: Santa Fe National Forest,
    Pecos Wilderness, Pecos Ranger District
Features: huge wildflower-studded meadow,
    trout fishing, easy access to camping spots

The high meadows of the Pecos Wilderness make for scenic midsummer walks with few peers. Either Beattys Flats or Mora Flats make worthy destinations; better yet, combine the two into a multiday trip into the heart of the wilderness. The journey takes hikers through long grasslands painted with extraordinary wildflowers and leads to the Pecos River and smaller streams where hungry trout willingly sip flies on the fast currents.

The extensive open area along the Pecos River is named Beattys Flat in honor of a former resident who built a cabin in the meadow in the early part of the twentieth century. An account of the way things used to be is colorfully told in the long-out-of-print *Beatty's Cabin* by Elliott Barker. Look for a copy of this gem before heading out on the hike. Mora Flats is a huge valley split by several picturesque mountain streams. The direct route from Iron Gate to Mora Flats makes an easy destination for an 8-mile round-trip overnight into the Pecos Wilderness and is suitable for beginning backpackers or families. The grades are gentle, the views spectacular, the fishing excellent, and the camp spots plentiful in the flats. Hikers must camp at least 200 feet from all streams.

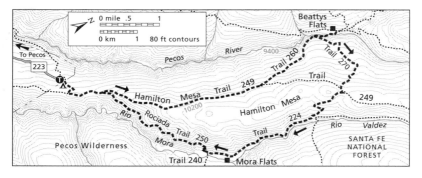

The Hamilton Mesa Trail on the way to Beattys Flats

To reach the trailhead from Santa Fe, take I-25 east to the Glorieta/Pecos exit 299. Turn left, pass over the interstate, then turn right to travel on NM 50 for 6 miles to a T intersection with NM 63 in Pecos. Turn left and continue about 18 miles to FR 223. Bear right onto this bumpy road that requires a high-clearance vehicle or a carefully driven car. In 4.3 miles, park at the trailhead at Iron Gate Campground. A small parking fee is required.

Head through the gate at the trailhead and begin a gentle climb on the Hamilton Mesa Trail 249. A single switchback takes you up to the ridgeline where the trail swings left. Enjoy viewpoints into the canyon of the Rio Mora as you continue along the rocky ridge and through an aspen stand. In 0.7 mile, bear left to stay on the Hamilton Mesa Trail and begin a moderate climb that stays on the east side of the ridgeline except for a brief stretch along the forested summit. Another few minutes under tall Douglas firs will bring you to a gate and into a huge meadow where wild iris, sunflowers, and dozens of other wildflowers bloom. Continue across the meadow for a few minutes. Close to the top of the ascent, near a stand of aspen, ignore a social trail right and bear left.

The next mile is among the prettiest stretches of trail in all of New Mexico. The huge open meadow offers never-ending views of the surrounding high peaks of the Sangre de Cristos. Finding twenty-five species of wildflowers—including star-eyed grass, three types of wild onion, tall sunflowers, and the uncommon orange skyflower—wouldn't be unusual in midsummer. Pass through several wooded patches before reaching a trail junction at mile 3.5. The trail straight ahead (Trail 249) goes to Pecos Falls; to go to Beattys Flat, take the left fork, Trail 260. Descend into the forest as the trail begins the drop to the Pecos River through steep pitches and level aspen stands. After another mile, with the river in earshot, bear left at the junction with Trail 270, pass through a gate, and drop the final half mile to Beattys Flats.

Cross the Pecos River on a stout bridge and enter the flat. Explore upstream to the limestone cliffs at the confluence with the Rito del Padre, or spend some time fishing for brown trout. No camping is permitted in the flat, but ample sites can be found upstream.

After spending time at Beattys, head over to Mora Flats. Recross the bridge over the Pecos River and retrace your steps up Trail 260 for a few hundred feet. At the junction with Trail 270, turn left (east) and climb over Hamilton Mesa, passing Trail 249. Two miles from the Pecos River, meet the Rio Valdez Trail 224, bear right and travel 2 miles downstream to Mora Flats. Bear right onto the Rociada Trail 250.

After enjoying the Mora Flats area, continue on Trail 250. The trail parallels the Rio Mora to the junction with Trail 240. Stay right as the trail begins to climb out of the canyon. Ascend a series of switchbacks to gain a long, winding ridge above the Rio Mora, passing through open stands of aspen along the way. In early summer, the ridge is covered with large, yellow false pine lupines, wild iris, Richardson's geranium, wild strawberries, and more—as many as fifty wildflower species may be found in bloom. It's a steady climb of 2.5 miles to reach the junction with Trail 249. Bear left and continue less than a mile to reach the trailhead.

11   PECOS BALDY LAKE

Distance: 12.5 miles, backpack
Difficulty: strenuous
Elevation range: 8,850 to 11,400 feet
Elevation gain: 2,800 feet
Best time of year: mid-June to early October
Water: Jacks Creek, Pecos Baldy Lake
Maps: USGS Cowles and Truchas Peak;
    USFS Pecos Wilderness
Managed by: Santa Fe National Forest,
    Pecos Wilderness, Pecos Ranger District
Features: views of highest peaks in the southern
    Sangre de Cristo range

Late summer is the ideal time to enjoy a glorious trip to one of New Mexico's premier alpine areas, the high country surrounding Pecos Baldy Lake. The long, strenuous trip to the lake puts hikers at the foot of the humpbacked Pecos Baldy Peak. In July and August the trail is lined with wildflowers, and in September golden aspens are on stage. Bighorn sheep frequent this area, too, but the lake and the surrounding mountain scenery are the highlights of this trip. Be prepared to share the trail with plenty of other hikers. Also, be sure to watch the weather and be ready to seek shelter during sudden thunderstorms in this exposed terrain.

Reach the trailhead by taking I-25 east from Santa Fe about 15 miles to exit 299 at Glorieta/Pecos. Turn left, cross the overpass, then turn right onto NM 50.

Pikas are common on the talus of the highest peaks of the Sangre de Cristos.

In 6 miles, turn left onto NM 63 and drive 20 miles to Cowles. Continue straight on NM 63 for 3 miles to parking for the Pecos Wilderness Area near Jacks Creek Campground. A small fee is charged for the parking area.

Trail 257, the route to the lake, begins at the north end of the parking area. The first mile gains 700 feet of elevation, so be prepared for an early workout. After steep switchbacks, the grade eases a bit along a ridgeline. At mile 2.6, at the junction with Trail 25, take the left fork and pass through grasslands and aspen stands on the west flank of Round Mountain. Follow posts north across the meadow. The views north along this stretch are superb.

At the end of the meadow, Trail 257 again enters conifer forest and makes a gentle drop to Jacks Creek. Hop across the stream and head up the canyon for about 0.25 mile before the trail swings away from the creek. At mile 4.5, Trail 259 angles right toward Beattys Flats. Take the left fork to stay on Trail 257. Resume the steep climb through shady forest and enjoy peeks of East Pecos Baldy around mile 6. One last steep section brings hikers within view of Pecos Baldy Lake. It's a short drop to the lakeshore, but camping is not permitted in the lake basin. Look for campsites in the trees to the north of the lake.

From the lake, consider climbing the 12,528-foot East Pecos Baldy. Take Trail 251 southwest from the lake. The trail climbs steeply up the south flank of the mountain before intersecting Trail 275. This route angles right from the main trail and makes quick work of the remaining 700 feet to the summit.

When it's time to head back, return to the trailhead by the same route.

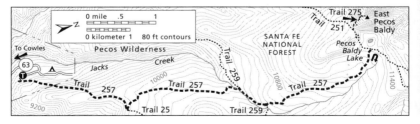

Opposite: *The canyon of the Red River near its confluence with the Rio Grande*

NORTHERN SANGRE DE CRISTO MOUNTAINS

12 | TRAMPAS LAKES

Distance: 10 miles, day hike or backpack
Difficulty: difficult
Elevation range: 9,100 to 11,400 feet
Elevation gain: 2,600 feet
Best time of year: mid-June to early October
Water: Rio de las Trampas
Maps: USGS El Valle and Truchas Peak
Managed by: Carson National Forest,
    Pecos Wilderness, Camino Real Ranger District
Features: picturesque canyon, high lakes

As it climbs 5 miles up the canyon of the Rio de las Trampas, the Trampas Lake Trail 31 stays within shouting distance of the cascading stream. The well-worn trail provides a long but reasonably gentle route to the lakes, which are nestled in a rock-lined bowl between Jicarilla and the Truchas peaks. Around the lakes, the entire horseshoe ridgeline stands above 12,400 feet. As late as 12,000 years ago, the high peaks of the Pecos Wilderness supported small glaciers and the upper canyon of the Rio de las Trampas exhibits the distinctive U shape of glacial valleys. The small stream—the "River of the Traps" in Spanish—takes its name from the days of the mountain men who came from Taos to trap beaver in the canyon. It is likely that Kit Carson trapped this stream early in his Western career.

    Reach the trailhead from Santa Fe by taking US 84/285 north to Española. When US 84/285 turns left, continue straight on NM 68 north. In 14 miles, turn right at the intersection with NM 75 near the town of Dixon. In another 14 miles, turn right onto NM 76. Continue 4.4 miles through the village of Chamisal and turn left onto FR 207 (before reaching the village of Trampas). Drive through El Valle to the end of FR 207, about 9 miles, and park at the primitive campground.

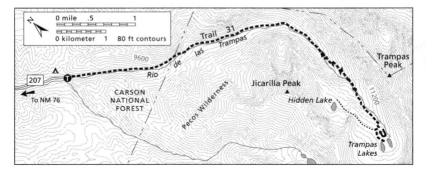

A streamside trail in the Sangre de Cristo Mountains

From the small campground at the trailhead, look for a trail sign on the left near the only structure in camp. Immediately head uphill and begin the steady ascent. In a few minutes, pass through a gate and continue climbing on the heavily forested slope above the canyon floor. This stretch is particularly lovely in July when the wildflowers are at their peak. Enter the Pecos Wilderness after 1 mile, then enjoy expanding views as the trail passes impressive piles of talus. Near mile 2.5, cross the stream on a log bridge and continue about 0.25 mile before another log leads back to the east bank.

Near an open hillside, hikers may have to negotiate a few downed trees within a huge blowdown before again finding a clear path. Pass a prominent avalanche chute on your right before the grade increases. Broad switchbacks help make the climb a bit easier on this last 1.5 miles of trail.

After making another stream crossing, enter a sloping meadow where the trail is often muddy. Near mile 5, a spur trail to Hidden Lake goes right. Bear left on the now faint main trail and follow the small outflow stream to the lakes.

Explore around the basin and enjoy the view from both lakes, then head downhill and return to the trailhead by the same route.

13 | SOUTH BOUNDARY TRAIL

Distance: 11 miles one-way, day hike or backpack
Difficulty: moderate
Elevation range: 7,250 to 10,250 feet
Elevation gain: 500 feet; 3,300-foot descent
Best time of year: late May to late October
Water: American Spring
Maps: USGS Shady Brook and Ranchos de Taos
Managed by: Carson National Forest,
 Camino Real Ranger District
Features: historic trail, views of Wheeler Peak
 Wilderness, quiet, solitude

The South Boundary Trail—so named because it runs parallel to the dividing line between the former Taos and Rio Grande del Rancho land grants—travels the length of the Fernando Mountains. The trail was blazed by ranchers in the early 1800s as a route to drive sheep from Taos to grazing areas in the high country. Traversing the north side of the ridge, the route is a long, shady walk through deep Douglas fir and spruce forest. The first 8 miles of the hike descend gently; the last 3 miles are very steep.

To do this hike as a one-way descent, set up a shuttle by leaving a vehicle at the El Nogal Picnic Area, 3 miles east of Taos on US 64. Continue east on US 64 for 10 miles beyond the picnic area and turn right onto FR 437. In 0.4 mile, stay on FR 437 by turning right, heading for Garcia Park. Climb steadily on this rough but easily passable road. At mile 6.7, Trail 164 joins the road. Continue on the road another 0.3 mile to Garcia Park where the trail splits off the road to the right at a trailhead signboard.

From FR 437, walk west through the open meadow of Garcia Park, climbing a small drainage. Meet a wide dirt track coming in from the right before intersecting an old forest road at mile 1. Turn left on the road (now identified as Trail 164) and continue through open stands of aspen, spruce, and fir. At mile 1.5, begin a gentle climb to skirt around Sierra de don Fernando, passing great views of the Wheeler Peak Wilderness to the right. At mile 2, begin descending around the northwest base of Sierra de don Fernando. At the bottom of the descent, at mile 2.6, angle left on a trail that crosses a small

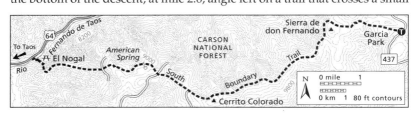

Meadows and aspen stands border the South Boundary Trail.

meadow, using rock cairns and trail markers as a guide. After descending from the top of a small knoll, the trail bears right at a large cairn.

Descending through a closed forest, the trail joins an abandoned road. At mile 3.1, bear left. From here the route is often marked with large rock cairns. At a fence in a few hundred yards, bear right off the old road and onto a trail. Begin a long, wonderful, ever-so-gently descending stroll through thick conifer forest, stands of aspen, and oak scrub.

At mile 5.7, enter a large meadow at the base of Cerrito Colorado, where several scenic campsites are located. At mile 7.2, the trail crosses to the south side of the ridge. Just beyond a small saddle, intersect a road angling back sharply to the left. Bear right as the trail follows the road, passing through drier oak-scrub woodland, then cross away from the road to the north side of the ridgeline. At mile 8.5, walk through a four-way intersection and continue straight on the main trail. Soon pass American (Bear) Spring. Beyond the spring, bear right as a trail enters from the left and continue straight.

At mile 9, a sign indicates that the trail goes right, but continue straight ahead on the road. In 0.2 mile, continue straight at a four-way intersection. From this point, the trail descends steeply on a rocky surface through open woods. At mile 10.4, reach a small saddle on the ridgeline. The trail drops to the south side of the ridge and becomes very steep. Turn through many switchbacks descending the north flank of the ridge. At mile 11, reach another trail junction, continue straight, and then make a sharp left. Cross the bridge over the Rio Fernando de Taos and enter the El Nogal Picnic Area.

14 | Cebolla Mesa/Big Arsenic Trails

Distance: 7.4 miles, day hike or backpack
Difficulty: moderate
Elevation range: 6,590 to 7,370 feet
Elevation gain: 1,300 feet
Best time of year: March to November
Water: Red River, Little and Big Arsenic springs
Map: USGS Guadalupe Mountain
Managed by: Carson National Forest,
　　Questa Ranger District; Bureau of Land Management,
　　Rio Grande Wild and Scenic River, Taos Field Office
Features: deep rugged canyon, large river, fishing

The Rio Grande has carved a gorge 60 miles long and up to 1,000 feet deep through the thick sheets of lava that emanated from the volcanoes of the Taos Plateau. The river within the gorge remains wild and free-flowing, fed by snowmelt in Colorado's San Juan Mountains and by thousands of springs

The Cebolla Mesa Trail drops 800 feet to the Rio Grande in the first mile.

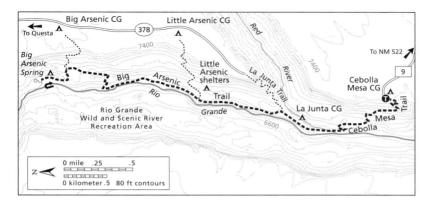

within the gorge itself. The basalt walls are steep, and house-sized boulders have tumbled from them to line the river or break the current as in-stream rocks. The polished rocks at streamside are slick, and the water off the banks is often ten feet deep. Ducks, mergansers, geese, and bald eagles are frequent sights along the river.

Several trails enter the gorge from the Bureau of Land Management's Rio Grande Wild and Scenic River Recreation Area north and west of Questa, but entering the gorge via Cebolla Mesa requires less driving from Taos. The well-maintained Cebolla Mesa Trail leads to the confluence of the Red River and the Rio Grande and some of the best fishing in the state. Plenty of campsites are available within the gorge; particularly attractive are the shelters and firepits at La Junta, Little Arsenic, and Big Arsenic primitive campgrounds.

To reach the trailhead from Taos, head north on US 64 about 4 miles to the junction with NM 522. Continue straight on NM 522 for about 16 miles to FR 9. Turn left onto this rutted dirt road, which, when dry, is passable to all vehicles. Drive the length of FR 9, bearing left at an intersection 1 mile from the highway, and arrive at the Cebolla Mesa Campground in 3.5 miles. The trailhead is clearly marked in the campground.

The Cebolla Mesa Trail 102 quickly drops from the rim on a series of steep switchbacks, passing through mixed vegetation that includes everything from yuccas to Douglas fir. Views of the river and the gorge are spectacular on the entire 1-mile descent. At the Rio Grande, a footbridge crosses the Red River into La Junta Campground; if the bridge is washed out or damaged, during low flows it is possible to wade across the shallow current. Across the bridge, take the left fork and wander through a maze of trails through the shelters, and then climb a low ridge that separates the two rivers.

Heading north, the trail stays on the low divide, offering views up the canyon of the Red River. In 0.3 mile from the bridge, the La Junta Trail branches right to climb to the rim. Bear left and immediately drop to the Rio Grande. Continue upcanyon, at times climbing to the bench above the river to avoid large rockfalls. Pass the Little Arsenic shelters, the Little Arsenic Trail leading to the rim, and 0.25 mile beyond the shelters, the spring just to the right of the trail.

At mile 3.5, the trail ascends steeply to avoid a massive rockfall that stretches to the river. From the bench above the river, the climb continues over a low mound of boulders. Just beyond, pass the trail descending from Big Arsenic Campground on the rim. Before the next descent back to river level, more shelters are visible on the flat below. Again along the river, enjoy the shade of the trees and shelters at Big Arsenic. The springs are on the opposite side of the flat. Return to the trailhead by the same route.

15 LOBO PEAK

Distance: 11 miles, day hike or backpack
Difficulty: strenuous
Elevation range: 8,400 to 12,115 feet
Elevation gain: 3,800 feet
Best time of year: late June to October
Water: Manzanita and Italianos creeks
Maps: USGS Arroyo Seco and Wheeler Peak
Managed by: Carson National Forest, Columbine-Hondo
    Wilderness Study Area, Questa Ranger District
Features: challenging climb, cool and shady trail,
    unique views

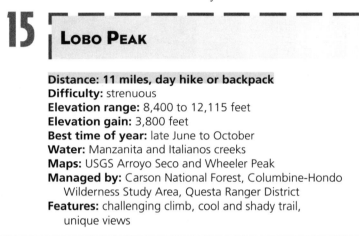
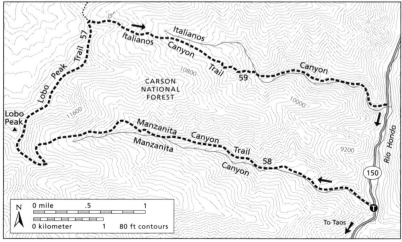

The top of Lobo Peak offers a 360-degree view.

At 12,115 feet, Lobo Peak is the highest point in the small range of mountains that lies between the Rio Hondo and the Red River. The mountains rise abruptly from the bordering canyons, forcing the trail to Lobo Peak to gain almost 4,000 feet in 4.5 miles. Lobo Peak's isolation from other high points makes the views from the top unique, taking in the Taos Plateau and Rio Grande Gorge to the west, the Latir Peaks to the north, and the Wheeler Peak area to the south.

From Taos city center, go north and west on US 64 for 4 miles to the junction with NM 150. Turn right, following the signs for Taos Ski Valley. Continue about 12 miles from US 64 (2 miles from Upper Cuchilla Campground) and park at the trailhead for the Manzanita Trail.

Start up the Manzanita Canyon Trail 58, which begins on a dirt road. Pass through a gate, then bear left to parallel the creek in Manzanita Canyon. At mile 0.8, where water from a spring drains along the route, the road becomes a true trail. In a few minutes, make the first of many crossings of the creek over the next 0.5 mile.

At mile 1.5, climb two switchbacks and parallel the stream higher on the slope. For the next mile, the grade steepens as the trail becomes almost like a staircase in places. At mile 2.6, the trail bends left to cross a dry drainage, then resumes the steep climb. Cross the base of a small talus slope, and then enter a clearing offering views of the ridge to the east. Reach another clearing at mile 3.7, this one offering views of the high ridgeline to the north. At an unmarked intersection, bear left, then begin walking a series of switchbacks to the top of a narrow ridge. Turn right with the ridgeline and enter a small meadow with great views in all directions. Continue along the ridge, watching carefully for the trail when it crosses open areas. At the junction with Lobo Peak Trail 57 at mile 4.5, go straight to reach the summit of Lobo Peak.

After enjoying the view from the summit, return to the junction of the Lobo Peak and Manzanita Canyon trails. Turn left (northeast) onto the Lobo Peak Trail, following a ridgeline in the direction of Gold Hill. At mile 5.5, skirt the base of a rocky crag before the trail becomes faint as it passes to the left of a small peak. The trail then drops steeply to a saddle.

At the saddle, turn right onto the Italianos Canyon Trail 59. Several quick switchbacks lead to a nice campsite near a small spring. Look carefully for the trail as it leaves the marshy area and climbs the toe of a small ridge. At mile 6.6, reach a meadow where the trail disappears, though a rock cairn visible on the other side of the clearing marks the route. Continue to drop through small meadows and open conifer forest, passing plenty of fine campsites along the way. After a brief flat stretch, descend through switchbacks at mile 8.1 to cross the main stream in Italianos Canyon. The trail remains wet for the next mile, crossing the stream many times. More campsites can be found between miles 9 and 10. At mile 10, exit the canyon and reach NM 150. Turn right and walk 1 mile to the Manzanita Trailhead.

16 | WILLIAMS LAKE

Distance: 4 miles, day hike
Difficulty: moderate
Elevation range: 10,190 to 11,150 feet
Elevation gain: 1,000 feet
Best time of year: mid-June to mid-October
Water: carry water
Map: USGS Wheeler Peak
Managed by: Carson National Forest,
   Wheeler Peak Wilderness, Questa Ranger District
Features: views of alpine lake and rugged peaks

Despite the state's relatively southern latitude, New Mexico's highest terrain was covered by glaciers until about 10,000 years ago. Hikers basking in the refreshing air of the alpine world surrounding the shores of Williams Lake will find it easy to picture the thousand-foot-thick sheet of snow and ice that filled the valley. The lake itself lies in a deep cirque completely surrounded by a jagged ring of peaks. Although the summit is not visible from the lake, Wheeler Peak—the state's highest point—forms the eastern rim of the cirque.

The 900-foot climb to Williams Lake over a gentle pass at 11,150 feet doesn't require a lot of huffing and puffing. The Williams Lake Trail is a popular midsummer stroll that is routinely accomplished by hikers from ages four to eighty.

In some ways, hiking to Williams Lake is easier than finding the trailhead. From Taos, take US 64 north about 4 miles to the intersection with NM 150. Turn right and drive toward Taos Ski Valley. Fifteen miles from US 64, drive to the very eastern end of the parking area for the ski area. Swing to the left and look for the sign for Twining Road. Turn right onto the unpaved road and continue 0.5 mile. Turn left onto Phoenix Switchback Road, then make a sharp right onto Kachina Road in another 0.3 mile. Climb along this main road another 1.3 miles to the hikers parking area at Deer Road.

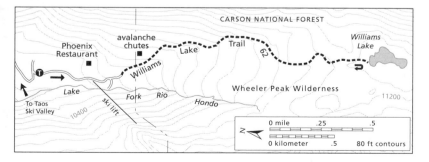

Looking across Williams Lake toward Wheeler Peak

Beyond the trailhead information board, follow the wide road heading south from the parking area downhill and past a small pond on the left. At the base of a ski lift and near the Phoenix Restaurant, continue uphill on the road, following a sign pointing to Williams Lake. In a few minutes, another sign for the lake points left. At about mile 0.4, a third sign again points left. Finally, at mile 0.7, bear right to leave the road and begin walking on Trail 62.

Walk along the edge of the forest past three impressive avalanche chutes where snapped-off trees tell the tale of recent slides. The climb is gentle but steady as the trail enters the moist spruce-fir forest where snow can linger into July. Pass through two boulder piles pushed downcanyon by the glaciers. Alpine wildflowers such as yellow Indian paintbrush, towering polemonium, and king's crown bloom along the trail. At mile 1.8, crest a low pass and suddenly find Williams Lake at the bottom of a huge bowl of rock. Drop to the lake and enjoy the grassy meadows on the south and west edges. After resting, return to the trailhead by the same route.

17 | GOLD HILL

Distance: 10 miles, day hike or backpack
Difficulty: strenuous
Elevation range: 9,430 to 12,711 feet
Elevation gain: 3,300 feet
Best time of year: late June to October
Water: Long Canyon
Maps: USGS Red River and Wheeler Peak
Managed by: Carson National Forest, Columbine-Hondo
     Wilderness Study Area, Questa Ranger District
Features: well-graded climb, cool shady trail, superb views

At 12,711 feet, Gold Hill qualifies more as a mountain than a hill, and hikers won't find any precious metal on the summit. And although Gold Hill doesn't quite make it on the list of the state's ten highest named peaks, the view from the summit rivals that of nearby Wheeler Peak. The routes to these two high points share the first 2 miles, but at Bull-of-the-Woods Pasture most hikers head right to Wheeler, leaving the left-hand trail to Gold Hill delightfully devoid of people.

The trailhead is located in the upper parking area at Taos Ski Valley. From the center of Taos travel north on US 64. At a traffic signal in 4 miles, turn right onto NM 150. Follow this winding road about 15 miles and reach the parking area at Taos Ski Valley. Bear right and continue about 0.3 mile past the parking lots to the upper parking area.

Look for the Wheeler Peak Trail 90 heading uphill from behind the wilderness information board. The track crosses a road and begins its steep ascent. In the first mile, ignore the winding trail marked for horses and stay on the steeper, wider hiking route. With the Rio Hondo to the right, ascend this steepest portion of the entire hike under a forest canopy.

One mile from the start, the Long Canyon Trail 63—the return route for this trip—heads left. A few yards beyond the intersection, Trail 90 swings left and begins another steep section. Continue straight and uphill and the trail joins an old mining road coming in from the right. The route swings south to again parallel the Rio Hondo, passing through narrow meadows with occasional views down the slope to the ski basin. Much of this section is unshaded, but the trail passes stands of aspen and summer wildflowers, particularly the chartreuse fireweed.

As you approach Bull-of-the-Woods Pasture 1.9 miles from the start, the route splits from Trail 90, which heads to the right. Bear left and in a few yards (before you reach the edge of the soggy pasture) turn left again onto the Gold Hill Trail 64. Begin the moderate, miles-long ascent of the end of the long ridge of which Gold Hill is the summit.

In the course of the next mile, the trail alternates between open meadows and stands of fir, climbing gradually up the quartzite-studded ridge. At mile 4.2, reach timberline and the tundra-clad ridge leading to Gold Hill. Follow the trail through the meadow to the ruins of a cabin near a small mine, where the view of Wheeler Peak is superb.

To continue on the now-faint trail, walk a few yards west, back toward the trees, looking for a sign marking the beginning of the Long Canyon Trail 63. A faint track in tall grasses leads to the sign. Once at the signpost, turn right and take the again easy-to-follow Gold Hill Trail 64 up to the ridge. Hikers who miss the route should simply follow the grassy ridgeline heading north.

Passing through scattered bristlecone pines, the trail gains the ridge. Again, the official trail fades, so head to the left of a false summit straight

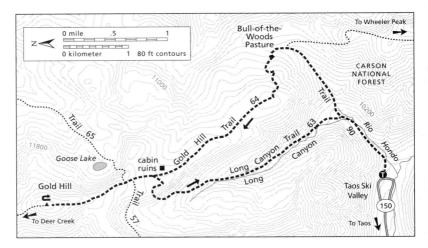

An old mining cabin on the way to Gold Hill boasts an outstanding view of Wheeler Peak.

ahead. The trail comes back into view near the junction with the Lobo Peak Trail 57 and skirts left of the false summit. Along the final half mile, the views to the west are especially grand. Goose Lake lies straight down to the right (east) of the ridge. Watch the ground, too, for signs of bighorn sheep.

A small rock shelter marks the summit and provides protection from the almost constant wind. The view of the rest of the world that stretches from the top reaches into Colorado to the summits of Conejos and Blanca peaks.

When it's time to leave, head back down the ridge to the sign "Columbine-Twining National Recreation Trail," for the Long Canyon Trail 63 located a few hundred feet west of the cabin ruins. The route is easy to follow downhill through grasses surrounded by stands of conifers. As the trail reaches the edge of the Long Canyon, it bears right, enters the forest, and curls toward the canyon's head. After a few minutes of walking across the steep eastern wall of the gorge, reach the canyon floor. Swing left to follow the canyon downhill, ignoring the track that continues straight and goes uphill.

It's a straight shot from here, following Long Canyon for 2 miles. The descent is often steep. The trail stays on the east side of the canyon floor and picks up a stream about halfway down. Springs along the way enliven the spruce-fir forest with splashes of color from wildflowers. Intersect Trail 90, turn right, and drop down, retracing your steps over the last mile back to the parking area.

18 WHEELER PEAK

Distance: 14 miles, day hike or backpack
Difficulty: strenuous
Elevation range: 9,430 to 13,161 feet
Elevation gain: 3,700 feet
Best time of year: late June to early October
Water: Middle Fork of the Red River
Maps: USGS Wheeler Peak; USFS Latir and
Wheeler Peak Wilderness
Managed by: Carson National Forest,
Wheeler Peak Wilderness, Questa Ranger District
Features: long walk above tree line, spectacular views

As the highest point in New Mexico, 13,161-foot Wheeler Peak is a popular destination for hikers. A well-worn trail with moderate grades leads to the summit, passing through the state's most extensive area of alpine vegetation. Eye-popping views extend in all directions from the long ridge leading to the peak; a small herd of bighorn sheep and the rare chance to see white-tailed ptarmigan add to the attractions.

A safe hike to Wheeler Peak requires a good deal of common sense. High elevation makes sunscreen mandatory on this trip, even on cloudy days. Snow remains on the upper trail into early or even late July, when the

Bull-of-the-Woods Pasture fills a broad saddle at the end of the ridge that culminates in Wheeler Peak.

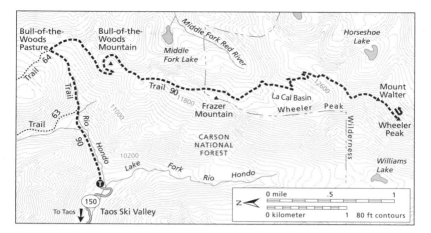

summer thunderstorm season makes it dangerous to be on the ridge. Start your hike early to get off the peak by noon. September is the best time to make the climb, but hikers should know the weather forecast before starting the trip; intense snowstorms can hit the mountains any time after late August. The trip to Wheeler Peak is a long one, and hikers should allow ten to twelve hours for the round-trip to the summit.

From Taos, go north and west on US 64 about 4 miles to the junction with NM 150. Turn right, following the signs for Taos Ski Valley. Continue about 15 miles and park in the upper gravel lot at Taos Ski Valley near a wilderness information board.

From the trailhead, follow the signs for Wheeler Peak Trail 90 and begin hiking northeast along the headwaters of the Rio Hondo. Follow the wide hiking route and ignore the winding horse trail. Intersect Long Canyon Trail 63 at mile 1, and stay on Trail 90 by following an old road along the north slope of the canyon, with views back to the ski area. At mile 1.9, reach Bull-of-the-Woods Pasture and the intersection with the Gold Hill Trail 64. Follow the road to the right, staying on Trail 90 and skirting the west side of Bull-of-the-Woods Mountain. The road climbs to the ridgeline and, at mile 2.9, meets an easy-to-follow trail leading up the ridge.

The trail, now above tree line, continues along the ridge, passing the summit of Frazer Mountain at mile 4.1. Descend into the headwaters of the middle fork of the Red River, which offers limited campsites and water at mile 5. The trail resumes the climb, passing the La Cal Basin. Another steep mile in thin air leads to the ridgeline. At mile 6.8, reach the summit of Mount Walter. Descend briefly to a saddle, then climb the final 0.25 mile to the summit of Wheeler Peak, where Trail 91 continues along the ridgeline before descending to Horseshoe Lake.

While keeping an eye on the weather, enjoy the view, which takes in the highest peaks of the Sangre de Cristos as well as parts of the Rio Grande Gorge. Return to the trailhead by the same route.

19

COLUMBINE CANYON TO HONDO CANYON

Distance: 12 miles one-way, day hike or backpack; optional 8-mile out-and-back hike
Difficulty: strenuous; easy for out-and-back trip
Elevation range: 7,950 to 12,711 feet
Elevation gain: 4,800 feet
Best time of year: mid-June to mid-October
Water: Columbine Creek, Placer Fork, Long Canyon
Maps: USGS Questa and Arroyo Seco; USFS Latir and Wheeler Peak Wilderness
Managed by: Carson National Forest, Columbine-Hondo Wilderness Study Area, Questa Ranger District
Features: old mining operations, quiet canyon with running water, alpine scenery

More than a century ago, miners blasted tunnels in the walls of Columbine Canyon, and the slopes bear the scars of the search for treasure. Throughout the Sangre de Cristo range around Red River, miners combed the canyons for silver and gold deposits. A few found gold in the gravels of Columbine Creek, and the lure of yellow metal still attracts prospectors to the stream. Although hikers can take a gold pan and try their luck, they are more likely to find a bonanza in the form of abundant wildflowers, luscious wild strawberries, or bronze native trout.

Hikers can take either of two approaches to a trip up Columbine Canyon. For a leisurely, round-trip summer stroll, head 3 or 4 miles up the canyon and enjoy its forest and meadows. For a challenging overnight hike, consider the staircase climb over the main ridge and down into the canyon of the Rio

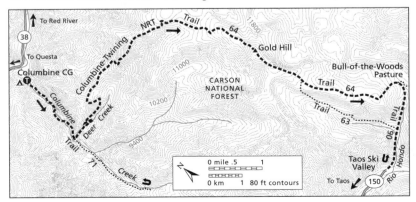

The trail toward upper Columbine Canyon passes through several meadows.

Hondo. This route, the Columbine-Twining National Recreation Trail, makes a relentless climb over the crest of the range, traversing an old miners trail that connected the camps at Columbine with the ones at Twining, known now as Taos Ski Valley.

For the 12-mile ridge hike, set up a shuttle from Taos by following the directions to the trailhead in the Taos Ski Valley as described in the Gold Hill Hike 17. Leave one vehicle, and in the other return to the traffic signal at the intersection of US 64, NM 150, and NM 522. Turn right onto NM 522 north and continue 20 miles to Questa. Turn right onto NM 38 and find Columbine Campground in 5 miles on the right.

Begin hiking in Columbine Campground at the signs for the Columbine-Twining National Recreation Trail. The route leads up the canyon bottom along Columbine Creek, which is graced with clear water dancing over a bed of pastel gravel. Along the trail are stately aspens too big for anyone to wrap their arms around. The path frequently swings along the base of talus fields piled against ragged cliffs. Both local species of columbine—the blazing little red and the exquisite blue Colorado—grow along the trail, but in July the sheer numbers of mountain parsley and wild geranium steal the show. Finding more than fifty species in bloom along the trail is not unusual. Wild strawberries are ripe in late July.

Cross three arching bridges before reaching the confluence with Deer Creek at mile 1.5. Hikers taking the easy route should continue up Columbine Canyon on Trail 71, in the direction of Lobo Peak. Just beyond a fourth bridge, a rocky meadow offers views to the ridgeline to the south and makes a good lunch stop or turnaround point.

To continue on the Columbine-Twining National Recreation Trail, turn left at mile 1.5 and head east up Deer Creek, following signs for Gold Hill. The trail continues along the canyon bottom for a half mile before starting a steep ascent through ponderosa pine forest. The trail is narrow and on a steep slope, so use caution while climbing the switchbacks. After gaining 1,500 feet, reach the ridgeline at mile 3.5. Another 2 miles of steady climbing through conifer forest along a ridge leads to the foot of Gold Hill and a meadow with great views back into Deer Creek. This area offers the most protected camp spots on the rest of the route.

Fern-leafed lousewort in Deer Creek Canyon

After a short, wooded stretch, burst out into the meadows of Gold Hill, reaching the summit at mile 7.4.

After enjoying the view, head down the south flank of Gold Hill on Trail 64. Descend quickly, passing the Long Canyon Trail 63. At mile 10.5, enter Bull-of-the-Woods Pasture. Turn right onto Trail 90 and descend along the Rio Hondo to Taos Ski Valley.

20 | HEART LAKE AND LATIR MESA

Distance: 12.4 miles, day hike or backpack
Difficulty: strenuous
Elevation range: 9,200 to 12,600 feet
Elevation gain: 3,800 feet
Best time of year: mid-June to late September
Water: Lake Fork, Bull Creek, Heart Lake
Maps: USGS Red River and Latir Peak; USFS Latir and
    Wheeler Peak Wilderness
Managed by: Carson National Forest,
    Latir Wilderness, Questa Ranger District
Features: grand views above tree line, alpine lake,
    running water

At the close of the most recent Ice Age, glaciers melted from the highest peaks of the Sangre de Cristo range and left behind a dozen small lakes in cirques at the heads of the valleys and amid the jagged skylines that form their backdrops. Located in the Latir Wilderness, Heart Lake is only 5 miles from the trailhead and is backed by sweeping mesas that reach above 12,000 feet. For casual hikers, it is an easy climb to the lake; strong day hikers and backpackers can make a grand loop past the lake onto the alpine ridges of Latir Mesa, where sweeping views reach from the Latir Lakes below to the summits of distant Colorado.

A few cautions: Navigating this route above Heart Lake requires skill with maps, and a compass or GPS. The trails fade in the high meadows, and routefinding is necessary over Latir Mesa and to the Bull Creek Trail. The loop trip traverses more than 4 miles of terrain above timberline, so hikers must take care when planning a summer trip into this area.

It is a good idea to be off the ridges by noon, before thunderstorms have the opportunity to build. An alternative is to wait until September, but at that time hikers must be prepared for chilly nights. Camping is not permitted within 300 feet of Heart Lake or in the meadow surrounding Baldy Cabin. Farther along the route, some nice forested sites are available just below the initial steep drop into the Bull Creek drainage.

To get to the trailhead at Cabresto Lake, drive 0.25 mile on NM 38 from the intersection of NM 522 and NM 38 in Questa. Turn left onto NM 563 and

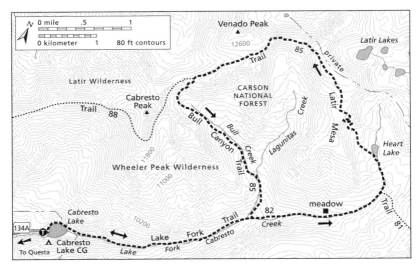

travel 2.1 miles, then turn right onto gravel FR 134. Cross into Carson National Forest and drive 3.3 miles to FR 134A. Turn left (north) and continue 2.1 miles to Cabresto Lake and campground. This road is rough in places, so a high-clearance vehicle is recommended, although sedans carefully driven can make the trip.

The Lake Fork Trail 82 starts by skirting to the left (west) of Cabresto Lake, then makes a long, steady climb parallel to Lake Fork of Cabresto Creek. The first 2 miles traverse conifer forest with cork-bark fir dominating the slopes. After passing through several small meadows, meet the Bull Canyon Trail 85, about 2.5 miles from the start. Bear right, cross Bull Creek, and continue along the Lake Fork Trail 82.

After climbing the only switchback on the trail, enter a blue spruce forest. At mile 3.5, find a long meadow with excellent campsites on both sides of Lake Fork. In 0.5 mile, the trail reenters the forest and climbs a low ridge. At mile 4.2, bear left toward Heart Lake at the junction with Baldy Mountain Trail 81. In a few minutes, enter a small meadow and bear right to parallel small streams on both the left and right. As the trail peters out, again pick up the main trail to the left of the streams. From here it is a short distance to Heart Lake.

To reach Latir Mesa, head to the southwest shoreline and find a sign indicating Trail 85 and the way to Latir Mesa. Climb along a ridgeline to get excellent views of Heart Lake, and ascend a steep talus slope to gain the flanks of Latir Mesa. Here the trail fades and hikers must do some routefinding. Head toward the rounded summit of the mesa where the Latir Lakes come into view. Do not cross onto private land on the north side of the ridge.

Skirt the flanks of a summit, indicated as peak 12,692 on the map, then stay close to the ridgeline as it swings around the head of Lagunitas

Heart Lake with July snow on Latir Mesa

Fork to a saddle at the foot of Venado Peak. From the saddle, stay on the slopes of Virgin Canyon, keeping a row of low rocks on your left. A sign near the valley bottom points toward Cabresto Peak. Ascend this easier-to-follow trail up the slopes of Virgin Canyon to the top of the ridge and to a saddle and the junction with Trail 88. Angle left to follow the arrows to Bull Canyon Trail 85 and walk down the steep head of the canyon. In 0.5 mile, skirt a meadow and watch for campsites along the forest edge. The trail drops steeply for 2 miles to the intersection with the Lake Fork Trail. Turn right and walk downhill to Cabresto Lake and the trailhead.

21 | Sawmill Park

Distance: 11 miles, day hike or backpack
Difficulty: moderate
Elevation range: 9,660 to 11,000 feet
Elevation gain: 1,500 feet
Best time of year: late May to late October
Water: Sawmill Creek
Maps: USGS Wheeler Peak and Eagle Nest; USFS Latir and
   Wheeler Peak Wilderness
Managed by: Carson National Forest,
   Wheeler Peak Wilderness, Questa Ranger District
Features: easy hike into a long, high meadow

The 3-mile-long meadow by Sawmill Creek is one of New Mexico's easiest-to-reach high-country destinations. The grades of this trail are gentle

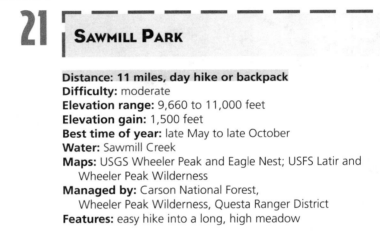
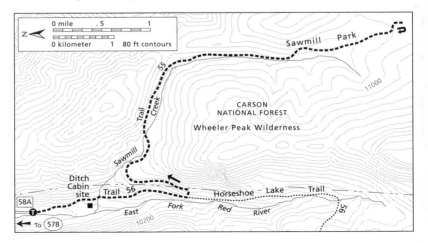

enough for beginning backpackers. Idyllic campsites are located at the west end of the meadow and in the basins of several side drainages that enter from the west. Most visitors to the Wheeler Peak Wilderness head for the rim country to the west; it is likely that hikers will have Sawmill Park to themselves.

From the east end of the town of Red River on NM 38, take NM 578 south for 6.4 miles to the end of the pavement. Bear left, cross a bridge, and immediately bear right to take the gravel FR 58A. Continue through private land on the rough road. After about 0.8 mile, bear left at a fork, following the signs for the East Fork Trailhead. Park at the East Fork Trailhead, 1.4 miles from the paved section of road.

Begin hiking on an old road angling uphill into the trees. Climb steadily for 0.4 mile to reach a small meadow, the site of Ditch Cabin. Cross Sawmill Creek on a small bridge, then begin a long, well-graded climb parallel to the East Fork of the Red River.

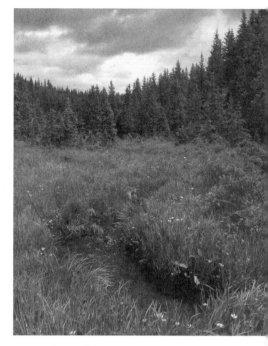

Sawmill Creek as it passes through Sawmill Park

At a well-marked intersection 1.4 miles from the start, turn sharply left onto Sawmill Park Trail 55. This trail continues the easy climb up the east wall of the East Fork Canyon, crossing into the Wheeler Peak Wilderness. Once over the ridge, the trail again meets Sawmill Creek, following the creek upstream to enter the meadows of Sawmill Creek. Pick up the tread of the trail near the trees at the north edge of the meadow. From here, the trail follows the meadow, with small but deep Sawmill Creek meandering through the tall grass and wildflowers blooming all summer long. Stay on the trail to prevent damage to the meadow. Watch for deer, elk, and snowshoe hare in the forest openings.

About 3 miles from the start, the meadow and trail swing south. The valley narrows and widens several times before reaching Sawmill Park, 4.9 miles from the start. The trail is easy to follow to a lone Douglas fir tree standing at the meadow's edge. From the tree, follow the meadow south as it slopes up to a saddle. Here the meadow is always wet and alive with white marsh marigolds. At the saddle, a fence marks the boundary of private property. Return to the trailhead by the same route.

22 | HORSESHOE LAKE

Distance: 13.5 miles, backpack
Difficulty: strenuous
Elevation range: 9,450 to 11,950 feet
Elevation gain: 2,800 feet
Best time of year: late June to mid-October
Water: forks of the Red River, Horseshoe and Lost lakes
Maps: USGS Wheeler Peaks: USFS Latir and Wheeler Peak
   Wilderness
Managed by: Carson National Forest,
   Wheeler Peak Wilderness, Questa Ranger District
Features: alpine scenery, high lakes, fishing, wildlife

Horseshoe and Lost lakes lie in rugged bowls at the foot of the highest ridge in New Mexico. The trail to the lakes is surprisingly gentle, threading through deep conifer forest up and above the canyon of the East Fork of the Red River. Ample campsites are available along the way, and this beautiful area invites more than a day trip. Both lakes host good populations of trout and are popular destinations for anglers. From Horseshoe Lake it is a short trip to the summit of Wheeler Peak, but extending the hike in this manner should be attempted only as part of an overnight trip. Hikers can eliminate the road portion of this hike with a short, 2-mile shuttle by leaving a car or a mountain bike at the Middle Fork Lake Trailhead, then driving to start the hike at the East Fork Trailhead. See Hike 21, Sawmill Park, for driving directions to the East Fork Trailhead.

   Begin hiking on an old road

Horseshoe Lake is backed by the highest ridge in New Mexico.

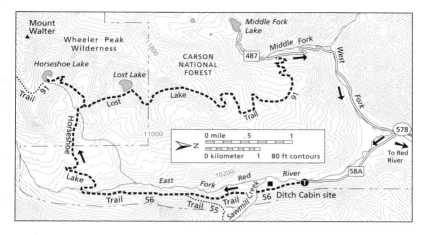

angling uphill into the trees. Climb steadily for 0.4 mile to reach a small meadow, the site of Ditch Cabin, and cross Sawmill Creek. The trail begins a gentle ascent through mixed conifer forest, rich in wildflowers—calypso orchids, false Solomon's seal, Colorado columbine, monkshood, and cow parsnip—all summer long.

At mile 1.4, pass the intersection with the Sawmill Park Trail 55 to the left and continue up the canyon of the East Fork. At mile 2.6, drop down to cross the East Fork on a bridge. The trail now climbs several broad switchbacks, wandering through forest, meadow, and talus, with Red Cone often visible on the ridge to the left. As the trail crosses a small ridge, the high ridgeline that includes Wheeler Peak and Mount Walter stretches out in front. After crossing a bridge, reach a trail junction at mile 4.0. Turn left to begin the climb to Horseshoe Lake, about a mile from the junction. Camping is not permitted within 300 feet of the lake.

Backtrack down from Horseshoe Lake to the main trail. At the junction, turn left, heading toward Lost Lake. The trail loses elevation and crosses two wide talus slopes. A half mile from the trail junction, reach Lost Lake. Hikers can choose among many fine campsites located at least 300 feet away from the lake, which holds plenty of cutthroat and rainbow trout.

Continuing down the Lost Lake Trail 91 from the lake, pass an old trail branching to the right, then leave the Wheeler Peak Wilderness. The trail now offers superb views to the north and east as it heads north through forest and talus. At mile 7, the trail begins to switchback down from the ridge and enters a dense conifer forest. Over the next 3 miles, the trail drops 1,500 feet to the intersection with Middle Fork Lake Road (FR 487). Bear right and walk down the narrow road, which continues to switchback down the slope. At mile 10.5, cross a bridge over the West Fork of the Red River. Turn right onto the road parallel to the Middle Fork, soon passing the Middle Fork Lake Trailhead. Continue on the road just over a mile to reach NM 578. Bear right, cross a bridge, and immediately bear right to walk on FR 58A. Continue through private land on the road, heading straight 0.2 mile from the bridge. After about 0.8 mile, bear left at a fork, following the signs for the East Fork Trailhead. Reach the East Fork Trailhead 1.4 miles from NM 578.

23 | COMANCHE CREEK

Distance: 7 miles, day hike
Difficulty: easy
Elevation range: 9,250 to 9,700 feet
Elevation gain: 500 feet
Best time of year: late May to late October
Water: Comanche Creek
Map: USGS Comanche Point
Managed by: Carson National Forest,
    Valle Vidal Unit, Questa Ranger District
Features: rocky-sided valley, mountain vistas, fishing,
    historic features

The valley of Comanche Creek is quintessential Valle Vidal, a region defined by open and expansive grasslands, shimmering creeks, and islands of conifer

The La Belle Lodge stands at the site of the gold-mining camp of La Belle.

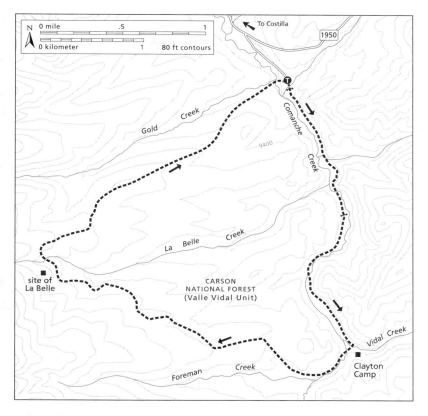

forest. This route follows Comanche Creek 2 miles before climbing to grand views from the mesas above. Near the site of La Belle, a once-thriving gold-mining community near the head of La Belle Creek, the route follows the traces of abandoned roads back to Comanche Creek. Rumor has it that these were the very roads taken by Tom Ketchum, one of the last train robbers, when he rode from his hangout in Valle Vidal to Saturday night dances in La Belle, his identity unknown to the local townsfolk. Note that carrying a map, along with a compass or GPS receiver, will be helpful in navigating this trip.

To reach the trailhead, take NM 522 north of Taos 40 miles to NM 196 at Costilla. Turn right on this paved, then all-weather gravel road. Seventeen miles from NM 522, at the Carson National Forest boundary, the road becomes FR 1950. Six and a half miles beyond the forest boundary, bear right on an un-marked dirt track heading from FR 1950 down toward Comanche Creek. Park at the wide turnout before the gate, about 0.5 mile from FR 1950.

From the parking area, walk along the old road that parallels Comanche Creek, immediately passing through a gate. At mile 0.5, at the mouth of

Open grasslands are the defining feature of Valle Vidal.

La Belle Creek, walk beneath some dramatic outcrops of granite before cross-ing the stream and climbing to another gate. Two more stream crossings lead to the junction with Vidal Creek at mile 2.3. To the left are the cabins and barns of Clayton Camp. The road crosses Vidal Creek and in a few yards, Comanche Creek. Continue parallel to Comanche Creek for another 0.4 mile to the junction with Foreman Creek.

At the faint junction, the main trail up Comanche Creek bears left across a boggy area; bear slightly right onto a faint road that turns up a small grassy drainage heading northwest. The route follows the traces of the road through an expansive meadow with views in all directions. Climb to a low ridge, passing a small ruin to the left. On the ridge, the faint road turns left to follow the crest. Look back to the east for a glimpse of a huge, grassy bowl. This valley is Valle Vidal, from which the entire area takes its name.

About 3.5 miles from the start, the road bears slightly to the right, now heading northwest. Descend through a drainage and climb to another ridge. The road follows along the edge of the forest to reach the site of La Belle at mile 4.4. The La Belle Lodge is the dominant structure, but the ruins of cabins, headframes, and flues are scattered through the area. After exploring La Belle, follow an abandoned road as it crosses La Belle Creek and climbs gently up the next ridge. Gain the top of the ridge at mile 5.5, then enjoy a long descent with views to the Costilla Range to the north. At mile 6.9, cross Comanche Creek near its confluence with Gold Creek, and close the loop with a few steps to the trailhead.

24 McCrystal Place

Distance: 6 miles, day hike
Difficulty: easy
Elevation range: 8,150 to 8,550 feet
Elevation gain: 500 feet
Best time of year: late May to late October
Water: McCrystal Creek
Maps: USGS Van Bremmer Park and Ash Mountain
Managed by: Carson National Forest,
  Valle Vidal Unit, Questa Ranger District
Features: impressive homestead ruins

In the late nineteenth century, the sprawling Maxwell Land Grant covered more than a million acres of the northern Sangre de Cristo Mountains. That such a huge piece of prime real estate was not in the public domain was too much for some neighbors to accept. Many small ranchers established homesteads on the grant, believing that eventually the land would be rightfully declared open to the public. The grant managers called them squatters.

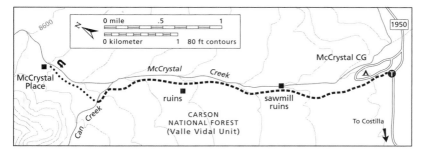

A wagon at the McCrystal Place

John McCrystal moved his family to a small valley watered by a narrow stream draining off Costilla Peak. Despite knowing that the land belonged to the Maxwell Grant, he boldly built his house and ranch and soon became a leader among the anti-grant men. As the courts upheld the rights of the grant, pressure on the ranchers increased. In 1890 McCrystal was forced to settle with the grant and purchased 320 acres for $960.

The old road to the McCrystal Place travels 3 miles along McCrystal Creek, offering a solid view of homesteading around the turn of the century. Even though the ranch is in ruins, one can see why it was worth fighting for. Cattle still graze the rich meadows along McCrystal Creek; timber is plentiful in the surrounding hills. The peaceful view from McCrystal's yard extends many miles to the south.

To reach the trailhead, take NM 522 north of Taos 40 miles to NM 196 at Costilla. Turn right on this paved, then all-weather gravel road. Seventeen miles from NM 522, at the Carson National Forest boundary, the road becomes FR 1950. Continue about 20 miles to McCrystal Campground. Park off the road near the campground entrance.

From the campground entrance, walk west along FR 1950 for about 0.25 mile to a dirt road angling to the northwest and parallel to the campground road, which is just on the other side of a fence. Bear right, pass through a gate, and stroll through the shady pine forest, watching for tassel-eared Abert's squirrels. After about a mile, the trail meets up with McCrystal Creek to the right. The trail now parallels the creek, passing the large ruins of a sawmill along the way.

At mile 1.5, the road enters a large marshy meadow. A bit farther on, pass a stone foundation to the right and the remains of a wooden structure on the left. At mile 2.6, the road swings to the west to parallel Can Creek. Follow the road for a few yards, then head straight across an extensive meadow, crossing Can Creek on the way.

In a few minutes, reach the remains of the large main house and several smaller structures of the ranch. The ruins are fragile and dangerous: Stay out. Explore the ranch and enjoy the view down the valley to the mountains beyond, then return to the trailhead by the same route.

25 | North Ponil Creek

Distance: 7 miles, day hike
Difficulty: easy
Elevation range: 7,750 to 8,000 feet
Elevation gain: 300 feet
Best time of year: late May to late October
Water: North Ponil Creek
Maps: USGS Van Bremmer Park and Abreu Canyon
Managed by: Carson National Forest, Valle Vidal Unit,
  Questa Ranger District
Features: scenic meadow, ghost town

Walking the long, flower-laced meadow beside North Ponil Creek is a delightful trip a hundred years back in time. Despite the 2002 Ponil Fire, the small valley is much as it was before lumbermen pushed a railroad through its serene grasslands, but the traces of human use are still much in

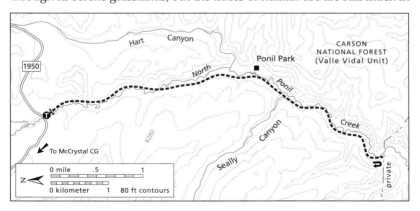

evidence. The Cimarron and Northwestern Railway traveled 22 miles into the mountains from the town of Cimarron to Ponil Park, the broadest part of the meadow, which soon became a bustling railroad and lumber town. The railroad connected Ponil Park, the center of operations in the woods, to a series of lumber camps in the canyon below. Perhaps as many as two hundred people lived there in 1910, working the rails, in the sawmills, or as lumbermen. The surrounding forest never provided as much timber for mine supports and railroad ties as the company had anticipated, so the line was torn up in 1921.

To reach the trailhead, take NM 522 north of Taos 40 miles to NM 196 at Costilla, nearly to the Colorado border. Turn right on this paved, then all-weather gravel road. Seventeen miles from NM 522, at the Carson National Forest boundary, the road becomes FR 1950. Continue about 21

The remains of at least a dozen cabins are found at Ponil Park.

miles to park at the wide turnout on the left, 1 mile beyond McCrystal Campground.

Begin hiking on the south (right) side of FR 1950, on a double-track behind a "Road Closed" sign. The track leads downcanyon, parallel to the diminutive North Ponil Creek. In several hundred yards, pass around a gate and continue down the wide meadow. The landscape outside the meadows is a mosaic of rapidly recovering burned areas and mixed conifer forest. Throughout the summer, hikers will be accompanied by the buzz of dozens of broad-tailed hummingbirds as they visit penstemons.

After 1.5 miles, the trail crosses the stream and follows the boundary of burned and unburned pine forest on the west side of the valley. At mile 2.1, Hart Canyon joins the North Ponil valley from the left. Ruins of the old town are visible across North Ponil Creek. Continue down the west side of the valley, passing a small railroad trestle and then two cabin ruins. Here the trail parallels the railroad. After Seally Canyon enters from the right, the trail runs along the top of the railroad grade, with rotting or burned ties lying along the route. Continue to walk on the old railroad for another mile until reaching the national forest boundary at a fence. Turn around and return on the same trail.

On the return trip, cross to the east side of the valley near the trestle. Look for at least a dozen ruins and a small cemetery. Please respect these reminders of the past and leave them undisturbed. After enjoying the town, continue back up North Ponil Creek 2 miles to the trailhead.

26 | LITTLE HORSE MESA LOOP

Distance: 6-mile loop, day hike
Difficulty: moderate
Elevation range: 7,550 to 8,250 feet
Elevation gain: 800 feet
Best time of year: May to late October
Water: carry water
Map: USGS Raton
Managed by: Sugarite Canyon State Park
Features: scenic meadow, ghost town

One of New Mexico's most scenic state parks, Sugarite is centered on the canyon of the same name. Gambel oak and ponderosa pine paint the canyon walls in a mosaic of green. Turkey and deer are common in the oaks and grasslands, and signs of elk, bobcat, and black bear are common in the forests. As for wildflowers, the park is loaded with unusual species such as the orange-flowered calico bush, Colorado columbine, and Canada anemone.

Deep cracks form along the edge of Little Horse Mesa.

When ranchers worked the land in the late 1800s, they called the canyon Chicorica, a name that lives on in the creek flowing in the valley today. The name Chicorica may be a corruption of the Spanish *achirocia* (the wild chicory plant), or it may date back to when Comanches lived in the area and named it for the "abundance of birds" on the mesas. Anglo coal miners had trouble twisting their tongues around the Comanche word. Before long, Chicorica was corrupted into Sugarite, which is properly pronounced *sugar-REET*.

The park owes its existence to black and dusty coal. The most recent sea to cover New Mexico receded about 60 million years ago, leaving thick swamps in its wake. The decay of millions of swamp trees accumulated as muck, which was later squeezed by the earth into coal. Deposits were discovered near Raton Pass in 1821 by the Long Expedition, but it wasn't until 1909 that it was economically feasible to begin mining operations in Sugarite Canyon. The Chicorica Coal Company developed the diggings and the accompanying coal camp. Starting with about 500 residents, the town of Sugarite doubled in size over the next twenty years, but faded away as the demand for coal fell.

Sugarite Canyon State Park is located a few miles northeast of Raton. From that city, take exit 452 from I-25 and head east on NM 72. In 3.7 miles, bear left onto NM 526. The park entrance and visitor center are 1.7 miles up NM 526. Stop and pay the small day-use fee before continuing up the canyon. The trailhead is 4 miles beyond the park entrance.

Three trails connect to form a varied 6-mile loop that circles the volcanic ramparts of Little Horse Mesa. The circuit, along with a short spur trip, offers views of the sandstone and coal walls of Sugarite Canyon,

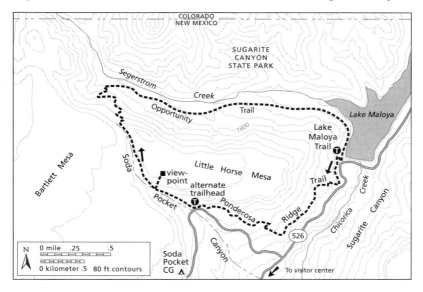

the rolling grasslands of the mesa tops, Lake Maloya, and the secluded Segerstrom Creek.

Begin at the small parking area on NM 526 at the west end of the dam that backs up Lake Maloya. (Note that hikers can also begin the loop at the horse corral near the entrance to Soda Pocket Campground.) A sign points the way to the Ponderosa Ridge Trail, the first leg of the journey. Head left on the trail as it winds through pine forest. Steep, eroded switchbacks lead to a level bench that offers views down Sugarite Canyon. A mile from the start, another steep pitch in the trail leads to a second bench. Weaving in and out of meadows, the trail descends to the road to Soda Pocket Campground and the head of the Opportunity Trail at mile 2.

From the Opportunity Trailhead, head northwest on the now rocky trail as it ascends Soda Pocket Canyon on a moderate grade. Gambel oak shades much of the narrow trail. At 2.4 miles from the start, hikers can take the 0.25-mile-long Little Horse Mesa Trail to the right. This trail makes short work of the ascent to the mesa top, where views of the sloping top of Bartlett Mesa and the old volcano Bobblers Knob sit to the north. Return to the Opportunity Trail and continue upcanyon. The trail soon smooths out until it reaches a lovely meadow beneath the cliffs of Bartlett and Little Horse mesas.

About 3 miles from the start, the trail reaches a pass and begins to descend through open forest. Switchbacks lead down the slope to the bottom of Segerstrom Canyon at mile 3.9. Bear right and proceed downcanyon with the sound of the flowing stream nearby. The trail passes through tallgrass meadows and stands of oak for the next 1.5 miles. At a broad meadow near the end of the canyon, look to the left for the rounded Bobblers Knob on the cliff above.

At mile 5.4, bear right at the junction with the Lake Maloya Trail. Follow the old road along the lakeshore back to the trailhead.

27 | CAPULIN VOLCANO RIM TRAIL

Distance: 1 mile, short day hike
Difficulty: easy
Elevation range: 7,900 to 8,182 feet
Elevation gain: 300 feet
Best time of year: year-round
Water: at visitor center
Map: USGS Folsom
Managed by: Capulin Volcano National Monument
Features: huge pile of volcanic cinders, spectacular long-range views

The Great Plains may seem an unusual setting for volcanic activity, but the Raton-Clayton volcanic field covers more than two hundred square miles

Lava flows from the base of Capulin Volcano are best seen from the rim of the crater.

and holds about one hundred volcanic centers from which lava has flowed during the past 8 million years. These volcanoes mark the easternmost limit of recent volcanic activity in the United States.

Capulin Volcano is the centerpiece of a small national monument located in extreme northeastern New Mexico. The nearly perfect cinder cone was set aside as a classic example of this type of volcanic vent in 1916. The cone—built up by small bits of lava forcibly ejected from the central vent—is surrounded by four lava flows that oozed from cracks at the base. Each of the flows is visible from the crater rim; together they appear as waves of dark green vegetation rippling from the mountain. During the eruptions that occurred from 8,000 to 2,500 years ago, the sticky, chunky lava never flowed far from the volcano. Much of the Raton-Clayton volcanic field can be seen from the trail that travels the crater rim. Most impressive are the lava-capped mesas to the north and west, and the immense shield volcano called Sierra Grande to the southeast.

Reach Capulin Volcano by taking exit 451 from I-25 at the city of Raton. Go east on US 64/87 about 28 miles to the town of Capulin. Turn left onto

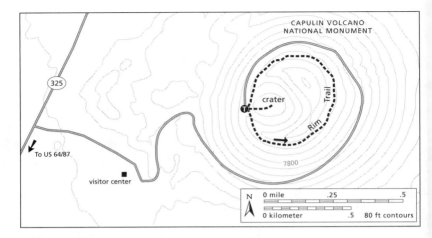

NM 325 and follow the signs about 4 miles to the national monument entrance. From the visitor center, take Crater Rim Drive as it corkscrews to the western edge of the crater and a small parking area.

The Rim Trail heads to the right (east) from the southern end of the parking area. The route is paved the entire way, but steep grades make comfortable walking shoes a must. Begin by heading south, circling the crater in a counterclockwise direction. Just below are the lobes of the second lava flow, delineated by sweeping lines of trees. The view south from the summit takes in the old volcanoes. Watch for the aerial displays of turkey vultures as they play on the air currents within the crater. The trail also provides an opportunity to look at the ways the junipers hold together the cinders of the cone.

Before getting back in your car, take a short spur trail that leads down into the bottom of the crater. The view from the bottom offers an interesting vantage point, providing a measure of understanding about how the surrounding pile of cinders and rocks was formed.

Opposite: *The Valle Jaramillo from the Cerros del Abrigo Trail*

JEMEZ MOUNTAINS AND BANDELIER NATIONAL MONUMENT

28 | Ojitos Wilderness

Distance: 4.5 miles, day hike
Difficulty: easy, but some routefinding required
Elevation range: 5,650 to 5,920 feet
Elevation gain: 400 feet
Best time of year: year-round
Water: carry water
Maps: USGS Collier Draw and Ojitos Spring
Managed by: Bureau of Land Management,
    Albuquerque Field Office
Features: colorful badlands, unusual rock formations

New Mexico's treasure chest of natural features is so full of gaudy baubles that one can easily overlook the smaller gems. The Ojitos Wilderness is such a place, usually passed over by those heading to the nearby, better-known Jemez Mountains.

At the Ojitos Wilderness, the soon-to-be-adobe layers of the Morrison formation are eroded into ridges with fantastic shapes. Hikers will find

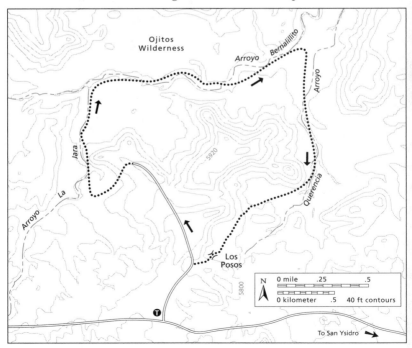

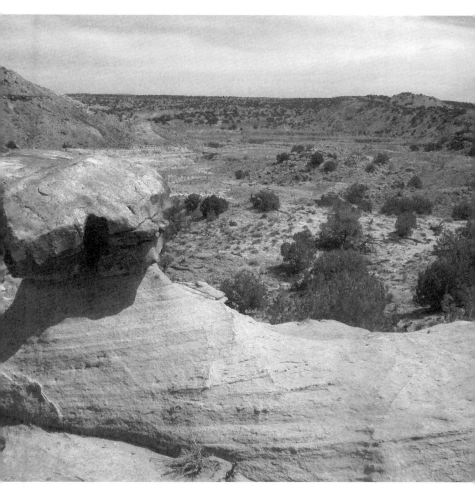

A sandstone hoodoo overlooking Querencia Arroyo

everything from toadstool rocks to banded mud castles. The stone castles are complete with pointed turrets and ramparts studded with shining stones polished smooth by waves on the shore of an ancient sea. Careful observation reveals petroglyphs, geodes, and other special treats.

To get to the area, take I-25 to the US 550 exit, about 20 miles north of Albuquerque and 40 miles south of Santa Fe. Head west, leaving the highway about 2.3 miles south of the town of San Ysidro. Turn west onto a dirt road and immediately take the left fork. Stay on the road through the Zia Pueblo reservation and in 6 miles cross a cattle guard to enter public land. Continue on the all-weather gravel road and park near a closed road heading north, which is located about 12 miles from the highway.

The open vegetation and rolling terrain of the Ojitos Wilderness invites wandering and that's a good thing: there are no trails in the area. Wander with a map and compass or GPS unit, or try the following suggestion.

From the parking area, walk north on the dirt road heading along a ridge. Follow the road about a half mile as it skirts along the rise. Watch for weird cylinders of rock that look like massive dinosaur bones. Whenever practical, descend the left (south) side of the ridge into the wide drainage, Arroyo La Jara. At or near the arroyo bottom, turn right and head downstream. Enjoy the miniature badlands eroded into the soft mudstone of the valley.

After about 0.25 mile in the wash bottom, and about 1 mile from the start of the hike, meet the larger Arroyo Bernalillito. Turn right and continue walking in the sandy wash. Along the way are more badlands, tunnels of mud, and a variety of colorful stones along the gravel bars. Pass an intersection with another arroyo from the north. After about 1.5 miles, Arroyo Bernalillito intersects Querencia Arroyo in a broad plain. Turn sharply right and head up the Querencia drainage. Stay close to the cliffs to the right (west) as the route winds through a confusing maze of washes. Pass through an area of rounded rocks, then over the pass labeled Los Posos on the map. Come to the dirt road that was used as the first part of the trip. Turn left and return to the parking area.

29 TENT ROCKS CANYON TRAIL

Distance: 3 miles, day hike
Difficulty: easy
Elevation range: 5,740 to 6,375 feet
Elevation gain: 400 feet
Best time of year: mid-March through N
Water: carry water
Map: USGS Cañada
Managed by: Bureau of Land Management, Albuquerque Field Office; Cochiti Pueblo
Features: very narrow canyon, strangely shaped rocks

Tent Rocks Canyon is a narrow slice through tuff ejected from small volcanoes at the edge of the massive Jemez Volcano. In places the walls of the canyon are 200 feet high, yet a child's arms can span the width wall to wall. The canyon takes its name from the surrounding weird towers of tuff capped by harder, more erosion-resistant rocks. These cap rocks offer some protection to the crumbly tuff directly beneath, resulting in a hoard of conical spires shaped roughly like tepees.

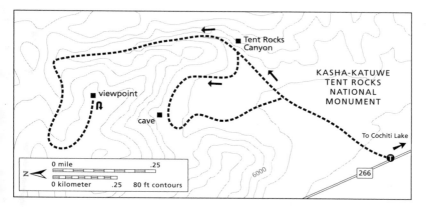

Tent Rocks Canyon and the surrounding rock spires have spawned New Mexico's newest national monument, Kasha-Katuwe Tent Rocks National Monument. Jointly administered by the Bureau of Land Management and Cochiti Pueblo, the 5,300-acre area has two trails that lead into the wonderland, one along the base of the cliffs, another into the canyon.

Take I-25 south from Santa Fe or north from Albuquerque to the Cochiti exit 264. Go west on NM 16 for about 8 miles to a T intersection. Turn right onto NM 22, heading for Cochiti Dam. Go past the spillway and, at the base of the dam, turn left with NM 22 as it heads toward Cochiti Pueblo. In 1.8 miles, at the end of NM 22, turn right onto FR 266. This dirt road is bumpy but passable to any vehicle. At 4.8 miles, turn right at the sign for Kasha-Katuwe Tent Rocks National Monument. Park in the small lot on the right. Note a small fee is charged for day use of this area. The monument is open from 8:00 AM to 5:00 PM from November 1 to March 31, and from 7:00 AM to 6:00 PM the rest of the year.

Begin hiking the Tent Rocks Canyon Trail at the BLM parking area. Follow the sandy trail, marked with National Recreation Trail signposts, about 100 yards to a junction and bear right. A bit less than 0.5 mile from the start, the trail leads into an arroyo. Bear left and walk up the sandy bottom into a narrowing canyon. Just before reaching the mouth of the canyon, the trail splits at mile 0.6; the left fork is the cliff trail, but for now go right into the canyon.

The trail passes between high walls of banded volcanic deposits as the canyon alternates between narrow and open sections. Short stretches are a squeeze for an adult with a day pack. At one point, hikers must crawl under a boulder to continue, but this only adds to the fun.

At mile 1.2, a primitive trail continues 0.25 mile to a viewpoint above, climbing the steep slope on loose rock. From the viewpoint, backtrack to the mouth of the canyon. Just outside the canyon at mile 2.1, turn right onto the cliff route and climb steeply out of the arroyo. After 200 yards, drop into a broad amphitheater surrounded by banded cliffs. The trail follows the base

Kasha-Katuwe Tent Rocks National Monument was set aside to protect the tepee-shaped rocks found on the flanks of the Jemez Mountains.

of the cliffs, passing a cave that shows signs of use by Ancestral Pueblo people. Just past the cave, descend into a narrow arroyo. At the bottom, turn left and walk down the arroyo. In 100 yards, cross a larger arroyo and continue as the trail skirts the base of the western side of the amphitheater back to the parking area.

30 | CERRO PICACHO

Distance: 8 miles, day hike
Difficulty: difficult
Elevation range: 6,580 to 8,113 feet
Elevation gain: 2,000 feet
Best time of year: May 15 to November
Water: Sanchez Canyon
Maps: USGS Cañada and Cochiti Dam
Managed by: Santa Fe National Forest,
    Dome Wilderness Area, Jemez Ranger District
Features: wild canyon scenery, running water, isolated peak

At 5,200 acres, the Dome Wilderness is the smallest wilderness area in the southwest. The Dome sits on the more remote edges of the adjacent

Bandelier Wilderness and offers considerable solitude and scenery to adventurous hikers. Named for St. Peters Dome, the highest point in the area, the wilderness area encompasses portions of the isolated Sanchez Canyon, a scenic gem with colorful walls, lush vegetation, and a desert waterfall. The dome of Cerro Picacho offers outstanding views of the southern portion of the Jemez Mountains as well as of the finger mesas of Bandelier National Monument. FR 289, the approach road, is closed each year from winter to May 15, so this is a summer and fall hike.

Reach the trailhead by taking I-25 south from Santa Fe or north from Albuquerque to the Cochiti exit 264. Go west on NM 16 for about 8 miles to a T intersection. Turn right onto NM 22, heading for Cochiti Dam. Go past the spillway and, at the base of the dam, continue straight when NM 22 turns left. Head into the village of Cochiti Lake and pass the local shopping plaza. Continue straight for 2.8 miles and turn right onto FR 289. Head up this rough road, entering the Santa Fe National Forest in 2.2 miles. At a hairpin turn in another 1.3 miles, park near the sign for the Dome Wilderness.

Begin hiking on the St. Peters Dome Trail 118. The trail heads north for a few hundred feet before dropping quickly into the bottom of Eagle Canyon. Immediately begin climbing out of the canyon on a rocky trail. Don't watch for birds of prey here; the canyon was named for Joseph Eagle, a promoter of early mining operations in the area. Enter the Dome Wilderness and pass through an abandoned pumice pit that was mined for the ejecta from the most recent volcanic eruption in the Jemez Mountains only 50,000 years ago. In a few minutes, begin a second descent, this one into Sanchez Canyon. At mile 1.2, reach the canyon bottom, where a permanent stream flows. Just below the trail, the flow drops off the high waterfall that gave the canyon its Pueblo name, "arroyo of the place of the waterfall."

Make a gentle climb out of the canyon heading east and ascending a ridgeline on what is probably an ancient route. At mile 2.1, reach the junction with the Cañada-Capulin Trail that heads for Turkey Springs. Bear left to stay on Trail 118, which is now fainter and more overgrown, but still

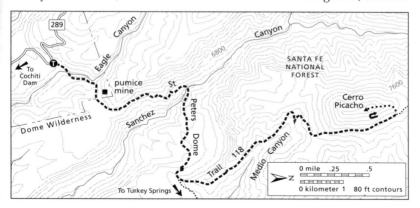

Tent rock tuff formations at the foot of Cerro Picacho

easy to follow. Climbing a low ridge, the view to the east encompasses the 5,000-acre San Miguel Fire of 2009. Over the ridge, the trail drops gradually along the upper reaches of Medio Canyon, heading northwest. Pass through open stands of ponderosa pine with low tent rocks (tepee-shaped towers of volcanic rock) surrounding the head of the drainage. Climb out the head of the canyon to a saddle 3.3 miles from the start and enjoy views of St. Peters Dome and the post-fire woodlands on its flanks. A steeper climb leads to another saddle in 0.6 mile. Enjoy the view from this point, or leave the trail and pick a route up the south ridge of Cerro Picacho. A 600-foot ascent through woodlands leads to the summit and a grand view in all directions. Return to the trailhead by the same route.

31 | RED DOT AND BLUE DOT TRAILS

Distance: 7.5 miles, day hike
Difficulty: moderate
Elevation range: 5,480 to 6,440 feet
Elevation gain: 1,150 feet
Best time of year: year-round
Water: Pajarito Springs
Map: USGS White Rock
Managed by: Los Alamos County
Features: White Rock Canyon, Rio Grande,
petroglyphs, springs

The Rio Grande carved White Rock Canyon through thick lava flows emanating from the volcanoes of the Cerros del Rio volcanic field to the east. Two

Ancestral Pueblo people adorned many of the smooth rock faces in White Rock Canyon with petroglyphs.

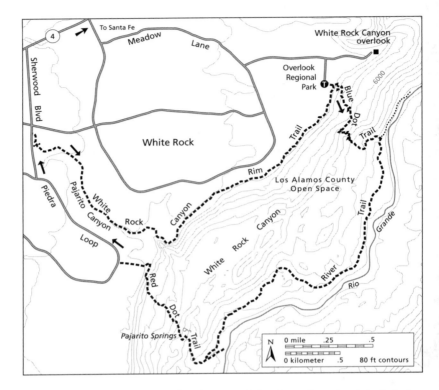

spectacular trails, unimaginatively named for the color of painted circles that mark the routes, lead into the canyon. The trails are stair-step affairs, descending successive blocks of lava that slumped from the cliffs as the Rio Grande wore its way down through the rocks. These are ancient trails that were used by Ancestral Pueblo people to travel from villages on the mesas to agricultural fields within the canyon.

From Santa Fe, go north on US 84/285 for 12 miles to NM 502 and bear left. Continue 8 miles and bear right onto NM 4 to the town of White Rock. At the traffic signal on the north edge of town, turn left onto Rover Boulevard. Make the first left onto Meadow Lane, traveling 0.7 mile to the entrance to Overlook Regional Park. Turn left on Overlook Road and continue past several athletic fields. Opposite a park maintenance shed, turn right. Continue to the rear of the parking area to the trailhead sign. Note that the park closes at 10:00 PM.

From the trailhead, follow the trail marked with rock cairns through a small drainage. In about 100 yards, the Blue Dot Trail starts at a gap in a fence. Turn left, dropping through a cleft in the rim, and begin the quick descent to the Rio Grande. From here the trail is much easier to follow: when in doubt, look for the blue dots painted on the rocks. Dropping from the topmost lava flow, the trail turns many tight switchbacks and crosses two broad benches. Just above the river, the trail enters a juniper woodland and becomes soggy with water from a few of the many springs that discharge into the river within the canyon.

At a trail junction near the river, the left spur leads in 0.25 mile to a sandy beach at streamside. To continue on the loop, turn right onto the River Trail, which begins with a long, sandy stretch. As the river comes in view again, the trail is squeezed between the river and a long ridge. Follow the trail around the end of the ridge, climbing to a bench covered with river cobbles.

After the trail again drops back to river level, cross the flow from Pajarito Springs using one of the many possible routes at mile 2.7. Pick up the Red Dot Trail on the other side, turn right, and head up the small stream. The trail recrosses the stream within the next couple hundred feet. With the stream to the left, watch to the right for a steep trail and climb over a ridge. In a few minutes, reach the pools of Pajarito Springs. This is a good place to rest before the long climb out of the canyon.

The trail from the springs is very steep. On the way up, take your mind off the hard work by enjoying the expansive view and by watching for elaborate petroglyphs on the rocks. About halfway up, the trail crosses a level bench, then completes the steep route to the rim. Out of the canyon, turn left and follow the trail to the paved Piedra Loop, 3.7 miles from the trailhead.

To return to Overlook Park, turn right on Piedra Loop and walk about 0.6 mile to Sherwood Boulevard. Turn right, then in 200 yards, turn right again at a gate on a dirt road where a small sign to the right marks the beginning of the White Rock Canyon Rim Trail. Follow the Rim Trail as it winds through the juniper woodlands of the mesa top. Many intersecting trails lead off in all directions; stay on the main route by heading generally east, keeping Pajarito Canyon on the right and White Rock Canyon ahead. After 1 mile on the Rim Trail, reach the edge of White Rock Canyon and bear left. Follow the trail 1.5 miles along the canyon rim back to Overlook Park.

32 | FALLS TRAIL

Distance: 4.8 miles, day hike
Difficulty: moderate
Elevation range: 5,380 to 6,060 feet
Elevation gain: 700 feet
Best time of year: March to December
Water: carry water
Maps: USGS Frijoles; Trails Illustrated Bandelier National Monument
Managed by: National Park Service, Bandelier National Monument
Features: colorful hike through volcanic landscape with two high waterfalls

Most visitors to Bandelier National Monument stay in Frijoles Canyon and tour the main pueblo, Tyuonyi, but the Monument offers plenty of back-country adventures, too. A spectacular introduction to the volcanic scenery at Bandelier is the Falls Trail. The route follows Frijoles Canyon downstream from the visitor center to the Rio Grande in White Rock Canyon. Along the way are stands of old-growth ponderosa pine, colorful deposits from under-water volcanic eruptions, and two high waterfalls. The best time to enjoy the falls is during spring runoff in March.

The entrance to Bandelier National Monument is located on NM 4 outside of Los Alamos. From the intersection of NM 502 and NM 4 east of Los Ala-mos, travel 13 miles west on NM 4; from Los Alamos, take NM 501 west of town for 6 miles to NM 4, turn left, and then continue 6 miles to the entrance station. The trailhead for the Falls Trail is the backcountry parking area just across Rito de los Frijoles (also called Frijoles Creek) from the visitor center.

Walk east along the parking area road for a few hundred feet to the trail entrance. Head down Cañon de los Frijoles, more commonly called Frijoles Canyon, with the creek below and never out of earshot. The hillside above the trail is piñon-juniper woodland and below the trail are tall ponderosas, massive cottonwoods, and an occasional white fir growing well below its normal elevation range. Orange cliffs top both sides of the canyon, but the

A hiker on the upper portion of the Falls Trail

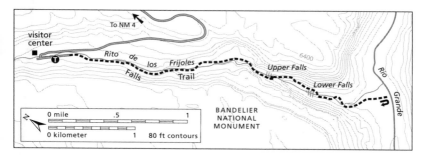

trail soon descends into a gorge of black basalt. The trail crosses the stream on bridges as it winds through open stands of pine on the canyon floor.

At mile 1.5, the gorge suddenly narrows and a banana yucca growing at trailside guards the entrance into another world. At the crest of a rise, the trail reaches the portal to White Rock Canyon. Unseen, the creek far below plunges over rocks, and the vista is filled with reds, oranges, and tans. Switchbacks lead to a viewpoint back up the inner gorge to the long threads of Upper Falls. More twists in the trail bring you to the canyon floor with towering walls of banded volcanic rocks in all directions. The trail descends on a narrow shelf to a view of Lower Falls, then again reaches the canyon bottom. Cottonwoods and box elders shade the trail as it winds along the stream. Watch for beaver sign as the trail enters the floodplain of the Rio Grande. In a few minutes, the trail crosses a river terrace once flooded by the backwaters of Cochiti Reservoir. The normally muddy river marks the turnaround point.

33 | FRIJOLES CANYON

Distance: 7.5 miles one-way, day hike
Difficulty: easy
Elevation range: 6,100 to 7,600 feet
Elevation gain: 1,500-foot descent; 300-foot climb
Best time of year: mid-March through mid-November
Water: Rito de los Frijoles
Maps: USGS Frijoles; Trails Illustrated Bandelier
    National Monument
Managed by: National Park Service,
    Bandelier National Monument
Features: wildlife, cliff dwellings, running water,
    picturesque canyon

People have used Frijoles Canyon (officially called Cañon de los Frijoles) as a route into the Jemez Mountains for centuries, first the Ancestral Pueblo residents in the lower canyon, then their Pueblo descendants. Today the

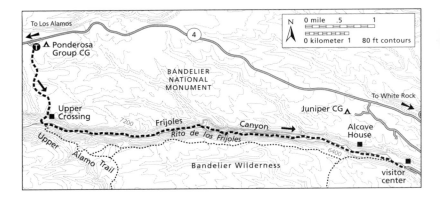

canyon is a quiet, sheltered place with year-round running water, making it a haven for wildlife. Elk are commonly spotted on the plateau above the canyon floor; mule deer are plentiful in the canyon itself. The entire canyon is shady, even in midsummer. The upper canyon supports tall Douglas fir, which gives way to ponderosa pine as the canyon cuts deeper into the rocks. Although the lower end of the Frijoles receives heavy visitation, the upper canyon sees few hikers.

This one-way, downhill hike requires setting up a short shuttle. Park a vehicle at the Bandelier Visitor Center, located 10 miles west of White Rock off NM 4. Return to the Bandelier National Monument entrance and turn left (west) onto NM 4. Continue west 6 miles to the Ponderosa Group Campground and park at the well-marked trailhead for the Upper Crossing.

Begin hiking downhill on a trail that soon joins a fire road entering from the right. Follow the signs to Upper Crossing at a minor intersection at mile 0.4, then enter the Bandelier Wilderness just above the edge of Frijoles Canyon. The trail drops 400 feet on several steep switchbacks to reach the bottom of Frijoles Canyon at mile 1.5. Cross the creek on a log bridge and immediately come to a three-way trail junction with the Upper Alamo Trail. Turn left onto the Frijoles Canyon Trail, heading toward the visitor center and paralleling the Rito de los Frijoles. The trail stays close to the stream with several crossings on stepping stones or bouncy log bridges.

About 3.5 miles from the start, an interesting side canyon enters from the left. Just after this junction, walk through the narrows of Frijoles Canyon where the walls are only a dozen feet apart. From this point, the trail crosses the shallow stream more than a dozen times.

The easy, shaded stroll continues until another narrow section of canyon forces the trail up and over a steep ridge. Cliff dwellings appear in the canyon wall to the left, but hikers must stay on the trail. About 6.5 miles from the start, the trail meets the Alcove House Trail coming up from the visitor center. Alcove House sits 140 feet above the canyon floor and can be reached via several long ladders; it is a worthwhile side trip. Continue back on the gravel path to the parking area near the visitor center.

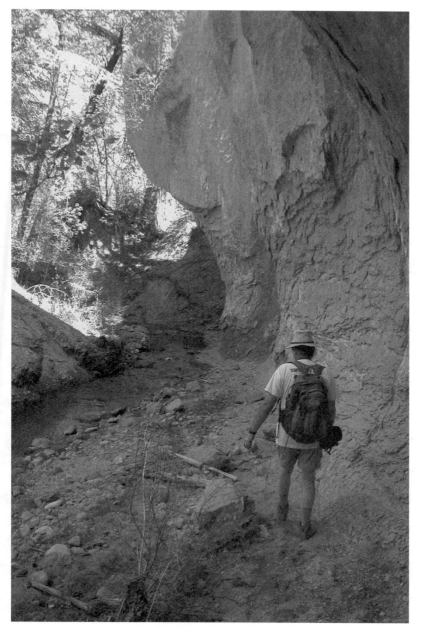

Tiny Rito de los Frijoles carved the walls of Frijoles Canyon through more than 300 feet of soft volcanic tuff.

34 YAPASHI PUEBLO

Distance: 12-miles one-way, day hike or backpack
Difficulty: difficult
Elevation range: 5,970 to 7,580 feet
Elevation gain: 2,500 feet
Best time of year: mid-April to October
Water: Rito de los Frijoles, Upper Alamo Crossing,
  Capulin Canyon
Maps: USGS Frijoles; Trails Illustrated Bandelier
  National Monument
Managed by: National Park Service, Bandelier National
  Monument
Features: stunning views, large junipers,
  Ancestral Pueblo village

The best way to see a large portion of the Bandelier backcountry is to set up a short shuttle and hike one-way from Upper Crossing to the Bandelier Visitor Center via the Upper Alamo Trail. Park a vehicle at the visitor center, return to the Bandelier National Monument entrance, and turn left (west) onto NM 4. Continue west 6 miles to the Ponderosa Group Campground and park at the well-marked trailhead for Upper Crossing.

In the Bandelier backcountry, canyons are cut between fingerlike mesas radiating from the hand of the Jemez Mountains. This hike drops into and out of three steep canyons, accumulating an elevation gain of almost 2,000 feet. The roughest, steepest climb is at Lower Alamo Crossing near the end of the hike. The trip can be very hot in summer, with little shade available for long stretches.

This long trek invites an overnight stay and permits are available at the Bandelier Visitor Center. No camping is permitted in Upper Alamo or Frijoles canyons, and no fires are allowed in the backcountry: use only gas stoves for cooking.

Yapashi Pueblo is one of the largest pueblos on the Pajarito Plateau. Hikers will find standing walls made of tuff-blocks, kiva depressions, and red and brown pottery scattered throughout the pueblo. To protect this ancient structure, stay off the walls and out of the kivas, and leave potsherds where you find them.

Begin hiking on a trail and fire road through the open ponderosa pine forest. The trail swings to the right at about 0.4 mile from the start. About a mile from the start, drop into the head of a small drainage and follow a series of steep switchbacks to the Upper Crossing of Rito de los Frijoles and the cool shady bottom of the Frijoles Canyon.

Decorative pottery pieces are rare and should be left untouched if discovered.

After crossing the small stream on a log bridge, follow the trail a hundred feet to a junction. Bear right to follow the Upper Alamo Trail, following the arrow pointing toward Yapashi Pueblo. The path angles up the south slope of the canyon. (The Frijoles Canyon Trail also goes to the left, but it stays in the canyon bottom.) Climb out of the canyon on several switchbacks, reaching the top at mile 2. The low plant growth and tall standing tree snags on the mesa are evidence this area was hard hit by the 1977 La Mesa Fire. In many locations, the backdrop of the Jemez Mountains show signs of the more recent Cerro Grande Fire. After the trail drops into and out of a small drainage, bear left at the junction with the Alamo Springs Trail. At the next intersection at mile 3.1, bear right as the Frijoles Rim Trail goes left, and pass another branch of that trail angling back to the left in a few hundred yards.

The route now drops slowly into Upper Alamo Canyon via a small side drainage. The trail reaches Alamo Canyon directly below several small, colorful tent rocks halfway up the canyon wall. Cross Alamo Creek at a delightful spot about 4 miles from the start. The trail turns downstream in the bottom of Alamo Canyon for 0.25 mile before climbing to the mesa above. Bear left at the junction with a trail marked for Capulin Canyon. From here the trail descends through open pine forest along a small drainage. At mile 6.3, the trail meets the edge of an escarpment, offering more long-range views to the east. Drop down several rocky switchbacks before bearing left at another trail junction at mile 7.3. The trail to the right leads to water and fine campsites in Capulin Canyon.

Continue east on the top of a ridge where at first the trail is confused by a network of side trails. Gradually the main trail becomes easy to follow.

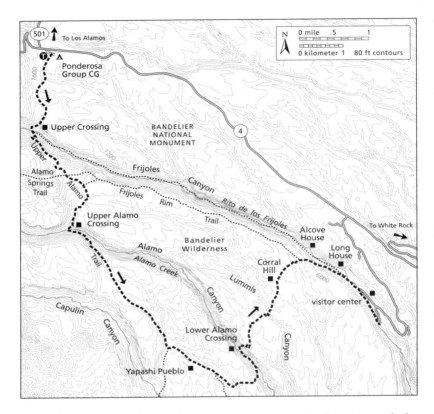

About 0.5 mile beyond the side trail leading to Capulin Canyon, reach the low mounds of Yapashi Pueblo. Explore around the perimeter of the pueblo before continuing down the trail.

From Yapashi, follow the ridge top before dropping down into and out of a small canyon. While traveling through open juniper pine woodland, pass the junction with the Lower Alamo Trail to the right. Climb a low ridge, then drop 500 feet to Lower Alamo Crossing. The canyon bottom is shaded by pine and box elder, with flowing water during spring. Make a short hitch west up the canyon bottom under towering orange cliffs. The staircase climb to the next mesa is the hottest, toughest part of the hike, but shady ponderosa pines dot the rim.

Heading north toward Frijoles Canyon, cross a small drainage, then the larger Lummis Canyon. Beyond the foot of Corral Hill, make one last climb to the edge of Frijoles Canyon. About 10.5 miles from the start, meet the Frijoles Rim Trail and bear right. (For those doing a loop hike, turn left; it is 6.5 miles back to the trailhead.) In a few hundred feet, enjoy views into Frijoles Canyon and look across the canyon for the ladders to Alcove House. The trail now angles down the south wall of Frijoles Canyon, offering views of Long House along the way, and soon reaches the trailhead near the Bandelier Visitor Center.

35 CERRO GRANDE

Distance: 4 miles out-and-back, day hike
Difficulty: moderate
Elevation range: 8,990 to 10,160 feet
Elevation gain: 1,400 feet
Best time of year: May through November
Water: carry water
Map: USGS Bland
Managed by: National Park Service, Bandelier National
  Monument
Features: 360-degree views, fall aspens, elk

In the Jemez Mountains, geography and geology combine to create an unusual plant community that adds a distinctive feature to the scenic quality of the range. Volcanic soils on young peaks can support dense mixed-conifer forest and do so on three sides of the summits. The intense southwestern sun beats directly on the south-facing slopes, resulting in warm, dry conditions much of the year. Forest vegetation has difficulty growing on the south slopes, and many of the highest peaks in the eastern Jemez support extensive, roughly triangular grasslands on their sunniest side. Cerro Grande (Big Hill) has one of the largest montane grasslands in the Jemez.

Historically, fire played a role in maintaining the grasslands, holding the trees at bay by killing small seedlings that established themselves on the forest-grassland border. With 100 years of fire suppression, the hilltop meadows are shrinking in size. One of the objectives of a 2000 prescribed fire was to reintroduce fire to the system and push back the forest. The prescribed burn, renamed the Cerro Grande Fire, escaped and six days later entered the town of Los Alamos, destroying more than 400 homes and transforming Cerro Grande into a well-known landmark.

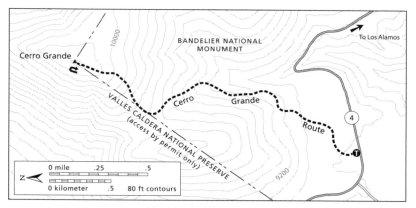

Signs of the 48,000-acre fire are hidden from the summit, but not much else in northern New Mexico is. The view reaches south to the Sandia Mountains and east to the Sangre de Cristo Range. But the scene to the west encompasses the great valleys of the central Jemez, including the peak's alter ego, Valle Grande (Big Valley). From this point on the eastern rim of the Valles Caldera, the extent of the volcanic collapse is readily apparent. It is a landscape unlike any other in the state.

The Upper Frijoles Addition of Bandelier National Monument was opened to public access in 2005, and Cerro Grande is its premier destination. Park managers opted not to build trails in the area, but there is now a well-worn, marked route from the trailhead to the summit.

Reach the trailhead from the intersection of NM 4 and NM 503 west of Los Alamos by heading west on NM 4, immediately climbing the Pajarito fault. The road winds a path up the rim of the Valles Caldera. At mile 6, turn into the Cerro Grande parking area in Bandelier National Monument on the right.

Pass through the gate near the information kiosk and begin walking the smooth, well-trodden trail through an aspen meadow. Throughout the summer, the meadow is dotted with beautiful cinquefoils, harebells, and several species of fleabane. The trail is flat and boggy at first, then it begins a sharp ascent along a linear meadow. As the trail makes several short, steep climbs, watch for yellow diamonds on the trees marking the route. The trail soon drops into a major drainage, crosses the bottom, and then ascends more or

less straight up the slope. After a quarter mile of steep pitches, at 1.4 miles from the start, the trail enters at the foot of a long meadow that extends north to the summit.

Pass through tall bunch grasses and watch for wildflowers hidden in the meadow. It is a moderate climb of about 0.6 mile to the summit. The view becomes increasingly grand as you approach the peak, but the view from the very top beats all. To the west are the *valles* of the Valles Caldera, and to the south is an all-encompassing view of the rugged southern half of the Jemez Mountains. After enjoying the view, return to the trailhead by the same route.

A sheepherder carving on an aspen on Cerro Grande

36 | GUAJE RIDGE

Distance: 9.5-mile loop, day hike
Difficulty: difficult
Elevation range: 7,025 to 8,790 feet
Elevation gain: 2,200 feet
Best time of year: May through November
Water: carry water
Map: USGS Guaje Mountain
Managed by: Santa Fe National Forest, Española Ranger
District
Features: close-up look at post-fire recovery,
long-range views

The 2000 Cerro Grande Fire left 48,000 acres of the Jemez Mountains covered with black trees and gray ash. On a human time scale, recovery after a crown fire is slow, but the natural processes begin almost immediately after the ground cools and constitute a relentless progression of revegetation. This loop through the heart of the Cerro Grande burn area is an education in the destructive powers of a crown fire, the nature of post-fire erosion, and the spectacular recovery ability of a forest. The trail starts in Rendija Canyon, where the constantly changing stream channel still is choked with gravel washed from the steep mountainsides in the first year following the fire. As the route reaches Guaje Ridge, it offers unobstructed views of the Valles Caldera rim and most of northern New Mexico. The loop is a tribute to the trail users of Los Alamos, who as volunteers completely reconstructed the trails that they once thought were lost forever.

Reach the trailhead from downtown Los Alamos by taking Trinity Drive west. At the intersection with Diamond Drive at the medical center, turn right onto Diamond. Continue 1.4 miles to 35th Street on the left. Turn left and drive to the T intersection with Arizona Avenue. Turn left and go 0.3 mile to the trailhead parking and information kiosk on the right.

Start walking uphill on the Mitchell Trail through a meadow dotted with pine saplings planted immediately following the Cerro Grande Fire. In 0.2 mile, continue straight as the Perimeter Trail heads left. Cross a dirt road and drop into Rendija Canyon. Pass the return leg of the trip, the Perimeter Trail, to the right. The trail now follows Rendija Canyon for about a mile. The canyon that once supported stately ponderosa pines now has a luxurious growth of native grasses and wildflowers, along with a generous dose of thorny New Mexico locust. Head steadily up the canyon on a rolling trail to mile 1.1 where the trail suddenly leaves the canyon bottom and begins a winding climb to Guaje Ridge. The trail is steep and eroded in

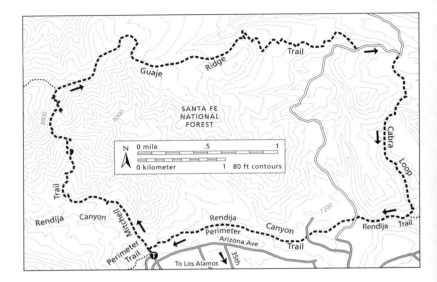

spots as it traverses ridges of fallen burned trees. Reach a false summit at mile 1.8, and then contour the head of a large drainage to the reach Guaje Ridge at mile 2.5.

At a sign commemorating the trail builder, turn right onto the Guaje Ridge Trail. Pass through a decade-old aspen forest, then enjoy views to the east and south. After a steep downhill, the grade moderates into a rolling descent with close-up views of Caballo Mountain. Tall New Mexico locusts offer sparse but welcome shade during this stretch. As the trail descends along the ridgeline, it passes through flat grasslands, slickrock rims, and in the fall, fields of purple asters.

At mile 5.5, intersect a wide road atop a saddle. Bear left onto the road for 0.4 mile to the intersection with the Cabra Loop at a second saddle. Turn right and immediately right again to descend through a small bowl. The Cabra Loop undulates through the terrain with wonderful views to the east. At a trail intersection at mile 6.5, make a sharp turn to the right to drop along a drainage. In a few minutes, reach a grove of ponderosa pines and continue down the floor of the canyon. The trail climbs over a low ridge before switchbacking down to meet the Rendija Trail at mile 7.5.

Turn right to head up the Rendija Trail. Continue straight at the first trail junction and then plunge into the rocky crack that gave Rendija its name. After post-fire floods, the trail has become a short scramble over rocks for a few hundred feet. Past the rocks, continue up the canyon floor to a sign marking the Rendija Trail's exit from the canyon. In a minute, reach a road, turn left for a few yards, then turn right onto the Perimeter Trail just before the road crosses the streambed.

*More than 1,000 hours of volunteer work brought back the Guaje
Ridge Trail after the Cerro Grande Fire.*

The Perimeter Trail heads up shady Rendija Canyon. The trail crosses a gravel road where a sign points the way to continue, then in another quarter mile reaches a paved road. Follow the sidewalk fifty feet to the left, cross the street, and follow the distinct trail past the housing area. At the first trail junction, angle right onto a wide trail parallel to the canyon floor. Follow the Perimeter Trail another 1.3 miles to meet the Mitchell Trail. Turn left and descend a short way to the trailhead.

37 | CABALLO MOUNTAIN

> **Distance: 14 miles out-and-back, day hike or backpack**
> **Difficulty:** strenuous
> **Elevation range:** 8,620 to 10,440 feet
> **Elevation gain:** 4,200 feet
> **Best time of year:** May through November
> **Water:** Guaje Canyon
> **Map:** USGS Guaje Mountain
> **Managed by:** Santa Fe National Forest, Española Ranger District
> **Features:** wild canyon and mountain country, views of the Rio Grande rift, wildlife

Although the summit of Caballo Mountain is closed to public access, the landmark meadow on its south flank provides one of the most extensive views in the Jemez Mountains. The view across the Rio Grande rift to the Sangre de Cristo Mountains is ample reward for the long, steep climb to the top. The journey to Caballo is made more challenging by the fact that the trail crosses Guaje Canyon—a 900-foot ascent on the return. The trip leads through several high meadows, which are prime elk habitat, and offers viewpoints into the Valles Caldera National Preserve along the way. In fact, the view into the

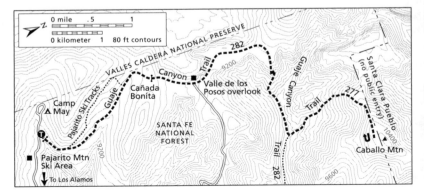

Entering the meadow atop Caballo Mountain

Valle de los Posos near mile 3 makes a fine destination for those looking for a shorter hike. Maps show a second route to the mountain from the bottom of Guaje Canyon, but after the Cerro Grande Fire, this route became impassable.

The trailhead is located at the Pajarito Mountain Ski Area. From Los Alamos, take NM 503, Trinity Drive, west through town. From the security gates, continue west on NM 503 for 1.3 miles to the road signed for the ski area. Turn right and head steeply uphill to the ski area parking lot. Park at the west end of the parking area just before the road narrows and drops downhill.

Begin walking on the gravel road leaving the west side of the parking area. In 100 feet, the Cañada Bonita Trail (also know as the Guaje Canyon Trail) 282 heads to the right. In a few yards, pass around a gate and continue on an old road. At the top of the first hill, at mile 0.4, bear left onto the Pajarito Ski Tracks. Follow the well-worn path through tall Douglas firs and aspens, ignoring the many minor ski trail junctions. At mile 1.4, the trail swings west and parallels the edge of Cañada Bonita, an extensive bunchgrass meadow that in summer is dotted with Mariposa lilies, Indian paintbrush, and other wildflowers. At mile 2.1, cross the meadow, climb to a saddle, and then drop to reach another gate. In a few minutes of walking on a dirt road, reach the Valle de los Posos overlook, where the view reaches across the Valles Caldera National Preserve.

The trail continues at a signed junction a few yards north of the overlook. Leave the road and angle left onto a narrower road. The route now traverses north on rolling hills through mixed conifer forest. At mile 4, swing to the east, then begin a steep descent on twisting switchbacks to reach the floor of Guaje Canyon at mile 4.7. Travel downcanyon about 0.4 mile, enjoying the sound of rushing water. Watch for a rock cairn that marks the beginning of the Caballo Trail 277.

Turn left onto the Caballo Trail and begin the steep ascent up the northwest flank of the mountain. At first the trail parallels a deep drainage to the left, and then it winds along the flanks of two ridges as it rapidly gains elevation. The first mile of the trail gains about 1,200 feet before the grade moderates in a densely overgrown forest. Here the trail wiggles around deadfall before resuming the steep pitch that leads to the summit meadow. Wander out into the meadow, but stay south of the Santa Clara Pueblo boundary. After a well-deserved rest, return to the trailhead by the same route.

38 CERROS DEL ABRIGO TRAIL

Distance: 6.5-mile lollipop loop, day hike
Difficulty: moderate
Elevation range: 8,750 to 9,600 feet
Elevation gain: 900 feet
Best time of year: May through September
Water: carry water
Maps: USGS Valle Toledo; Cerros del Abrigo Trail Map
    at Valles Caldera National Preserve website
Managed by: Valles Caldera National Preserve
Features: grand views of the Valles Caldera, rock glacier

In the heart of the Jemez Mountains, the Valles Caldera National Preserve includes six major grassland valleys. The valleys are located in an immense volcanic collapse crater, the Valles Caldera. The *valles* were well-known for their scenic beauty, and for ninety years efforts to transform the ranchland into a public park failed. Finally in 2000, a political compromise created the Valles Caldera National Preserve. The enabling legislation required the former ranch be an experiment in public land management, and that it remain a working ranch as more traditional recreational activities took place. The preserve is managed by a board of trustees who have to date taken a unique approach to access to public land. Access fees are charged for very specific activities, and private vehicles are not permitted beyond the recreation staging area. Only a few hiking trails are open and visitors must ride a shuttle to trailheads. Hikers are required to stay on the established trails, and no overnight use is permitted. The result is hikers can enjoy a scenic walk with the knowledge that only a limited number of other visitors are on the preserve.

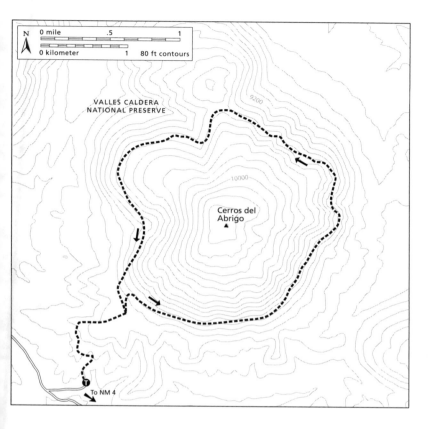

The Cerros del Abrigo Trail uses old logging roads to circumnavigate one of the small volcanic domes in the Valles Caldera. It is a hike with a modest climb followed by level walking for most of the journey. Along the way, the old road offers an outstanding view of each of the major *valles* in the preserve and is one of the most scenic hikes in New Mexico. Permits for hiking Cerros del Abrigo and other trails are available on the Internet or by phone. Only a limited number of days and reservations are offered, so it is a good idea to make your reservations several months in advance. Visit the website for the Valles Caldera National Preserve (see "Sources of Additional Information" at the back of this book) for the latest information and to make your trip reservations.

When your hike day arrives, head west from Los Alamos on NM 501 to the intersection with NM 4. Turn right onto NM 4 and head west. NM 4 winds up the rim of the Valles Caldera. Pass the Cerro Grande parking area in Bandelier National Monument at mile 6. About 12 miles from NM 501, turn right into the preserve. Continue about 2 miles on a well-graded gravel

A rock glacier along the Cerros del Abrigo Trail

road to the staging area and park. Check in at the visitor station, and ride the shuttle to the trailhead (about twenty minutes).

Begin walking uphill in a small valley. The trail soon swings to the west and begins a steady but moderate climb through second-growth forest of Douglas fir and aspen. In 0.9 mile, enter an open ponderosa pine stand and watch for a sign directing you to the right. Continue the climb, slowly traversing to the south side of the Cerros del Abrigo. Along the way, watch for views into Valle Jaramillo and smaller grasslands. The path levels out at about mile 1.5 and stays on this contour as it crosses to the hill's east flank. Here are views of the Valles Caldera rim and the peaks Cerro Grande, Pajarito Mountain, and the boulder-faced Cerro Rubio.

Continue around to the north face of the mountain and expansive views of the Valle Toledo. Cross a low saddle at mile 3.7, and then begin the slow descent from the contour you have been following. At mile 5, cross the foot of a rock glacier, a large field of angular volcanic boulders. In a few minutes, reach the intersection first encountered at mile 0.9. Bear right to continue downhill to the drop-off point where a van awaits to take you back to the staging area.

39 | VALLE GRANDE TRAIL

> **Distance: 2 miles out-and-back, day hike**
> **Difficulty:** easy
> **Elevation range:** 8,650 to 9,050 feet
> **Elevation gain:** 400 feet
> **Best time of year:** May through September
> **Water:** carry water
> **Maps:** USGS Bland (trail not shown on map); Valle Grande
> Trail Map at the Valles Caldera National Preserve website
> **Managed by:** Valles Caldera National Preserve
> **Features:** views from the edge of an extensive montane
> valley, elk

The Valle Grande is the largest of the montane valleys lying within the Valles Caldera. It is a grass-filled bowl formed by a series of lakes that puddled inside the collapsed volcano. The grand grasslands are a result of a combination of soil conditions, wildfire, vegetative competition, and high altitude. From the highway that passes along its edge, the *valle* seems huge. But only by sitting within the bowl can the true size of the *valle* be comprehended. Looking up at the surrounding walls of the caldera adds the proper perspective and provides a unique view of this scenic location. Early mornings in September, the air is often filled with the calls of bugling elk. This short hike leads to a spot a few hundred feet within the Valle Grande. It is one of two of the Valles Caldera National Preserve's free, spontaneous hikes. No reservations or access fees are required. However, the preserve's regulations state that hikers must stay on the trail at all times.

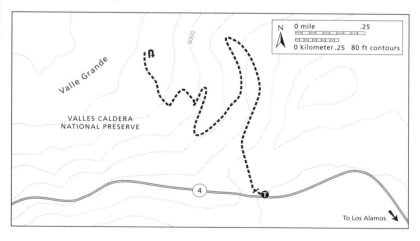

Elk herds are a common sight in the Valle Grande.

Reach the trailhead from the intersection of NM 4 and NM 501 west of Los Alamos by heading west on NM 4, immediately climbing the Pajarito fault. Pass the Cerro Grande parking area in Bandelier National Monument at mile 6. At the top of a rise at mile 6.8, enter the Valles Caldera National Preserve. Turn left into an unmarked parking area just west of the preserve boundary.

Carefully cross to the north side of the highway where a wooden sign announces the beginning of the Valle Grande Trail. Turn left and walk along a fence line for a minute, then pass through a gate and continue north on the now wider trail. The smooth tread is atop an old road and gradually descends through mixed conifer forest with monster Douglas firs, aspens, and ponderosa pines. Along the gradual descent, keep an eye out for the carvings on the aspens done by sheepherders. Swing through a gentle turn and continue down the now rocky path. Several broad switchbacks ease the downhill grade. As the trail passes through aspen stands, note the "high water mark" of browsing elk that shows they can reach only so high on the trees to tear off chunks of bark. About a mile from the start, the trail bursts out into an alcove of the Valle Grande. Suddenly, the entire *valle* lies ahead, lined with conifer-covered volcanic hills. Continue down the trail to a natural rock wall, and linger here to drink in the expansive view. When you've had your fill, make the gradual climb back to the trailhead on the same route.

40

EAST FORK OF THE JEMEZ RIVER

Distance: 4.6 miles one-way, day hike
Difficulty: easy
Elevation range: 8,120 to 8,580 feet
Elevation gain: 600 feet
Best time of year: mid-April through November
Water: East Fork Jemez River
Map: USGS Redondo Peak
Managed by: Santa Fe National Forest, Jemez National
  Recreation Area, Jemez Ranger District
Features: dormant volcano, fishing, wildlife,
  mountain meadows

In contrast to the many rugged hikes found in New Mexico, a stroll along the East Fork of the Jemez River is an easy, relaxing walk. The high-country stream flows within a rocky canyon in a deep conifer forest, yet the river also meanders through a series of open meadows filled in summer with a riot of wildflowers. The canyon is home to mountain wildlife, including mule deer, elk, bobcat, raccoon, and porcupine; birdsong fills the air at all times of day. The East Fork is well stocked with rainbow trout, and the most enjoyable hikes along the river include stops at the large pools for a bit of angling.

To set up a shuttle for a one-way hike, leave a car at the U.S. Forest Service East Fork western trailhead. From San Ysidro on US 550, travel north on NM 4, passing through Jemez Springs and past the intersection with NM 126. The well-marked western trailhead is about 5 miles from NM 126. From Los Alamos, go west on NM 501 to NM 4. Turn right and continue for 21 miles to the East Fork western trailhead. Once you have parked a car at the western trailhead, drive 3.5 miles east on NM 4 to the Las Conchas Trailhead, which is 0.25 mile west of the Las Conchas Fishing Access.

At the trailhead, the route descends wooden stairs from the parking lot to river level. Follow the trail as it heads downstream past tall cliffs of volcanic

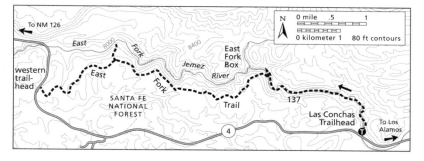

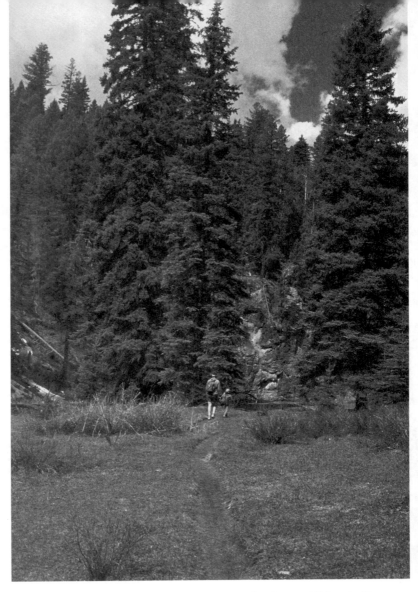

The popular East Fork Trail is a good introduction to hiking in New Mexico's high country.

rock and through alternating patches of forest and meadow. In the first mile, make five stream crossings on log bridges. Nice campsites are located along the river after the fourth bridge and beyond.

Cross three more bridges and reach the head of the East Fork Box in 2 miles. Here the main trail turns left and climbs to the canyon rim, but first take the short spur trail that leads along the river to views of the Box, a wild section of canyon. The main trail ascends on gentle switchbacks, then parallels the canyon on the mesa above. Continue west along the rim, parallel to a logging road that stays to the left. Much of this section of trail is a pleasant walk through open ponderosa pine forest.

At mile 4, a spur trail to the right descends again to the river. This trail branches about halfway down, the right fork dropping steeply to the bottom of the Box—a delightful and popular lunch stop—and the left fork leading to a trail along the river. Take both spurs and climb back to the main trail.

The last mile of trail descends slowly through a pine stand overcrowded with small ponderosas. Near the end, the trail merges with a wide logging road, marked as a ski trail with blue diamonds. Reach the west trailhead about 4.6 miles from Las Conchas, or 6 miles including the side trip to the river.

41   JEMEZ FALLS AND McCAULEY HOT SPRINGS

Distance: 5.6 miles out-and-back, day hike
Difficulty: moderate
Elevation range: 6,800 to 7,910 feet
Elevation gain: 1,200 feet
Best time of year: April to November
Water: carry water
Map: USGS Jemez Springs
Managed by: Santa Fe National Forest,
    Jemez Ranger District
Features: hot springs, tall waterfall, deep canyon

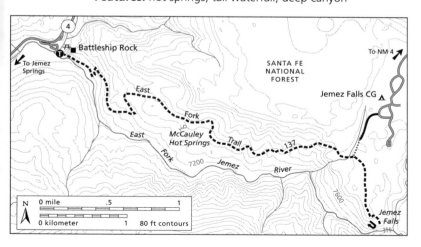

Scattered through New Mexico's national forests are dozens of hot springs where hikers can soak in naturally heated water bubbling out of the ground. One concentration of springs is located in the Jemez Mountains. McCauley Hot Springs are a delightful series of pools that lie in the Jemez backcountry on a bench above the East Fork of the Jemez River. An oval pool as big as a living room is the main attraction, but the warm outflow from the pond collects in three or four smaller rock tubs below. At about 92 degrees Fahrenheit, the water in every pool is delightfully relaxing.

The East Fork Trail 137 leads to the hot springs from two directions. Hikers can start at either trailhead and return via the same route, or walk through the entire canyon. The route described here heads from Battleship Rock Picnic Area to Jemez Falls and requires a modest climb of 1,200 feet. Consider the hot springs a reward on the return leg of the journey.

Reach Battleship Rock Picnic Area from Los Alamos by taking NM 501 to NM 4. Turn right onto NM 4 and head in the direction of Jemez Springs. Continue about 30 miles to the village of La Cueva, passing the Jemez Falls Campground at about mile 24. At La Cueva, bear left to stay on NM 4 and continue 3.2 miles to the picnic area on the left, where a small day-use fee is charged. The picnic area is reached from the south by traveling on US 550 to the village of San Ysidro. Turn right on NM 4 and continue about 6 miles beyond the town of Jemez Springs. The area closes at 7:00 PM, and no overnight parking is permitted.

Follow the trail signs for Trail 137 from an imposing wooden gazebo at the east end of the Battleship Rock Picnic Area. The trail stays close to the East Fork of the Jemez River for a quarter mile, and you should ignore a maze of fishing trails that lead right to the East Fork. Follow the main route as it ascends the south-facing canyon slope. The grade is steady as the trail climbs farther from the canyon bottom. After a mile of climbing, enjoy a long stretch of rolling terrain shaded by tall ponderosa pines. After an hour of walking, reach the largest of the pools at the hot springs. If you decide to make this your destination, enjoy the warm water. If you are continuing upcanyon, follow the winding path through warm pools and the warm outflow stream.

Beyond the last pool, the wide trail continues to ascend the canyon. As you head uphill, enjoy expanding views of outcrops of colorful tuff—welded volcanic ash—scattered among the pines. Gain the canyon rim about 2.5 miles from the start and traverse rolling hills. Stay on Trail 137 as spur trails to Jemez Falls Campground go left. Near the Jemez Falls parking area, walk down the trail toward the falls, following the signs pointing straight ahead at a trail junction. Descend a minor drainage for 0.3 mile to an overlook of the falls and enjoy the impressive drop of the East Fork over a volcanic cliff. When you are ready to return, backtrack to the main trail and retrace your steps to Battleship Rock on Trail 137.

42 | SAN PEDRO PEAKS

Distance: 16.5 miles out-and-back, backpack
Difficulty: difficult
Elevation range: 9,250 to 10,570 feet
Elevation gain: 1,400 feet
Best time of year: late June through late September
Water: Clear Creek, Rio de las Vacas
Maps: USGS Nacimiento Peak;
    USFS San Pedro Parks Wilderness
Managed by: Santa Fe National Forest,
    San Pedro Parks Wilderness, Cuba Ranger District
Features: unique plateau scenery, wildlife, solitude,
    good fishing

The San Pedro Parks Wilderness sits on a high granite plateau at the northwestern edge of the Jemez Mountains. The peaks average 9,500 feet in elevation. Damp granitic soils produce extensive meadows interrupted by open stands of fir and spruce, offering an expansive feeling not often

Most trails in the San Pedro Parks parallel streams.

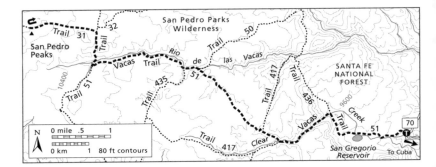

found high in the mountains. Although the hiking is easy, this unique landscape is little known and sees few visitors. It is the perfect summer escape from the crowds. The extensive trail network invites a couple days of exploration.

Elk and bear are frequently spotted in the meadows, and native Rio Grande cutthroat trout swim the clear waters of the Rio de las Vacas and Clear Creek. Because of the high elevation, snow lingers well into June and trails can be quite soggy until early July. Hikers should bring their best hiking boots and extra socks. Note that the trails often cross open bogs and can be difficult to follow; watch for wooden posts that mark the way.

Reach the San Pedro Parks Wilderness via NM 126 east out of Cuba or north from the village of La Cueva (north of Albuquerque and reached via US 550 and NM 4). Take NM 126 about 30 miles, mostly unpaved, from La Cueva. The road is passable to high-clearance vehicles except in winter and after heavy rains. From Cuba, take NM 126 east about 6 miles; all but the last 0.5 mile is paved. Turn onto FR 70, heading north. In 3 miles, park at the trail for the wilderness and San Gregorio Reservoir.

From the trailhead, walk a gentle uphill on the Vacas Trail 51. In 0.75 mile, skirt around the east side of San Gregorio Reservoir and make an easy crossing of Clear Creek. After reentering the conifer forest, swing east to rejoin Clear Creek at mile 1.7. Bear left along the edge of the picturesque Vallecito Damian, a steep climb up the canyon of Clear Creek. At mile 3, Trail 51 leaves the stream and climbs to a small wooded plateau as it passes junctions with Trail 417 first to the left and in a short distance to the right. Reach the Rio de las Vacas at mile 5 and cross to the east bank. At the intersection with Trail 50, turn left to stay on Trail 51. In 0.3 mile, again cross Rio de las Vacas and pass the Anastacio Trail 435 to the left. Along the next mile are numerous campsites with memorable views.

Near mile 7, turn right onto the Peñas Negras Trail 32 and climb a short drainage to a saddle. On top of the saddle, turn left onto the Rio Capulin Trail 31. Head uphill through rocky meadows toward the top of the plateau. The peaks are on a broad summit area that offers outstanding views in all directions. After enjoying the view, retrace your steps to the trailhead.

43 | WINDOW ROCK

Distance: 9 miles, day hike
Difficulty: moderate
Elevation range: 5,800 to 6,400 feet
Elevation gain: 800 feet
Best time of year: year-round
Water: carry water
Maps: USGS Chili and Mendanales
Managed by: Santa Fe National Forest,
Española Ranger District
Features: open spaces, large natural arch

In other parts of the Southwest, even modest natural arches have fanciful names like Backpacker Arch or Hellroaring Bridge. The generic name Window Rock downplays the interest in this attractive hole in rock that might have gone by the name Dragons Mouth. One of northern New Mexico's largest rock spans, Window Rock is punched through a thin ridge of hardened lava. From below, the black, gnarled stone around the opening looks like nasty teeth ready to chomp whoever wanders by.

With a diameter of about ten feet, Window Rock can be seen from more than 5 miles away, but the arch is much more appealing up close. The view through the window of the surrounding mesas and distant mountains is worth the extra effort required to get behind it.

To reach the trailhead, drive northwest from Española on US 84/285. Continue straight on US 84 when US 285 splits off to the right and note your mileage. In 3.2 miles from US 285, and halfway between mileposts 200 and 201 on US 84, watch for a yellow cattle guard on the left (south) side of the highway. Turn onto the road with the cattle guard and park off the highway near a Forest Service boundary marker.

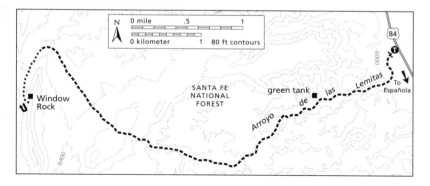

Window Rock

Begin the hike by walking through a gate and heading toward Arroyo de las Lemitas to the south (left as you pass through the fence). Several tracks lead to the arroyo; all parallel the highway and a powerline. Cross two smaller drainages before reaching the broad, sandy arroyo at mile 0.4. Turn right and trudge up the deep, soft sand of the arroyo bottom or along brief stretches of two-track road that appear now and then. Continue up the arroyo toward a lone sandstone tower and pass the spire and a green water tank at mile 0.9. A few minutes after passing a vertical rock wall with globs of sandstone at the base, the canyon abruptly turns right. At this point, about 1.4 miles from the start, bear left onto a sandy terrace and immediately watch for a steeply climbing old road leading out of the canyon. The road pitches slightly uphill for the next mile before descending into a broad valley. At mile 3.4, watch for the arch on the skyline to the left (south).

For a closer look at the window, hikers should avoid the erosion-causing trails up the front of the rock face and continue on the road past a stock pond to the shoulder of the ridge that holds Window Rock. Immediately turn left and follow a rocky road on the south side of the ridge for 0.25 mile. Although the arch is hidden from this rocky road, it is easy to find by climbing to the left and searching along the ridge.

After enjoying the view from the arch, return to the trailhead by the same route.

44 RIM VISTA TRAIL

Distance: 4.6 miles, day hike
Difficulty: moderate
Elevation range: 6,605 to 7,940 feet
Elevation gain: 1,200 feet
Best time of year: March to December
Water: carry water
Map: USGS Echo Amphitheater
Managed by: Carson National Forest,
    Canjilon Ranger District
Features: outstanding view of redrock country

The sedimentary rock layers of the Colorado Plateau create grand scenery from Utah to New Mexico. The rocks tell the story of shallow seas with dinosaurs roaming the shorelines, of freshwater lakes, and a massive sand dune desert rivaling the modern Sahara. Nowhere are these rocks more colorfully displayed than from the edge of the Mesa de los Viejos and an overlook simply called Rim Vista. The hike to the vista climbs from the red mudstones of the Chinle Formation to the top of the Dakota Sandstone, a climb through time of almost 100 million years. Little shade is available on this route, making it ideal in spring, fall, or winter, but to be avoided in summer.

From Española, travel north on US 84 about 37 miles to FR 151, almost 1 mile past the USFS Ghost Ranch–Piedra Lumbre Education Center. Turn left onto FR 151, a graded gravel road suited for all vehicles in dry weather. Seven-tenths of a mile from the highway, turn right onto a dirt track, which is signed for the Rim Vista Trail. In 0.2 mile, bear right at a Y intersection and park at the trailhead in another 0.1 mile.

Head west on Trail 15, immediately dropping into and out of a small arroyo. Climb around the end of a ridge to the top, passing in 0.2 mile a small knife-edged ridge with views to the right of swirling patterns in the

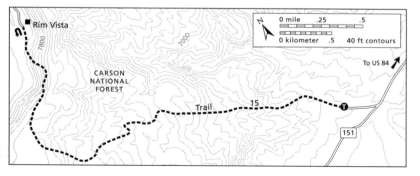

Entrada Sandstone. Continue a steeper climb on the south flank of the ridge. Beyond, blue diamonds mark the wide trail as it climbs a rocky section of slope through juniper-piñon woodland.

As the trail flattens out, climb a broad ridge dotted with sagebrush and large piñon pines. At mile 1.2, the trail swings south, then west again. In another mile, the gradual slope ends as the trail climbs a broad bench, then turns north to parallel the cliff of Dakota Sandstone above. The view becomes grander with each step, culminating at the vista at mile 2.2 where the trail meets the end of a rough road. On the mesa top, pick a rock to sit on and take a well-deserved break to enjoy the long-distance views. From the vista point, the rocks of Ghost Ranch, Abiquiu Lake, the Jemez Mountains, and the Sangre de Cristo Mountains are in view. Return to the trailhead by the same route.

The red sandstones of the Ghost Ranch area dominate the hike to Rim Vista.

45 | Ojitos Canyon Trail

Distance: 12 miles, day hike or backpack
Difficulty: difficult
Elevation range: 6,340 to 8,080 feet
Elevation gain: 1,800 feet
Best time of year: mid-March to November
Water: intermittent in Ojitos Creek, carry water
Map: USGS Laguna Peak
Managed by: Santa Fe National Forest,
    Rio Chama Wilderness, Coyote Ranger District
Features: colorful cliffs, secluded backcountry camping

A trip into Ojitos Canyon is a hiker's hike, a trip taken more for the sheer joy of walking and being in the backcountry than to reach a destination. The trail is one of northern New Mexico's only completed sections of the Continental Divide Trail. It follows Ojitos Canyon through colorful cliffs of Mesozoic rocks in the little-used Rio Chama Wilderness. The trail is well marked with Continental Divide Trail markers. Backcountry campsites are abundant in the canyon and near the trail's end on Mesa del Camino. A trickle of water will be found in the stream most of the year. Watch for chunks of white quartz, gypsum, and petrified wood, all common in the red Chinle mudstones along the first 2 miles of the trail.

From Española, travel north on US 84 about 37 miles to FR 151, about 1 mile past the USFS Ghost Ranch–Piedra Lumbre Education Center. Turn left onto FR 151, a dirt road suited for all vehicles in dry weather. Continue about 8.5 miles to Skull Bridge on the Rio Chama and park.

Cross the Rio Chama on the bridge and continue through a gate on the dirt road heading south. In 200 yards, the road swings west as the trail continues straight; look for pointed posts inscribed with the Continental Divide Trail symbol. After entering the Rio Chama Wilderness, the trail passes along the wide mouth of Ojitos Canyon through open sagebrush country backed

Ojitos Canyon was the site of a long irrigation ditch complete with flumes for stream crossings.

by red, tan, and yellow cliffs. Follow the trail as it turns left, entering a gap; then proceed around a mudstone mesa and over a low saddle before dropping back into the main canyon.

Immediately after passing through another hikers gate at mile 2.1, bear right and watch for the next trail marker. The path now closely follows the canyon bottom, where running water is found most of the year. Much of the trail follows the route of an abandoned acequia, and metal flumes from the old ditch appear at several stream crossings.

At mile 4.5, while on the east bank of the stream, the trail leaves the canyon bottom and begins to climb the wall of Mesa del Camino on a long series of steep switchbacks. Here the trail passes through an open forest of ponderosa pine and Gambel oak, offering views of the Ojitos Canyon. About 0.75 mile up the switchbacks, watch for a view through the trees of the canyon country below and of the San Juan Mountains on the distant horizon. Near the top of the climb, the trail leaves the wilderness and reaches a sloping bench at about 8,000 feet. The trail skirts the northwest edge of the bench, ending at a dirt road a couple hundred feet below the flat summit of Mesa del Camino. To the left is a protected campsite. From the end of the trail, hikers can bushwhack straight up to the summit of the mesa, or take the more moderate course of following the road to the north about a mile to a saddle that offers excellent views both to the west and east. Return to the trailhead by the same route.

Opposite: El Morro stands high above the surrounding plains.

Previous page: *Petroglyphs on flat ground are among the unusual features in the Ojitos Wilderness.*

Above: *The trail to Williams Lake passes several glacial rock fields.*

Below left: *The Blue Dot Trail drops from the canyon rim to the Rio Grand*

Below right: *Sheepherders frequently recorded their passage on the aspens surrounding the Valle Grande.*

Above: *Yellow aspen leaves and deep blue skies are signs of fall in New Mexico.*

Below: *A bee fly sucks nectar from a Rocky Mountain yarrow.*

Opposite: *Frijoles Canyon slices through the orange volcanic ash that erupted from the Valles Caldera about one million years ago.*

Above: *Lava flows form the cliffs of Little Horse Mesa.*

Below: *Mesquite pods in Yucca Canyon* (Photo by Jessica Martin)

Above: *Dry arroyos offer access passages to the De-Na-Zin Wilderness.*

Below: *Nambe Lake sits in a cirque along the crest of the Sangre de Cristos.*

Above: *Hamilton Mesa offers some of the best views of the high peaks of the Sangre de Cristo Mountains in the Pecos Wilderness.* (Photo by Joel Pearson)

Below: *The limestone ledges of Devils Den Canyon are one of the interesting features of the Guadalupe Mountains.*

Above: *The once thriving community of Ponil Park was built overlooking the grasslands and peaks of the Valle Vidal Unit of the Carson National Forest.*

The rock work at Peñasco Blanco is exquisite.

Opposite: *On Mesa del Camino, the view stretches north to the San Juan Mountains.*

Above left: *Shooting stars*

Above right: *The East Fork Trail offers spring hiking with a touch of snow.*

Below: *The trail network in the Big Tubes area crosses a natural lava bridge.*

Above: *The grassy mesas of Valle Vidal offer outstanding vistas in all directions.*

Below: *Hoodoo rock formations are common in the Ojitos Wilderness.*

Above: *St. Peters Dome from the approach to Cerro Picacho*

Opposite: *The grassy valley of the San Francisco River between the Frisco Warm Spring and the Frisco Box*

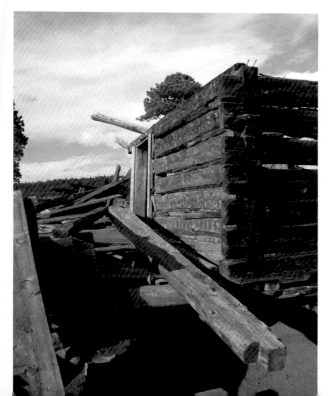

The main ranch house at the McCrystal Place dates back to around 1900.

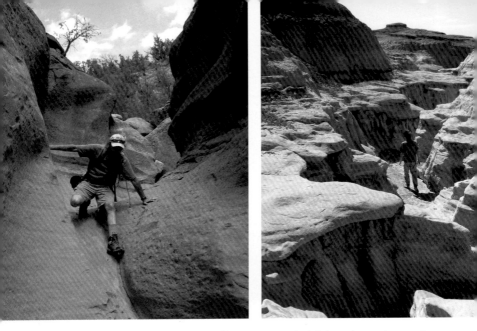

Above left: *Chavez Canyon offers gymnastic hiking through a series of narrow chutes.*

Above right: *Hikers can spend days exploring the convoluted miniature canyon in the Bisti Wilderness.*

Below: *A collared lizard perches on a trail marker on the Zuni-Acoma Trail.*

Above: *Gypsum sand dunes at White Sands National Monument*
(Photo by Jessica Martin)

Below: *Window Rock developed through a narrow ridge of lava
in the foothills of the Jemez Mountains.*

Next page: *Strange rock towers form where the Dakota sandstone
meets the Morrison formation.*

NORTHWEST PLATEAU AND ZUNI MOUNTAINS

46 CHAVEZ CANYON

Distance: 3 miles or more out-and-back, day hike
Difficulty: easy, but a scramble
Elevation range: 6,430 to 7,300 feet
Elevation gain: 900 feet
Best time of year: March to November
Water: none
Maps: USGS Laguna Peak and Navajo Peak
   (route not shown on maps)
Managed by: Santa Fe National Forest,
   Rio Chama Wilderness
Features: colorful cliffs, slot canyon

Hard sandstone and sporadic but intense rainfall can combine to create sinuous natural routes through seemingly impenetrable cliffs. Following water's course, hikers can navigate the red and white bands of rock on the trailless scramble into Chavez Canyon. The route features three short-but-sweet slot canyons and invites hours of wandering along the stream channel. However, take heed of the scoured rock: when water flows in the canyon, it is no place to be hiking. Check for the most recent weather forecast before journeying into the canyon, and be watchful for storms in the high country above that could send a flash flood through the gorge in a matter of minutes.

To reach the trailhead, take US 84/285 north from Española. Stay on US 84 when US 285 splits off to the north. About 37.5 miles from Española, and about 1 mile north of the USFS Ghost Ranch–Piedra Lumbre Education Center, turn left onto FR 151. This gravel road is passable to all vehicles in dry weather but may be slick when wet. Follow FR 151 as it winds along the Rio Chama for 12.5 miles. Here Chavez Canyon crosses the road and there is parking for two vehicles on the right.

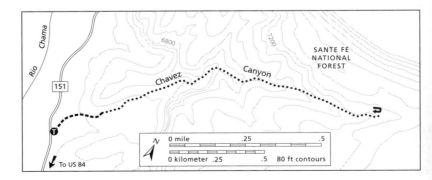

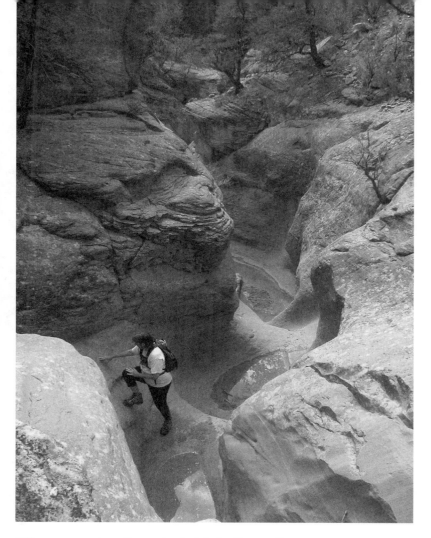

Hikers can explore three short slots in Chavez Canyon.

Begin by walking about 200 feet north on the road toward the Christ in the Desert Monastery visible just ahead. Watch for an unmarked trail heading to the right. The distinct trail heads toward the broad mouth of Chavez Canyon. The trail climbs gradually as it approaches impressive red and white cliffs to the north and south. In 0.5 mile, drop into the canyon bottom and work your way up the streambed. The route is rocky and the going is slow, but the canyon is filled with interesting features on all scales. The swirling layers in the sandstone dominate the long view; closer in are patterns of mud cracks, unusual wildflowers, and abstracts painted by flowing water with seedpods, pebbles, and silt.

At mile 0.7, reach the first of the slots. Trust the friction of your boot soles to work up through the potholes and slickrock. At mile 1.1, come to a split in the canyon. Explore both arms to the pour-offs a short way up. Continuing in the channel beyond this point requires climbing skills, but there is an easy way around the left fork by climbing the rock scree to the north for about 100 feet up and then continuing right to parallel the stream. You can reenter the canyon bottom above the pour-off in about 200 feet. Another few minutes brings you to a second narrows that ends in another cliff face. With caution, you can again skirt to the north to regain the canyon bottom above the pour-off. The canyon above this point offers slickrock stairs, balanced rocks, and a close-up look at the cliffs of Mesa de los Viejos. Exploring the full length of the canyon takes at least a half day. When you have finished your explorations, return to the trailhead via the same route.

47 | KITCHEN MESA

Distance: 4.6 miles, day hike
Difficulty: easy, except for one short climb
Elevation range: 6,540 to 7,140 feet
Elevation gain: 600 feet
Best time of year: late April to November
Water: carry water
Map: USGS Ghost Ranch
Managed by: Ghost Ranch Presbyterian Center
Features: redrock scenery, wide open vistas

The Ghost Ranch area, with its naked redrock landscape, is more characteristic of northern Arizona or southern Utah than it is of New Mexico.

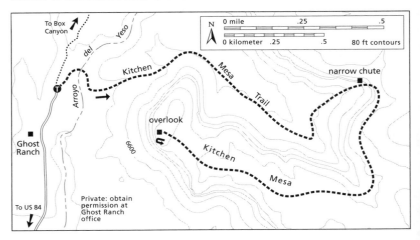

The brick-red mudstones of the Chinle Formation—massive river delta deposits from the age of the early dinosaurs—dominate Ghost Ranch. Above the Chinle are soaring cliffs of yellow-brown Entrada Sandstone capped by gray lake deposits of the Todilto Formation. The trip to the top of Kitchen Mesa takes hikers into the heart of this wilderness of stone, leading to breathtaking views of rocks, cliffs, and Abiquiu Lake to the south.

The Kitchen Mesa Trail traverses private land owned by the Ghost Ranch Presbyterian Center, which is very receptive to use of the trail by responsible hikers. Before hitting the trail, hikers must check in at the office and tell the staff of their plans to visit Kitchen Mesa.

From Española, take US 84/285 north, staying on US 84 when US 285 splits off about 5 miles from town. Continue about 35 miles from Española, through Abiquiu to the gravel road on the right marked for the Ghost

Hikers must climb this narrow chute to reach the top of Kitchen Mesa.

Ranch Presbyterian Center. (This is not the same as the USFS Ghost Ranch–Piedra Lumbre Education Center, which is about 1.5 miles beyond the Presbyterian Center.) Turn right and drive 1 mile to a road fork; follow the signs left to the office and ask for permission to hike the Kitchen Mesa Trail. Drive back to the fork, turn left, and continue slowly through the Center. About 1 mile from the office road turnoff, park in a large area just before a "No Vehicles Beyond This Point" sign.

The Kitchen Mesa Trail is marked with blue coffee cans. Find the first can by walking up the road (north) from the parking area for about 100 yards, then turn right to cross a small stream in Arroyo del Yeso. Climb to the bluff above the stream and walk the easy-to-follow trail across a sagebrush flat. Around a small hill, the trail passes in the shadow of Kitchen Mesa 400 feet overhead. Yes, the end of this trail is only 0.25 mile from the beginning!

The trail suddenly climbs and descends a steep, open slope of red Chinle mudstone, then bears right into a broad canyon. At mile 0.7, the trail crosses the canyon bottom, then climbs up the slope on the north side of the canyon.

One mile from the start, the trail crosses a slick stretch of loose rock where caution is required. The route climbs steeply up the rocks; follow the blue cans, painted blue arrows, and the path worn into the rocks. On the last section of the ascent, hikers must climb a narrow chute and boost themselves up through a fissure in the rock to reach the top of the mesa. Fortunately, well-placed hand- and footholds make the short climb easier than it first appears.

Once up the crack, the trail is almost on the mesa top. Bear right and cross the head of an arroyo, then make a final climb. The trail again bears right at the top of the mesa. From the 2-mile point, the trail crosses an eerie, barren white landscape: the gypsum lakebeds of the Todilto Formation. Walk to the end of the mesa and enjoy the expansive view. Bright sun and wind can make the last exposed 0.5 mile of trail unpleasant, so retreat to the edge of the junipers to find some shade for lunch or a rest stop. Return to the trailhead by the same route.

48 | BOX CANYON AND MESA MONTOSA

Distance: 10 miles, day hike
Difficulty: moderate
Elevation range: 6,540 to 7,980 feet
Elevation gain: 1,800 feet
Best time of year: March to November
Water: carry water
Map: USGS Ghost Ranch
Managed by: Ghost Ranch Presbyterian Center;
  Carson National Forest, Canjilon Ranger District
Features: redrock cliffs, fossils, spectacular box canyon
  and pour-off

Mesa Montosa is part of the northern boundary of the basin of Mesozoic rocks surrounding the Rio Chama. On the way to the mesa top, a short side trip leads to Box Canyon. The spur dead-ends at a pour-off—a normally dry waterfall—about 200 feet high and with a noticeable overhang. In the Box, hikers are surrounded on all sides by yellow rock cliffs. Throughout late fall to early spring, seeps in the cliff face are frozen, decorating the alcove with pillars of ice. Beyond Box Canyon, the trail climbs through time as well as altitude, beginning with Jurassic Entrada Sandstone, which is the cliff-forming rock of the canyon walls. The yellow, green, and purple muds of the Morrison Formation form a broad bench above the cliffs. Finally, the trail climbs the next cliff, the Cretaceous Dakota Sandstone.

This hike begins on the private Ghost Ranch Presbyterian Center at the same trailhead as the Kitchen Mesa Trail (Hike 47). Follow the same directions for access and securing permission to hike.

In winter huge columns of ice form at the pour-off in Box Canyon.

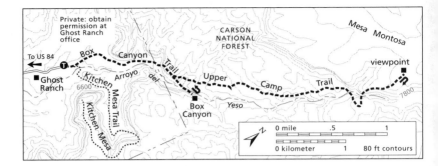

From the parking area, begin walking on the road marked for Kitchen Mesa and Box Canyon. In a hundred feet, the Kitchen Mesa Trail turns right. Continue straight and follow the road as it skirts the base of a monolith of Entrada Sandstone. Just after crossing an irrigation ditch, take the right fork, dropping down along the bottom of Arroyo del Yeso.

Heading upstream on a wide trail, cross under a flume, which is part of the old irrigation system for the ranch below. The trail now stays close to the stream, crossing it many times in the shade of cottonwoods. At a trail junction at mile 1.2, take the right fork marked for Box Canyon. The primitive trail stays close to the stream, crossing it many times. After several minutes, come to a small oasis where two canyons meet, and enjoy the small pools and waterfalls. Continue up the main canyon for 200 yards to the massive alcove and the high pour-off. The last section of trail requires a bit of scrambling over rocks.

After enjoying the alcove, backtrack to the earlier trail junction. Turn right onto the Upper Camp Trail. The trail climbs above the canyon floor before dropping into a side canyon. Next, the trail climbs steeply out of the canyon to a viewpoint overlooking Box Canyon. Crossing a sagebrush flat, the trail levels for 0.5 mile before climbing to another bench. On the bench, the trail swings west before climbing up a small drainage, which is easy to miss. The trail swings back to the east, now paralleling the high cliff of brown Dakota Sandstone to the left.

At mile 4.4, the trail again crosses the Arroyo del Yeso before climbing around a knoll. This steep section of trail offers great views of the Dakota cliff winding off to the west. Reach a low saddle and begin dropping into the upper Arroyo del Yeso. Before reaching the canyon bottom, bear left on a faint trail that crosses the canyon and climbs the opposite canyon wall on an old road. Several branches of the trail climb the hill: select any one. The old road contours around a point of Mesa Montosa, then climbs to the mesa top. Look for a road to the right that leads to the point of the mesa and long-distance views of the Jemez Mountains, the Rio Chama Canyon, and Abiquiu Lake. After enjoying the view, return by the same route.

49 | CRUCES BASIN

Distance: 8 miles, day hike or backpack
Difficulty: moderate
Elevation range: 9,150 to 9,800 feet
Elevation gain: 900 feet
Best time of year: late May through November
Water: Beaver, Diablo, and Cruces creeks
Maps: USGS Toltec Mesa; USFS Cruces Basin Wilderness
Managed by: Carson National Forest, Cruces Basin
  Wilderness, Tres Piedras Ranger District
Features: rolling mountain scenery, solitude

The Cruces Basin Wilderness is a small gem in Carson National Forest near the Colorado border. Open meadows, clear streams, long vistas, and bold granite outcrops characterize the high plateau. The long, dusty access road discourages most prospective visitors, so hikers are likely to enjoy their trip in relative solitude.

The lack of developed trails helps keep the Cruces Basin Wilderness a lonely place. Hikers must follow unofficial, angler, or game trails. The

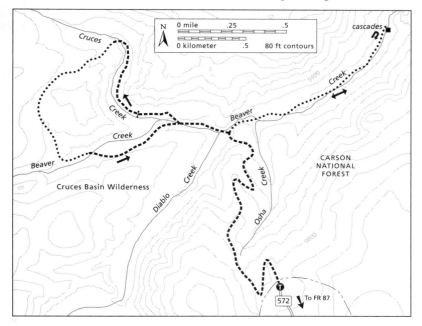

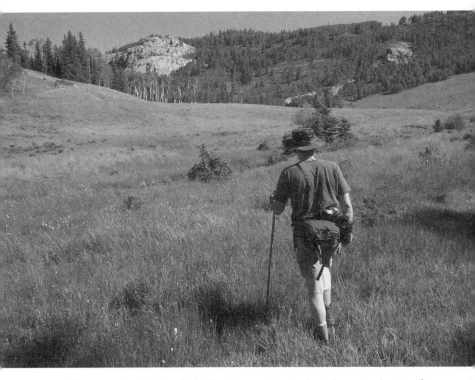

Hikers won't find trails in the Cruces Basin, but there is plenty of room to roam. (Photo by Joel Pearson)

described loop requires the ability to read a topographic map and find a route through trailless meadows and forest. Plan to spend several days here exploring from a base camp somewhere along the described route. Campsites and water are plentiful in the valleys of all three creeks. Numerous primitive campsites found along FR 572 just outside the wilderness make excellent overnight stops before a trip into the basin.

Entry to the Cruces Basin Wilderness is from Tres Piedras, about 33 miles west of Taos on US 64 and 55 miles north of Española via US 285. From Tres Piedras take US 285 north about 11 miles to FR 87 and turn left. FR 87 is a long gravel and dirt road passable to any vehicle when dry, but sections of the road can be impassable for days following heavy rains. Follow FR 87 through several junctions, passing FR 87A in 21 miles. A mile beyond FR 87A, turn right onto FR 572, heading uphill. FR 572 is rough and impassable when wet. When the road is dry, a carefully driven car can make the 2 miles to the trailhead.

Begin hiking the well-worn trail heading downhill from behind the wilderness information sign (ignore the fainter trail that follows an old road along the ridge). Drop into the head of Osha Canyon. In a long meadow at mile 1.2, come to a trail junction. Bear left and away from Osha Creek onto the branch leading back into the forest and over a saddle near the end of a ridge.

At the saddle, enjoy wonderful views of the three main streams of the Cruces Basin. To the left is Diablo Creek, and straight ahead are Beaver and Cruces creeks. The trail drops on loose rock to the junction of Diablo and Beaver creeks. From here the trail is less distinct, frequently disappearing in the wet meadows surrounding the streams. Before crossing Beaver Creek, turn right and head down the spacious valley for about a mile, passing deep pools and long riffles along the way. The valley comes to an abrupt end where the stream suddenly plunges 800 feet over a long string of cascades. Enjoy the view from the top of the pour-off, and then return to the point where you first met the valley floor. Cross to the north side of Beaver Creek and continue up the valley. From here the trail is less distinct, frequently disappearing in the wet meadows surrounding the streams. Head up the right side of Beaver Creek, passing some active beaver lodges along the way.

At mile 3.6, the valley splits with Beaver Creek to the left and Cruces Creek to the right. Follow the faint trail past the stream confluence and up Cruces Creek, soon passing through a gate. Just beyond are several shady sites for a base camp. The stream meanders through the broad meadow, turning west and passing beneath a huge wall of granite. Near the base of the rock wall, the trail crosses the stream and parallels the left bank, climbing more steeply. At mile 4.2, around the west side of the granite wall, the trail enters another extensive meadow. At this point, pick up the small stream that meets Cruces Creek in the meadow and follow the smaller stream as it heads west. Watch for blooms of pink shooting stars and purple bull elephant heads along the banks.

Follow the small stream as it heads uphill and into the forest. In 0.5 mile from Cruces Creek, about 4.8 miles from the trail start, the stream enters a narrow meadow and soon forks. Take the left fork, heading south, staying in the meadow. A faint trail near the edge of the trees leads up the meadow toward a saddle. As the trail reaches the marshy saddle, cross a fence line and look for a small, normally dry drainage heading southeast down the other side. Walk parallel to the drainage, dropping steeply through deep forest into the canyon of Beaver Creek. In 0.25 mile, the drainage enters a large meadow with views of the surrounding canyons and ridges. Drop through the meadow to the bottom and meet Beaver Creek. Pick up a trail on the north slope of the canyon that follows Beaver Creek downstream, rounding a massive granite outcrop that has bent the course of the stream to the north.

After a few minutes walking along Beaver Creek, the canyon opens into a broad meadow. Parallel the stream on faint trails down to the junction with Cruces Creek and pick up the trail used before to ascend the valley. Backtrack past the confluence of Diablo and Beaver creeks, and then make the moderate climb up Osha Creek to return to the trailhead.

50 CONTINENTAL DIVIDE TRAIL, SAN LUIS MESA

Distance: 10 miles out-and-back, day hike
Difficulty: easy
Elevation range: 6,350 to 6,700 feet
Elevation gain: 800 feet
Best time of year: March to May, September to November
Water: carry water
Maps: USGS San Luis and Arroyo Empedrado
Managed by: Bureau of Land Management,
    Albuquerque Field Office
Features: views of volcanic necks, badlands topography,
    strange-shaped rocks

The rangelands of the Rio Puerco watershed are a lonesome landscape that readily displays the paradox of the importance of water in shaping the land in the arid Southwest. Deeply incised arroyos fragment the terrain into thousands of isolated islands of rock. Sheer walls of sandstone border the islands and stretch on for miles. Dark, almost sinister volcanic necks—the throats of dead volcanoes now exposed by erosion of the softer sandstone—punctuate the scene. It is an eerie land that holds many beautiful secrets.

The segment of the Continental Divide Trail along the heights of San Luis Mesa provides exquisite views into the Rio Puerco Basin, and offers close-up looks at the interesting boundary between the erosion-resistant Dakota sandstone and the softer mudstones of the Morrison formation below. The combination of grand scenery and intimate geology makes this a great day hike in an isolated area. Access is easy via paved roads, but the nearest services are many miles away at San Ysidro to the south and Cuba to the north.

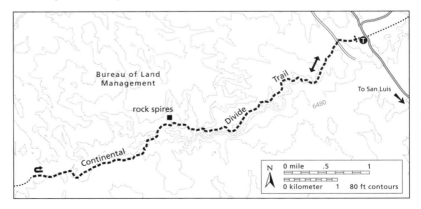

The Continental Divide Trail is well-marked with emblems and rock cairns.

Reach the trailhead for this section of the Continental Divide Trail via the paved CR 279, which is located at a well-marked intersection off US 550 about 19 miles north of San Ysidro and 22 miles south of Cuba. Head west from the highway on CR 279 toward San Luis. Pass through the village of San Luis and at about 8.5 miles from US 550, turn right onto the paved Torreon Road. In 3.6 miles, just before a five-way intersection at the top of a pass, watch for green pass-through gates on both sides of the road. Park on the west (left) side of the road at the green gate.

The trail segment has a very inauspicious start. Head west through the green gate and enter a disturbed patch of ground littered with trash and crossed by numerous dirt tracks. Stout rock cairns lead the way through the mess, with the rumbling sound of a hidden pipeline pump station filling the air. Follow the cairns as they lead under a powerline and across a gravel road at mile 0.3. Cross a pipeline scar, and then ascend through sagebrush to a rim of sandstone. Once at the top, hikers will quickly forget the first half mile of trail as they enter a quiet, expansive landscape.

After a few hundred feet of traveling through piñon-juniper woodland, approach the rim of the mesa. The largest volcanic neck in the area, Cabazon Peak, dominates the view for the next 2 miles, and a dozen other sculptured necks are visible to the south and west. The trail swings west as it traverses a bench with a long drop to the left and an intricate sandstone wall to the right. Enjoy both the sweeping views and the nooks, crannies, and hoodoos in the nearby sandstone. Through the next mile, the trail stays near the cliff edge, offering continually changing vistas. Near mile 1.7, meet a dirt track coming in from the right; join it for a quarter mile, then follow the cairns as they lead off on a trail to the left. New views open to the sandstone mesas to the north and west.

The nature of the route changes at mile 2.7 as the trail drops off the north side of the rim and enters the jumbled rocks of the contact between sandstone and mudstone. Pass impressive rock towers at mile 3.2, cross a narrow pass, and then drop to the base of the south-facing cliff. Continue west on the flats at the base of the cliff, passing through contorted rock formations. After a mile on the flats, the trail enters a broad pass where hikers should turn around and return to the trailhead.

Hiking in a bowl of weird hoodoos in the Bisti Wilderness

51 | Bisti Section, Bisti–De-Na-Zin Wilderness

Distance: 3 to 10 miles, day hike
Difficulty: easy, but requires routefinding skills
Elevation range: 5,750 to 6,000 feet
Elevation gain: 300 feet
Best time of year: March through November
Water: carry water
Map: USGS Alamo Mesa West
Managed by: Bureau of Land Management,
   Bisti–De-Na-Zin Wilderness, Farmington Field Office
Features: badlands topography, strange rocks

In art-rich New Mexico, the Bisti–De-Na-Zin Wilderness is the only gallery dedicated to a mud swamp. The duck-billed dinosaurs who lumbered across the muck 70 million years ago would be flabbergasted to see what's become of their claustrophobic swamp. Gone are the braided streams, giant turtles, and tree ferns; in their stead are rainbow-colored slopes of shale—the erstwhile swamp mud—dotted with living matter turned to stone.

Today's Bisti Wilderness is a haunting pastel landscape of humpbacked mounds, rock-toadstool forests, and goblin stones. Dinosaur bones and petrified wood litter the surface. A maze of miniature canyons holds a variety of hues and erosional sculpting unmatched in New Mexico. Walking through the wilderness is like strolling through an exotic set from a futuristic sci-fi film.

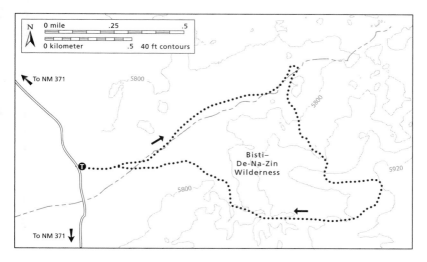

Large pieces of petrified wood are scattered about the badlands of the Bisti–De-Na-Zin Wilderness.

No trails slice through the wilderness, but the fun here is following the whims of the rocks and exploring places that look interesting. The topographic map will yield a few ideas for locations to check out. Use distinctive mounds of rocks as landmarks for navigation. Precious little shade is available within the rock wonderland, so head to the Bisti when temperatures are cool. Always wear plenty of sun protection and carry at least a quart of water per person.

Easiest access into the badlands is located south of Farmington. Take NM 371 south from Farmington for 36 miles. Turn left onto a gravel road that is signed for the Bisti Wilderness. In about 5 miles, watch to the left for a large parking area at the main access.

One possible route into the wilderness from this point is to follow the broad, sandy arroyo to the east. Walk on one of the social (unofficial, but well-traveled) trails leading up the canyon, or hike in the bottom of the arroyo. Either route leads into the heart of this amphitheater of clay and sand. After a mile, the terrain turns into a wonderland of interesting-looking crannies to explore. Hikers should wander where their fancy and the whimsy of the rocks take them. Look for narrow passages, crowds of what might be grotesque lawn ornaments, and mazes of rock. Exploring the entire perimeter of the main amphitheater would take more than a day. Use landmarks or the map to return to the trailhead.

52 ┌ De-Na-Zin Section, Bisti–De-Na-Zin Wilderness

Distance: 4 to 5 miles, day hike
Difficulty: easy, but requires some routefinding skills
Elevation range: 6,200 to 6,350 feet
Elevation gain: 200 feet
Best time of year: March through November
Water: carry water
Map: USGS Alamo Mesa East
Managed by: Bureau of Land Management,
 Bisti–De-Na-Zin Wilderness, Farmington Field Office
Features: badlands topography, strange rocks, isolation

The De-Na-Zin Wilderness is not as well known as its companion wilderness, the Bisti, but it offers six times the land area of similar wild scenery. Rocks deposited in swamps and forests on the edge of an ancient sea have eroded into fascinating shapes. The landscape is filled with lithic mushrooms, chocolate drops, turbans, and goblins. Also abundant within the wilderness are petrified logs, dinosaur bones, and mammalian fossils.

No established trails exist within the wilderness, but cross-country travel is easy. Wandering is encouraged, and the following route is only one of many possibilities for exploring. Hikers should be alert that there are private in-holdings within the wilderness, often with unmarked boundaries; fences usually mark the boundaries of grazing allotments. Visitors must stay off fragile formations and are prohibited from collecting rocks and fossils.

Several access points to the wilderness can be found along San Juan County Road 7500. Pick up CR 7500 at Huerfano Trading Post, about 40 miles south of Farmington on US 550 between mileposts 127 and 128. Turn

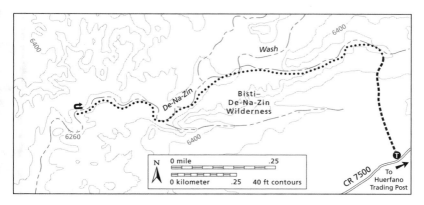

right (west) onto CR 7500 and drive about 12 miles to a parking area on the right that is signed for the De-Na-Zin Wilderness.

From the parking area, go through the fence on a dirt road heading north. Ignore a dirt track heading to the left as you drop gradually to reach an arroyo about 0.4 mile from the start. After this unpromising start, the scenery transforms as you turn left into the arroyo and walk in the sandy bottom. The arroyo soon drops into a shallow and narrow canyon. At mile 0.9 the canyon opens up into a broader gorge, and at mile 1.1 it intersects the larger De-Na-Zin Wash. Turn left to head down the arroyo. Walking is slow in the sand, but there is plenty of scenery to attract attention. Continue down the wash, exploring any or all of the interesting side canyons and alcoves found along the way.

Arroyos offer natural hiking corridors through the Bisti–De-Na-Zin Wilderness.

After following the convoluted course of the wash for 1.3 miles, watch for a tall spire of rock detached from the cliff to the left. Private land is just downstream, so hikers should turn around here and retrace their steps. If time permits, continue up the wash where hundreds of side drainages invite exploration.

53 | Pueblo Alto Loop

Distance: 5.3 miles, day hike
Difficulty: moderate
Elevation range: 6,100 to 6,475 feet
Elevation gain: 500 feet
Best time of year: year-round
Water: carry water
Map: Chaco Culture National Historical Park brochure
Managed by: National Park Service,
     Chaco Culture National Historical Park
Features: best views of large Chaco pueblos and
     remains of Chaco road system

In a state famous for its abundance of large Native American villages, Chaco Canyon holds the crown jewels. Visitors to the remains of multiple-story towns scattered along 6 miles of canyon floor are soon struck by the magical, mystical nature of the canyon. For whatever reason, the Ancestral Pueblo people, ancestors of the modern Pueblo groups living in New Mexico and Arizona, chose this canyon to build villages with hundreds of rooms.

At present, no paved roads lead to Chaco Canyon. From all approaches, at least 15 miles of rough gravel and dirt road await. When dry, the access roads are passable to any vehicle; they are all treacherous when wet. Visitors who have any doubts about road conditions should call the Chaco Culture National Historical Park (see "Sources of Additional Information" in back) for the latest information.

The easiest access to Chaco Canyon is from the north via US 550 and the route is well-marked with signs for Chaco Canyon. About 3 miles southeast of Nageezi (about 50 miles west of Cuba and 35 miles south of Bloomfield between mileposts 112 and 113), head south on San Juan County Road 7900. In 5 miles, turn right onto CR 7950. The pavement ends here and signs will lead the remaining 15 miles to the park entrance. Access from the south is over longer and rougher dirt roads leading from Navajo Highway 9. From Navajo Highway 9 at Seven Lakes Trading Post, NM 57 heads north 21 rough miles to the park.

Because of its remote location, a trip to Chaco Canyon requires some advance planning. Aside from the campground, no facilities are located in

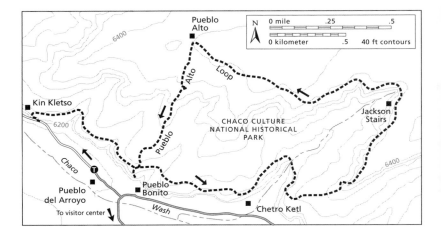

the park. Visitors must fill gas tanks before taking the long dirt roads into the park, and bring all the food and other supplies they will need. Food and gasoline can be purchased during the week at the trading posts along US 550 north of the park.

All trips into the backcountry, including the three described here, require a free permit available at the visitor center or at the trailhead. Removing or moving plants, rocks, or artifacts is prohibited. Leave all artifacts where they are found. To prevent damage to the fragile pueblos, stay off the walls. Even in the backcountry, stay on the designated trails. All trails close at sunset, so plan hikes accordingly.

The Pueblo Alto Loop is the most popular and diverse backcountry trail at Chaco Canyon. Modern visitors can easily sense the central role that Pueblo Alto played in Ancestral Pueblo commerce. Perched on the very top of the mesa, Pueblo Alto and its attendant smaller villages have a view of many places significant in the Ancestral Pueblo world, such as Mount Taylor to the south and the San Juan Mountains. Ancient roads from towns within the canyon to outlying sites as far as 40 miles away converge at Pueblo Alto.

To reach the trailhead, drive on the paved park road about 4.5 miles from the visitor center to the parking area for Pueblo del Arroyo. Begin walking west past the gate on the old, dirt park road for 0.3 mile. Directly behind Kin Kletso, a sign marks the beginning of the trail. Follow the well-worn, winding path up the talus along the cliff face, using caution. The trail soon enters and climbs a narrow crack in the rocks. Once on the first bench level of the mesa, follow the copious rock cairns as they lead east along the slickrock.

The trail parallels the cliff face, winding around the heads of several canyons. A half mile from the start of the trail, the return leg of the loop enters from the direction of Pueblo Alto to the left. Take a short, cairn-marked route to the right to the overlook of Pueblo Bonito almost directly below. Return

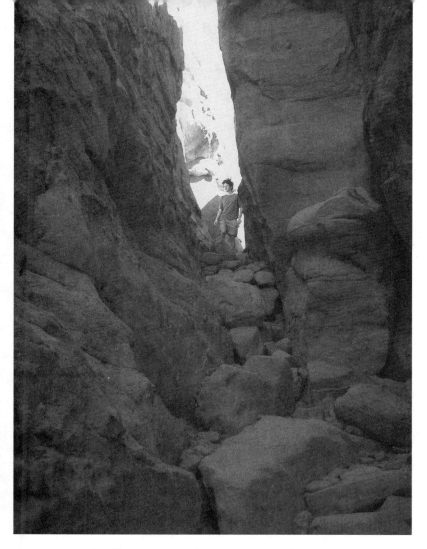

A narrow crack offers access to the mesa top on the Pueblo Alto Loop.

to the main route and turn right, continuing eastward along the slickrock bench. Climb a short spur of the mesa, and then descend along a cliff that offers views of Chetro Ketl.

The trail skirts the head of another box canyon and then follows a short segment of an ancient road alignment. The road is clear of loose rocks and is bordered by a low masonry wall. Round the end of this spur of the mesa and climb steeply northward to the next bench level. In about 200 yards, climb again through a narrow crack to the top of the ridge. After rounding the upper end of the canyon at mile 3, a marked viewpoint provides the best perspective on the Jackson Stairs, a precarious ancient route from canyon bottom to mesa top.

After a few minutes heading west on the slickrock, the trail climbs a sandy hill, leading in 0.5 mile to the remains of the Pueblo Alto complex. From the pueblo, the view encompasses hundreds of square miles to the north, extending from the La Plata Mountains in southern Colorado to Mount Taylor in the south. Line-of-sight connections can be made with pueblos to the north, a signal station in South Gap, Tsin Kletzin on the mesa on the opposite site of Chaco Canyon, and Mount Taylor to the south.

From Pueblo Alto, a sign points the way back to the trailhead. Head south for 0.5 mile, turn right onto the trail taken earlier, and then descend the crack to Kin Kletso and the old park road. Turn left on the road and walk back to the parking area.

54 | SOUTH MESA LOOP

> **Distance: 4.5 miles, day hike**
> **Difficulty:** moderate
> **Elevation range:** 6,140 to 6,675 feet
> **Elevation gain:** 800 feet
> **Best time of year:** year-round
> **Water:** carry water
> **Map:** Chaco Culture National Historical Park brochure
> **Managed by:** National Park Service,
>   Chaco Culture National Historical Park
> **Features:** lightly used trail, scenic overlooks, large intact pueblo

South Mesa and South Gap—a wide break in the south wall of Chaco Canyon—played a central role in the Chaco communication system, a complex series of line-of-sight connections between villages. The largest pueblos were probably sited near the South Gap due to the ease of travel through the gap into the canyon. A signal station near South Gap provided a visual link between Pueblo Alto and Pueblo Bonito. Perhaps no other village demonstrates the importance of the line-of-sight concept as well as Tsin Kletzin. Move the location of the town a hundred yards in any direction and visual connections with other Chaco sites are lost.

Driving directions to Chaco Canyon are found in the Pueblo Alto Loop (Hike 53) description. The South Mesa Trail begins at the parking area for Casa Rinconada, about 4 miles west of the visitor center on the eastbound side of the main park road. From the parking area, begin by following the Casa Rinconada interpretive trail. In fifty feet, bear right onto a gravel path heading toward Casa Rinconada. On the back side of the pueblo, find a post

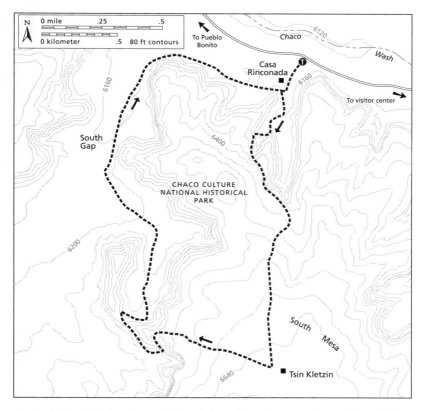

marked "South Mesa Loop." Turn left and continue on the main trail into the drainage to the east. Pass several room blocks before another signpost points to the route as it begins to ascend rocky ledges. Hike up the staircase ledges with ever-increasing views of Chaco Canyon unfolding behind you. A narrow crack in the rocks leads to a bench level that skirts to the west side of a box canyon. At mile 1, continue a gradual ascent on a sandy slope covered with bunchgrasses. Reach Tsin Kletzin at mile 1.5. Note the line-of-sight connections with Pueblo Alto to the north and the Chaco outlier, Kin Klizhin, through South Gap.

After exploring the pueblo, return to the signpost at the northwest corner and follow the trail marked for Casa Rinconada, 2.7 miles. The trail crosses the mesa top for a half mile before plunging off the cliff through colorful sandstones dotted with deep red iron concretions. Rocks lead the way as views of South Gap and the broad arroyos to the west open up. After crossing a narrow ridge, at mile 2.4 the trail switchbacks into a broad rincon, a drainage enclosed on three sides by rock walls. After winding through white, orange, and tan layers of sandstone, the trail reaches the floor of the rincon

Casa Rinconada from the South Mesa Trail

and bears left. Cross a faint road and reach the floor of South Gap. Turn right onto on old road and swing beneath the tall cliffs of South Mesa and wind back into Chaco Canyon. At mile 4.1, a sign points to the return trail back to Casa Rinconada. Walk the trail for 0.1 mile before turning left to retrace the first portion of the hike back to the trailhead.

55 | PEÑASCO BLANCO

Distance: 8 miles, day hike
Difficulty: easy
Elevation range: 6,050 to 6,290 feet
Elevation gain: 300
Best time of year: year-round
Water: carry water
Map: Chaco Culture National Historical Park brochure
Managed by: National Park Service, Chaco Culture National Historical Park
Features: large collection of petroglyphs, supernova pictograph, impressive Ancestral Pueblo village, expansive views

On the tan sandstone cliffs below the pueblo of Peñasco Blanco, the trail passes the most intriguing rock art to be found at Chaco Canyon. On a small

overhang along the south wall of the canyon, a red-painted crescent moon, large star, and handprint decorate the sandstone. Experts speculate the pictograph represents a supernova explosion that occurred in 1064, during the height of the Ancestral Pueblo culture in Chaco. Chinese astronomers left a written record of the sudden appearance of a bright new star located near the waxing moon. Ardent sky watchers, the Ancestral Pueblo people certainly witnessed the same event, and this unique rock painting may be their own pictorial record of the explosion.

For driving directions to Chaco Canyon, refer to the Pueblo Alto Loop (Hike 53) description. The trailhead to Peñasco Blanco is located along the main park road at Pueblo del Arroyo, about 4.5 miles west of the visitor center.

From the trailhead, walk the wide dirt road heading west and down the canyon. Pass Kin Kletso and continue to Casa Chiquita at 1 mile from the start. Follow the trail sign onto a wide, sandy trail running parallel to Chaco Wash at the base of the north wall of the canyon. After 1.5 miles of easy walking, look for an arrow pointing to a trail that travels against the very base of the cliff, where many petroglyph panels adorn the smooth faces of sandstone. A particularly striking panel—a tapestry design, bighorn sheep, and a human figure—is pecked high on the canyon wall, about 1.75 miles from the start.

After a large panel of rock art, the trail dips into a deep arroyo and immediately climbs out. Over the next mile, the trail angles away from the cliff to the center of the canyon, with several wide swings as it crosses deep drainages. About 2.7 miles from the start, the trail leaves the road, heading to the left to drop into Chaco Wash. Do not enter the wash when running water is present. At the base of the cliff on the south side of the wash, reach the supernova pictograph.

From the pictograph, the trail continues over the talus slope to the left of the rock art. The trail heads east along a rock ledge for a few hundred yards before rock cairns lead up the cliff face. Follow the ample cairns for another 0.5 mile as they lead up the ledges to bench level, with Peñasco Blanco in sight most of the way. The pueblo lies high atop the mesa, with outstanding views in all directions. After enjoying the pueblo walls and the scenery, return to the trailhead by the same route.

The supernova pictograph along the trail to Peñasco Blanco

56 | GOOSEBERRY SPRINGS TRAIL

Distance: 6 miles, day hike
Difficulty: difficult
Elevation range: 9,280 to 11,301 feet
Elevation gain: 2,100 feet
Best time of year: late May through early November
Water: carry water
Maps: USGS Mount Taylor; USFS Cibola National Forest
Managed by: Cibola National Forest,
    Mount Taylor Ranger District
Features: huge, open meadows; outstanding views

Mount Taylor is an extinct volcano rising high above the surrounding lava fields near Grants, New Mexico. The mountain is part of a much larger volcanic field extending to Arizona in the west and to jagged volcanic necks, tall spires of hardened magma, to the east. The mountain was built by periodic eruptions occurring from 4 to 2 million years ago. At the end of this period, the peak stood much higher than at present. Subsequent eruptions were of the explosive type and the sideways blasts tore the mountain apart, creating a high-rimmed crater draining to the east.

The Gooseberry Springs Trail climbs to the summit of the rim of the ancient volcano, 5,000 feet above the plains below, to take in a commanding view. This is a dry hike, with little or no water available at Gooseberry Springs any time of the year. The exposed meadows near and around the summit make this a risky place to hike during the summer thunderstorm season. This trail is best hiked in late May and June, after mid-September, or early on a summer's morning.

From Santa Fe Avenue in Grants, take NM 547 (First Street) north, following the signs for Mount Taylor. In one mile, turn right onto Roosevelt Avenue, and in another half mile stay on NM 547 by turning left onto Lobo Canyon Road. Continue about 12 miles to the end of the pavement and turn right onto FR 193. Travel this well-graded gravel road 5 miles to a small sign on the left marking the beginning of Gooseberry Springs Trail 77. (The junction of FR 193 and FR 501 is 0.1 mile beyond the trailhead.)

The first part of the trail climbs along a new segment of trail through the conifer forest parallel to a small drainage. In 0.5 mile, the trail crosses a grassy area and comes to a junction with the old trail. For the next half mile, old, new, and cattle trails create some difficulty in navigation. The old trail climbs on the north side of the drainage, and after crossing near the old/new junction, the new trail stays on the south side of the canyon. A low ridge to the south will keep hikers heading in the right direction until the two trails rejoin on the far side of an aspen grove about 1 mile from the start.

The Gooseberry Springs Trail crosses the extensive meadows surrounding Mount Taylor.

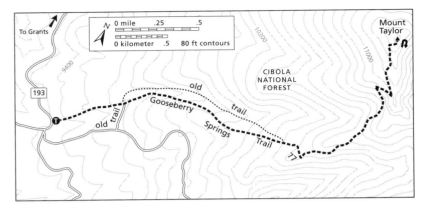

At mile 1.25, the trail leaves the forest and enters the extensive meadows surrounding the summit of Mount Taylor. Here the rutted trail rapidly gains elevation to cross a ridge about 1.7 miles from the start, with long-range views to the south and east. Swing north (left), climbing toward the summit visible straight ahead. The trail crosses the open meadow with a series of broad switchbacks. At mile 2.8, just below the summit, pass through a gate, then make the final climb to the top. From the summit, the horseshoe-shaped rim of the old volcano is clearly visible to the east. A trail continues to the north, leading down the mountain to FR 570; but, after enjoying the view, retrace your steps to return to the trailhead.

57 | BIG TUBES

Distance: 2 miles, day hike
Difficulty: easy
Elevation range: 7,600 to 7,640 feet
Elevation gain: 50 feet
Best time of year: mid-May through early July,
  mid-September to November
Water: carry water
Map: USGS Ice Caves
Managed by: Bureau of Land Management, El Malpais
  National Conservation Area; National Park Service,
  El Malpais National Monument
Features: lava tubes, lava flow features

The sprawling El Malpais National Monument and National Conservation Area are jointly administered by the National Park Service and the Bureau of Land Management. They feature some of the most recent lava flows in North America, perhaps as young as 3,000 years old.

Lava from the most recent eruption of Bandera Crater flowed more than 20 miles from the base of the cone almost to Grants. Within the flow is a 12-mile-long chain of collapsed and intact lava tubes. The tubes extending from Bandera Crater exhibit large and small holes in their ceilings: big holes are called skylights, smaller ones, windows. Below the openings, in a cool, wet habitat with plenty of sunlight, lives a unique community of green moss and insects. Help protect these biotic habitats by staying off the mosses. Come prepared to explore underground by bringing three sources of light, such as a battery-powered lantern, flashlight, and candle and matches.

Making the trip to the Big Tubes area requires some careful planning and a bit of luck. Although recent road improvements have made the journey easier, CR 42 is notoriously impassable when wet, with huge puddles blocking motorized access for weeks after prolonged rains. Make the trip only during dry spells: mid-May through early July and mid-September to November are best. Under dry conditions, the road is rough but passable to most vehicles, although high clearance is recommended. For the latest road conditions, contact the Northwest New Mexico Visitor Center in Grants (see "Sources of Additional Information" at back).

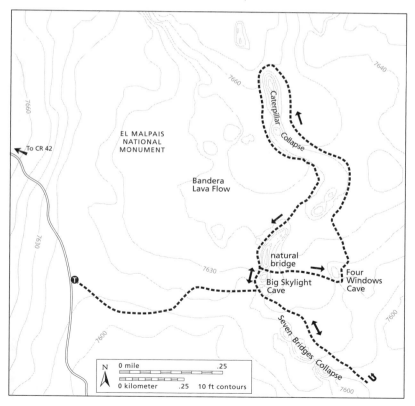

Four Windows Cave is the easiest lava tube to explore in the Big Tubes area.

From the west side of Grants, take NM 53 south toward El Malpais and El Morro national monuments for 26 miles (about 1 mile past the entrance to Bandera Crater and Ice Caves) to CR 42. Turn left and continue 4.6 miles on this rough road to Big Tubes access road. Turn left and drive 3.2 miles to the Big Tubes Trailhead. Pick up a brochure and cave map at the trailhead.

The rough trail to the Big Tubes is marked with large cairns. From the information board, find the first cairn and walk to it, then sight the next cairn. Continue in this stepwise manner over the Bandera Lava Flow, watching for the features of recent flows: blocky and jagged *a'a* lava; the smooth, ropy surface of *pahoehoe* lava; and pressure ridges can all be easily examined at close range along the trail.

Slow walking for 0.5 mile leads to the extensive tube and collapse area. Here a sign points to two trail branches, and hikers should plan to explore the entire network. From the sign, the trail left leads to Caterpillar Collapse and Four Windows Cave. Take a few steps up, staying on the south side of the collapse, to locate the cairned trail. Head to the natural lava bridge for a view into the yawning Big Skylight Cave.

A second sign points over the natural bridge and to Four Windows Cave, which is the most easily explored of the lava tubes in the area. Cross the bridge and follow the cairns a short 0.25 mile to the rim of another collapse. A cairn on the opposite rim marks an easy route into the trench. Enter the cave, but make certain to stay off the moss-covered rocks. Hikers with the proper equipment can follow the cave its entire 1,200-foot length. Having the detailed park service brochure and map will minimize the chance of confusion; it is surprisingly easy to become disoriented in the most remote part of the tube.

After exploring the cave, pick up the rock cairns leading from the entrance toward Caterpillar Collapse to the west. Follow the north rim of the collapse to its head, then swing east to follow the south rim back to the natural bridge. Retrace a few of your earlier steps to the first trail sign and this time follow the cairns along the right fork. First take a peek into the big skylight of the cave of the same name, and then continue several hundred yards to Seven Bridges Collapse. This long, interesting trench is spanned by a series of natural bridges. The trail leads into the collapse, where hikers can follow the trench for a short distance before reaching private property.

Return to the trailhead by retracing your steps to the first trail sign, then the half-mile trail back to the parking area.

58 Zuni-Acoma Trail

Distance: 7.8 miles one-way, day hike
Difficulty: difficult
Elevation range: 6,830 to 6,925 feet
Elevation gain: 400 feet
Best time of year: March through November
Water: carry water
Maps: USGS Arrosa Ranch and Los Pilares
Managed by: National Park Service, El Malpais National Monument
Features: lava structures, ancient trail, isolation

The Zuni-Acoma Trail spans overlapping lava flows from five volcanoes, following an ancient route that connects the two pueblos. Now part of the official route of the Continental Divide Trail (CDT), much of the route lies on solid, uneven rock, and the trail twists constantly as it traverses lava ridges

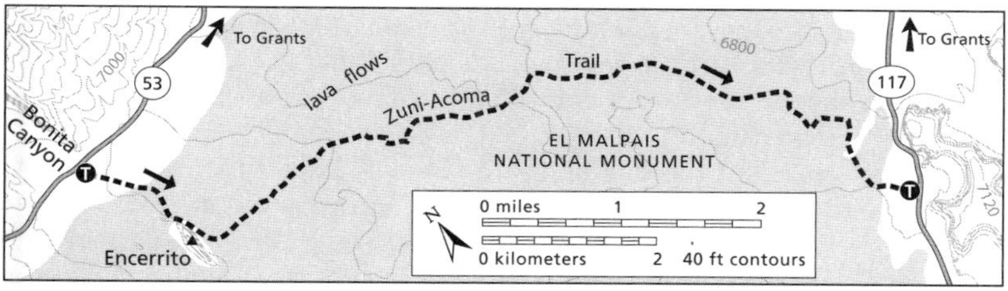

Fresh lava makes for rugged hiking on the Zuni-Acoma Trail.

and bridges. Make no mistake: despite the relatively short distance, it is a tiring journey. Allow five or six hours to complete the hike, and take plenty of water and sunscreen.

To walk the entire trail requires setting up a long car shuttle, but it's worth the extra effort. First, head south on NM 117, which is located at exit 89 off I-40, about 65 miles west of Albuquerque and 5 miles east of Grants. A little more than 15 miles from the interstate on NM 117, park in the marked lot along the highway.

Leave a car at this trailhead and return to the interstate. Head west to Grants and, on the west edge of the town, take exit 81 and travel south on NM 53. In 16 miles, park at the marked trailhead on the left.

Cross a small bridge over a fissure at the edge of the parking lot and drop off the lava to a double-track leading southeast across an open flat. After 0.5 mile, the trail abruptly meets the Twin Peaks lava flow. Climb to the surface of the flow and walk among scattered ponderosa pines. At this point, forward progress slows considerably. Hikers must divide their attention between looking down at the ankle-twisting terrain and looking up to watch carefully for the hundreds of rock cairns that mark the entire route. If you lose the way and can't find the next cairn, backtrack to the last trail marker and search again.

In a few minutes, the trail skirts the base of Encerrito, a low volcanic mound, and enters a sandy flat. At the junction with the main CDT, bear left to again meet the Twin Peaks lava. The next mile alternates crossing the rough lava and open grasslands. Watch for lava bridges, limestone blocks embedded in the lava, massive sheets of ropelike *pahoehoe* lava, and gnarled trees growing in pockets of soil within the lava. Some of these trees are thousands of years old.

At mile 2.8, the lava is notably more jagged and the vegetation more sparse. The trail now winds over the more rugged terrain of the Bandera lava flow. After another mile, meet the McCarty's lava flow. It will be obvious that this is the most recent flow along the trail. The rock is jagged, the vegetation scattered, and the trail incredibly twisted. Follow the cairns carefully across the 2 miles of this flow.

The last 0.5 mile of the trail traverses sandy islands between the lava flows. The trail ends at the eastern trailhead on NM 117.

59 | CHAIN OF CRATERS WILDERNESS

Distance: 20-mile one-way backpack, or 8-mile out-and back day hike
Difficulty: easy or moderate
Elevation range: 7,570 to 8,070 feet
Elevation gain: 500 feet
Best time of year: March through mid-May, September through November
Water: carry water
Maps: USGS Cerro Hueco and Cerro Brilliante
Managed by: Bureau of Land Management, El Malpais National Conservation Area
Features: cinder cones, volcanic bombs

Cinder cones are huge piles of material spewed from a volcanic vent. Nothing fancy—just bits of rock that were shot into the air and then fell nearby to form a conical mound. Most of the rocks are pebble-sized and called cinders;

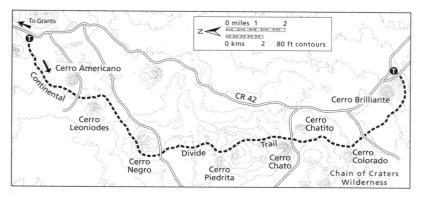

Much of the Continental Divide Trail in the Chain of Craters passes through juniper woodland with a cinder cone for a backdrop.

larger rocks shot higher may cool slightly on the trip down and form volcanic bombs, distinguished by their striated appearance. The resulting piles can rise several hundred feet, forming round hills with small craters in the center. The Chain of Craters Wilderness in El Malpais holds more than two dozen cinder cones that rise as much as 500 feet from the surrounding plain, and the Continental Divide Trail meanders through the chain for 20 miles. By setting up a shuttle, this relatively easy hike through the waterless piñon-juniper woodland and sparse ponderosa pine stands surrounding the craters makes an exciting two-day backpack; other hikers may simply want to explore the craters as an out-and-back trip from the northern parking area.

From the west side of Grants, take NM 53 south toward El Malpais and El Morro national monuments for 26 miles (about 1 mile past the entrance to Bandera Crater and Ice Caves) to CR 42. Turn left onto this sometimes muddy road and continue 5.5 miles to the Continental Divide Trail (north) parking area. To set up a one-way hike, continue on CR 42 another 15.5 miles to the southern trailhead, leave a vehicle, then return to the north trailhead.

From the north trailhead, begin hiking on the well-marked trail heading west. Ample cairns mark the route as it heads to skirt the west side of Cerro Americano, the highest cinder cone along the northern portion of the route. The trail crosses many dirt tracks and roads as it gently rises and falls over ancient lava flows. Along the way, tall ponderosa pines offer shade and pleasant rest spots. The red cinders of Cerro Americano form the backdrop as the trail stays close to the divide for the first 3.5 miles.

From the west flank of Cerro Americano, the next tall cinder cone, Cerro Leoniodes, comes into view. After crossing two dirt roads, the trail continues around the east side of Cerro Leoniodes. This is a good point to turn around for the out-and-back hike. To continue, swing to the southwest and climb over the west side of Cerro Negro. Around mile 7, pass small craters on the flanks of this cinder cone. From here, the trail heads due south and crosses through the center of an eroded cinder cone at mile 8.5.

The next 5 miles of the trail pass through the heart of the volcanic field. The hilly terrain supports numerous pine stands. Cinder cones, both dominant and barely recognizable, are everywhere along this section. Pass the C-shaped Cerro Piedrita near mile 10. At mile 13.5, pass between Cerro Chato on the right and its smaller neighbor, Cerro Chatito, on the left. Pass into more level country as the trail heads toward Cerro Colorado. The final 3 miles of trail skirt around the symmetrical Cerro Brilliante before reaching the southern trailhead.

60 NARROWS RIM TRAIL

Distance: 7.5 miles, day hike
Difficulty: moderate
Elevation range: 7,100 to 7,500 feet
Elevation gain: 400 feet
Best time of year: March through November
Water: carry water
Maps: USGS Arrosa Ranch and North Pasture
Managed by: Bureau of Land Management,
   El Malpais National Conservation Area
Features: stunning views of sandstone cliffs and
   rugged lava flows

The Narrows Rim Trail is a refreshing change of pace from the rugged, jagged lava flow hikes in the El Malpais area. This trail skirts the rim of the sandstone cliffs on the eastern side of the El Malpais, traversing sand and sandstone as it climbs gently through open woods. Along the entire length of the trail, hikers are beckoned away from the tread to the cliff edge to

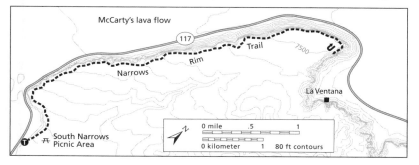

The rugged surface of the McCarty's lava flow is best seen along the Narrows Rim Trail.

drink in the views. Because the rim is located at the Narrows, a place where the lava from the McCarty's crater flowed within yards of the base of the sandstone walls, the view is straight down onto the almost-fresh lava. From above, cracks, squeeze-ups, pressure ridges, and frozen lava lobes are in plain sight and easy to recognize. To top it off, the trail ends at an overlook of La Ventana, one of the largest natural arches in New Mexico.

The Narrows Rim trailhead is located on NM 117 about 22 miles south of exit 89 on I-40. Turn left into the South Narrows Picnic Area and park.

The beginning of the trail is marked by a sign at the south end of the picnic area a few yards from the highway. Ascend some easy sandstone stairs, then begin a gradual but constant climb that follows the natural dip of the rock. The tread is mostly rock, but sandy stretches are frequent. The trail swings west and at mile 0.5 stays within a dozen yards of the cliff edge. Views of the McCarty's flow, the Chain of Craters, and the Bandera cinder cone field are numerous, and each lookout offers a unique perspective on the nearby lava.

After gaining about 300 feet in the first 1.5 miles, the trail levels off as it now swings back and forth away from the cliff. In spring, the sand is decorated by flowers on prickly pear, hedgehog, and pincushion cacti. At mile 3.4, the trail reaches the end of a point of rock and offers a new viewpoint looking north to the spires of Los Pilares and Mount Taylor. Another few minutes brings you to the end of the trail in a broad sandstone alcove opposite La Ventana. You will want to linger for a while before returning to the trailhead by the same route.

61 EL MORRO RIM TRAIL

Distance: 2 miles, day hike
Difficulty: easy
Elevation range: 7,210 to 7,430 feet
Elevation gain: 200
Best time of year: year-round
Water: carry water
Map: El Morro National Monument brochure
Managed by: National Park Service, El Morro
   National Monument
Features: historic inscriptions, pueblo village,
   desert waterhole

A hike doesn't have to last all day to be a New Mexico classic. The 2-mile trail from the El Morro National Monument visitor center to the mesa top provides an encompassing look at the history of the state. Along the way are a small pueblo, inscriptions from Spanish colonial times and the early years of American exploration, and some impressive geology—at least 10 miles of enjoyment compressed into a leisurely two-hour walk.

El Morro National Monument is an essential stop for those exploring the wildlands southwest of Grants. Take exit 81 from I-40 on the west side of Grants and head south on NM 53. Continue 41 miles to the El Morro entrance, turn left, and park at the visitor center. Pay the fee inside and pick up a copy of the interpretive guide that will add much to your understanding of the inscriptions.

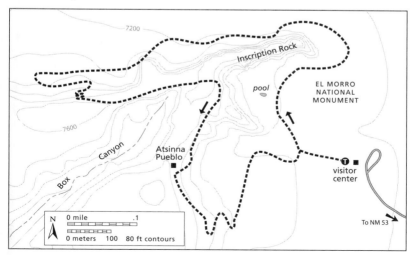

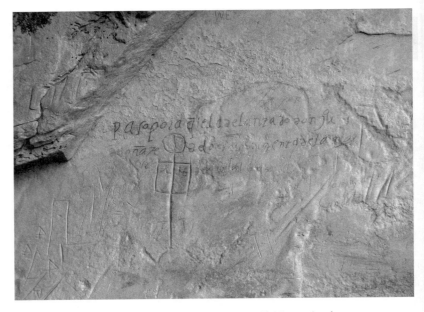

Spanish travelers recorded their passage at El Morro in the seventeenth century.

The paved trail begins at the back of the visitor center. Follow the trail right and, at the first two intersections, stay on the Inscription Trail at the foot of the bluff. Pass the deep green pool that attracted travelers to this spot, then walk along the cliff where hundreds of names and messages are carved in the smooth sandstone, dating from Juan Oñate in 1605 to railroad workers in the 1860s.

In 0.5 mile, round the tip of the mesa and climb past more inscriptions. In a few minutes, ascend several switchbacks to gain the mesa top where the view takes in the Zuni Mountains and some of the volcanoes in the nearby El Malpais National Conservation Area. Follow the double lines pecked into the slickrock sandstone around the head of idyllic Box Canyon. About 1.5 miles from the start, pass through the pueblo of Atsinna, an ancient town of more than 800 rooms. Beyond the village, the trail descends through the rocks to return to the visitor center.

Opposite: *The trail network at Dripping Springs Natural Area passes beneath the towering crags of the Organ Mountains.*

CENTRAL
MOUNTAINS

62 | CERRILLOS HILLS HISTORIC PARK

Distance: 5 miles, day hike
Difficulty: easy
Elevation range: 5,800 to 6,130 feet
Elevation gain: 600 feet
Best time of year: snow-free periods year-round
Water: carry water
Maps: USGS Madrid and Picture Rock
Managed by: Santa Fe County Open Space and
  Trails Division
Features: historic mining district, wide vistas, winter hiking

The oldest recorded mining operations in the Southwest were located at the nondescript mound of Mount Chalchihuitl in the Cerrillos Hills. At least 1,500 years ago, Ancestral Pueblo people used sharp sticks and shaped rocks to extract turquoise from the volcanic outcrops on the low mountain. Spanish colonizers at Santa Fe mined the colorful rock in the seventeenth century. In the 1880s, silver and zinc ores brought a new wave of miners to foothills above the Rio Galesteo.

Today, managed by Santa Fe County as open space, the Cerrillos Hills is a delightfully scenic spot with excellent hiking trails that make use of old mining roads. "Hills" is the operative word, for the terrain is rolling mounds separated by interesting canyons. Middle elevation, southern exposure, and open woodlands make this a premier winter-hiking destination. The 5-mile

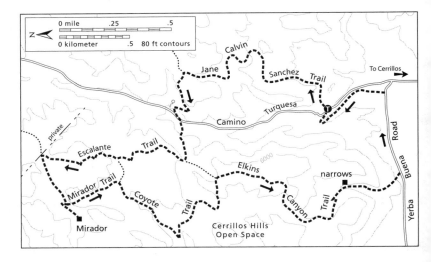

Many covered mines shafts are found in the Cerrillos Hills Historic Area.

hike through the historic district offers a glimpse at the hard work of miners, a desert spring, and outstanding views from two spur trails along the way.

To reach the trailhead, take exit 267 from I-25, which is located about 15 miles south of Santa Fe and 45 miles north of Albuquerque. Head east toward Waldo and Cerrillos on CR 57, a dirt road that is passable to all vehicles when dry. In 8 miles, enter Cerrillos and turn left at the intersection with CR 59 (don't cross the railroad tracks). In a quarter mile, bear left onto Camino Turquesa, following signs that point to the historic park. In 0.4 mile, turn left onto the entrance road for the parking area.

Walk back out to the road and cross to the trailhead for the Jane Calvin Sanchez Trail. Make a short, steep climb, then swing north over rolling hills dotted with juniper and piñon. The volcanic rocks are stained with red, which is often an indicator of a concentration of ores, and several covered mine shafts are along the route. At mile 0.8, bear left to stay on the Sanchez Trail and soon drop to a mineral spring where cattails and willows sprout from the damp ground.

At the spring, recross Camino Turquesa, and head down (left) the road for a hundred feet to meet the Escalante Trail. After another short, steep climb, gain a ridgeline with a backdrop of Grand Central Mountain. At mile 1.5, bear right to stay on the Escalante Trail and head for Mirador. In a few minutes, make a short side trip to the first of the viewpoints to take in the sweeping views to the south. Back on the main trail, turn left at a boundary fence and at mile 2.2, reach the spur trail to Mirador. Take the spur trail to the viewpoint and enjoy a rest stop with the middle Rio Grande Rift spread out before you.

To continue, return to the main trail, which is now called the Mirador Trail. Turn right and in 0.2 mile, bear right onto the Coyote Trail. Pass two mine clusters, make a long switchback turn, and at mile 3.3, turn right onto the Elkins Canyon Trail. The trail winds through tan and white hills for a mile before squeezing through a short narrows. Just out of the narrows, bear left and drop to a fence line along Yerba Buena Road. When the trail meets the road, bear left and walk along the road for 0.3 mile. Near Camino Turquesa, a trail sign points up an arroyo. Walk the arroyo for 0.2 mile to close the loop.

63 PETROGLYPH NATIONAL MONUMENT TRAILS

Distance: 7 miles for five trails, day hike
Difficulty: easy
Elevation range: 5,000 to 5,300 feet
Elevation gain: 300 feet
Best time of year: May to November
Water: at visitor center
Maps: National Park Service brochure and pamphlets
Managed by: National Park Service, Petroglyph National Monument
Features: spectacular petroglyphs

Petroglyph National Monument lies on the very edge of the sprawling western side of Albuquerque. Along a snaking escarpment of black volcanic boulders, the monument protects an extraordinary collection of more than 15,000 petroglyphs. The artists range from nomadic hunters who visited the site more than two centuries ago to ranchers who chased cows in the area

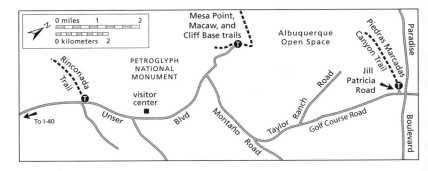

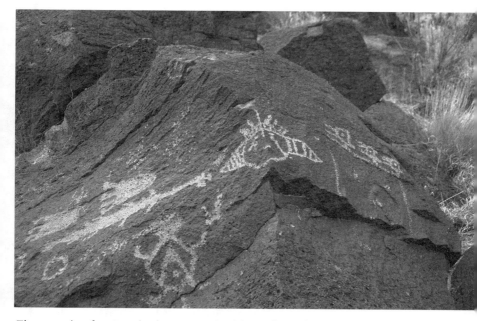

Thousands of petroglyphs are pecked into the volcanic rocks along the escarpment to the west of Albuquerque.

less than 100 years in the past. Most of the drawings, however, are from the Ancestral Pueblo people and are around 500 years old.

Petroglyphs are scattered across the edge of the mesa, but five trails lead hikers past concentrations of these intriguing aspects of Pueblo history. Viewing the rock art is best early in the morning when the sun is not so glaring on east- and south-facing slopes. Plan a visit for the first hours after the park opens at 8:00 AM. Take binoculars to spot glyphs high on the cliff and a pair of polarized sunglasses to make the art easier to see. The trails are sandy, flat, and easy.

Much of the monument lies adjacent to housing developments, and finding the official access points is sometimes an adventure in itself. The easiest way to explore the monument is from the south, starting at the Unser Boulevard exit off I-40. Head north on Unser for 2 miles to the trailhead for the Rinconada Trail on the left.

Head out the trail, which parallels the northern cliff of a huge amphitheater of rock. Clusters of petroglyphs are found along the way, each with a short spur trail leading to it. Follow the Rinconada Trail about 1.5 miles to its indistinct end, then loop along the arroyo to return to the trailhead or return by the same route. Hikers will undoubtedly be surprised when retracing their steps at how many petroglyphs they missed on the way out.

From the Rinconada Trailhead, drive north on Unser Boulevard and in 0.8 mile stop in at the visitor center. Pick up detailed maps of the trails, then continue north on Unser. At 1.4 miles beyond the visitor center, go straight on Unser at the intersection with Montaño Road. In less than a mile, turn right into the Boca Negra Canyon area where three trails await. The longest, the Mesa Point Trail, is about 0.5 mile long and has the greatest concentration of petroglyphs. The short Macaw and Cliff Base trails also pass amazing collections of rock art.

To reach the Piedras Marcadas Canyon Trail, return to the intersection of Unser and Montaño. Head east on Montaño 1.3 miles and turn left on Taylor Ranch Road. In 0.5 mile, continue straight onto Golf Course Road as Taylor Ranch Road bears left. At 3.9 miles from Unser, one block before the major intersection with Paradise Boulevard, turn left onto a small street, Jill Patricia. Park on the right side of the road just before the Las Marcadas housing development.

Walk the concrete path to the right along a retaining wall. Swing left and head uphill. At a fork in the trail, take the left branch and pass through a gate. Entering Albuquerque Open Space, follow the wide trail between the base of the cliff and the retaining wall. In less than 0.25 mile, a trail heads right. Take that trail as it winds close to the base of the cliff. The rocks here are decorated with an amazing assortment of masks, snakes, birds, and handprints. You can easily follow the trail for 1.3 miles before turning around.

64 | LA LUZ/TRAMWAY LOOP

Distance: 9.5 miles, day hike
Difficulty: strenuous
Elevation range: 6,500 to 10,300 feet
Elevation gain: 3,900 feet
Best time of year: May to November
Water: at tramway terminals, carry water
Maps: USGS Sandia Crest; USFS Sandia Wilderness
Managed by: Cibola National Forest, Sandia Wilderness, Sandia Ranger District
Features: spectacular, rugged country; one-way hike

The combination of the La Luz Trail and the Sandia Peak Tramway offers hikers a unique opportunity for a challenging one-way hike. The Sandia Mountains are a round-shouldered hump of granite and limestone that dominates the eastern skyline of Albuquerque. The La Luz Trail climbs 3,700 feet from the base of the Sandias to the crest at 10,300 feet. From the summit, hikers can return via the same trail or opt to enjoy a relaxing fifteen-minute

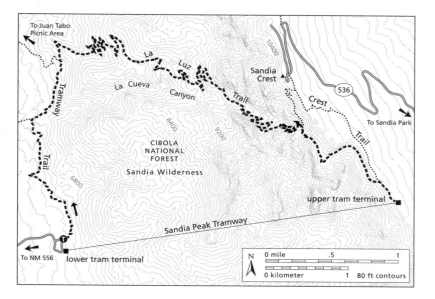

descent back to the base by riding the tram. As an alternative trip, hikers can take the tram to the top of the mountain and walk back down to the base, a trip that is still quite demanding. One-way tram tickets for hikers can be purchased at either terminal. The tram generally runs between 9:00 AM and 5:00 PM. Call (505) 298-8518 for the latest information.

The trailhead for the La Luz Trail is located at the Juan Tabo Picnic Area, but those interested in a loop hike need to begin at the Sandia Peak Tramway parking area and take the Tramway Trail to connect with the La Luz Trail 2 miles above its bottom terminus. This is a popular trail, crowded on weekends with hikers, climbers, and trail runners. The trail has a long history of rerouting and there are many places where old trails may confuse inexperienced hikers. The current trail is well worn its entire length. Note that the steep terrain limits the number of campsites along the way.

From Albuquerque, take I-25 north to the Tramway Road exit 234, NM 556. Head east on NM 556 for 6 miles, then turn left to stay on Tramway Road. One mile from the turn, enter the Sandia Peak Tramway grounds. After paying the nominal parking fee, park near the base of the tramway.

Begin hiking at the northeast corner of the parking lot at the information kiosk and sign for the Tramway Trail. Head into the granite boulder wonderland, immediately entering the Sandia Wilderness. The trail skirts the foot of the mountains, passing near homes and private property, so stay on the trail. In 1 mile, pass the La Cueva Trail to the left and cross La Cueva Canyon. Climb a narrow ridge directly above some large homes, then cross the ridge and bear right, dropping into another canyon. Here the many switchbacks of

The La Luz Trail crosses a talus slope dozens of times as it winds across the western face of the Sandia Mountains.

the La Luz Trail are visible across the canyon. At mile 2.6, immediately after crossing the bottom of the canyon, intersect the La Luz Trail and turn right.

Begin the long journey through "Switchback City," where the trail builders arguably went overboard to ease the grades of the next 800-foot climb. The trail now skirts the north side of a deep canyon on a shadeless slope before reaching a tunnel of vegetation in the canyon bottom. Climb the south wall of that canyon to an open saddle, then continue the ascent on the north slope of La Cueva Canyon. Several broad switchbacks through oak scrub lead to a saddle over a small spur ridge. Drop from the saddle into the conifer forest of upper La Cueva Canyon.

Cross the usually dry bottom of La Cueva Canyon at about mile 5. At this point the trail has gained 2,600 feet, with 1,300 feet to go. Take a deep breath and begin the steepest section of trail. The route is a long set of switchbacks that cross and recross a talus chute about a dozen times. Views of La Cueva Canyon and a huge granite slab to the right are impressive. One more set of broad meanders leads to a saddle and trail junction. The trail left goes to Sandia Crest; continue straight across the saddle on the La Luz Trail. Here the trail leaves the granite and travels along the base of a banded limestone cliff. This spectacular section of trail is perched on a wide ledge with nearby views of massive towers of granite. South Sandia Peak dominates the view in the distance.

At mile 9.3, reach the junction with the Crest Trail, which is usually crowded with tourists. To reach the upper tramway terminal, bear right across a wooden deck at the restaurant. The ticket window is in the U.S. Forest Service Visitor Center directly behind the tramway dock.

65 NORTH AND SOUTH SANDIA CREST/10K TRAIL

Distance: 9.5-mile loop, day hike
Difficulty: moderate
Elevation range: 9,400 to 10,670 feet
Elevation gain: 1,900 feet
Best time of year: May to October
Water: Media Spring
Map: USGS Sandia Crest
Managed by: Cibola National Forest, Sandia Ranger District
Features: isolation on the edge of a major city, views

In contrast to the steep western face of the Sandia Mountains, the east side of the range gently slopes from the crest, creating less demanding terrain for hiking and cross-country skiing. The North Crest Trail offers views of both sides of the mountain, traveling along the ridge above vertical granite crags, with a short side trail leading to North Sandia Peak. The 10K Trail, so named because it very roughly follows the 10,000-foot contour, drops through the sloping conifer forest of the east side of the range. Long-range views of the Rio Grande Rift can be found along this loop's final segment, the South Crest Trail.

Many viewpoints along the North Crest Trail offer long-range looks at the Rio Grande rift.

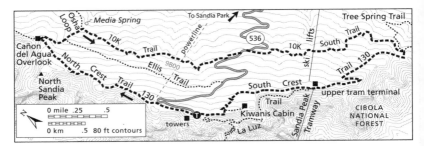

To reach the trailhead, go east from Albuquerque on I-40 to the Cedar Crest/Tijeras exit 175 and follow the signs for NM 14 north. In 6 miles, turn left onto NM 536. Continue 14 miles to the Sandia Crest and park in the large lot. A small day-use fee is charged for entering this area.

Begin by following the signs for the North Crest Trail 130, heading north from the end of the parking area. The trail skirts below a forest of radio and TV towers before entering the conifer woods and beginning to descend. Numerous short side trails lead to views to the west. In late May, the trail courses amid thousands of Canada violets, and in summer watch for Richardson's geranium and delphinium under the fir and spruce. Continue through conifer forest along the rim, passing an unmaintained side trail to North Sandia Peak at mile 1.5. This short trip leads to fantastic views of the granite spires and cliffs to the west. Along the main trail, make a short descent and reach the Cañon del Agua Overlook at mile 2. Find the 10K Trail at the edge of the clearing; watch for the blue diamonds that mark this as a ski trail. Turn right onto the 10K Trail and continue descending.

At mile 2.2, the trail crosses a broad road cut, a scar from a never-completed highway project. The Ellis Trail heads south along the road cut. Bear left to stay on the 10K Trail, and in a few minutes, pass a sign for Media Spring and the Osha Loop. Continue on the 10K Trail through the deep forest on a rolling trail, passing under a powerline at mile 3.6. Near mile 4, bear right to stay on the 10K Trail, which is still marked with blue diamonds. After a few hundred yards, reach a parking area along NM 536. Continue through the parking area, cross the highway, and pick up the 10K Trail on the other side. The trail immediately reenters the forest as it swings through open stands of conifer and aspen.

At mile 5, cross a ski run and soon pass under three ski lifts. The trail now drops through two drainages before contouring to the south to meet the Tree Spring and South Sandia Crest trails at mile 6.5. Turn right onto the South Crest Trail 130 and begin the long ascent back to the trailhead. The trail first passes on the north side crest line, then meets the cliffs of the crest at mile 7.5, where spectacular views await. The next stretch is a gentle climb to the top terminal of the Sandia Peak Tramway. Work your way through the small developed area on one of several trails, staying close to the rim. Beyond the tram, follow the signs toward Kiwanis Cabin. Just beyond where the trail skirts the bottom of a large meadow, pass the turnoff to Kiwanis Cabin and follow the signs pointing to the Crest parking area. Several gentle switchbacks lead back to the trailhead parking area.

66 PINO CANYON

Distance: 9 miles, day hike
Difficulty: difficult
Elevation range: 6,450 to 9,250 feet
Elevation gain: 2,800 feet
Best time of year: April to mid-May, mid-September
to November
Water: carry water
Maps: USGS Sandia Crest; USFS Sandia Wilderness
Managed by: Cibola National Forest, Sandia Wilderness,
Sandia Ranger District
Features: isolation on the edge of a major city, views

As the climate swings toward hotter and drier conditions, the effects can be seen all over New Mexico. In Pino Canyon, a few wet decades in the late twentieth century permitted cool-and-wet-loving Douglas fir to work down north-facing slopes into old ponderosa pine stands. An intense sequence of several drought years in the early 2000s stressed the Douglas fir and allowed insects to infect many stands. In Pino Canyon and other locations in the Sandia, entire mountainsides are now covered with dead trees. The trail up the canyon features a close-up look at this ecological change as the opened tree canopy focuses more sunlight on the forest floor and sun-loving species take hold.

The Pino Canyon Trail climbs from the city to the crest of the Sandias in 4.5 miles. It offers a shady route to the summit on an easy-to-follow and never rough segment of trail that has received loving care from volunteers. It is a popular weekend trek, so if possible, plan a weekday visit.

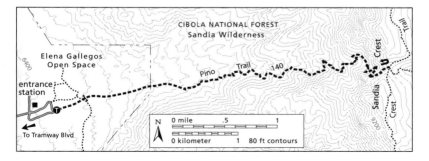

The Pino Canyon Trail heads into a huge rock bowl on the west face of the Sandia Mountains.

Reach the trailhead from Tramway Boulevard about 6 miles north of I-40 or about 7.5 miles south from exit 235 on I-25. Head east on Simms Park Road to the fee station about 1.5 miles from Tramway Boulevard. Pay the small fee and continue right on a one-way road. In 0.3 mile, park in the first parking area on the right.

Walk east along the road for a few yards to an opening in a fence marked for the Pino Trail 140. The first stretch is along wide, developed trail passing picnic shelters and resting benches. Scraggly juniper and spindly cholla grow in the thick carpet of grass as the trail ascends. At mile 0.4, cross a road/trail and continue climbing on the narrower Trail 140. Just short of a mile from the start, pass through a hikers gate at an information board for the Sandia Wilderness.

In the wilderness, the trail immediately enters thicker stands of juniper and tall piñon. Massive granite boulders draw hikers irresistibly from the trail for a short climb to the top. Shade is plentiful as the trail climbs through the forest, weaving in and out of ponderosa pine stands. Through the trees are glimpses of the granite towers of the central Sandias. In this stretch, the trail grade is a steady climb along a succession of ridges and swales.

At mile 2.2, drop from the nose of a small ridge and take in views of the route to the crest. A flat viewpoint at mile 2.5 offers grand views and a convenient rest or turnaround point. From here, the grade gets steeper as the route crosses several aspen-filled drainages. Another grand viewpoint at mile 3.5 provides a rest spot before the trail gains 800 feet over the next mile. The steep switchbacks end at the junction with the South Crest Trail 130. A short walk south along the crest will provide spectacular views to the east and west. After soaking in the sights, return by the same route.

67 | RIO GRANDE BOSQUE

Distance: 8.5 miles round-trip, day hike
Difficulty: easy, but some routefinding required
Elevation range: 4,990 to 5,040 feet
Elevation gain: 50 feet
Best time of year: year-round
Water: carry water
Map: USGS Los Griegos
Managed by: Rio Grande Valley State Park managed
by the Albuquerque Open Space Program
Features: winter hiking, view of the Rio Grande, unusual
ecosystem

The bosque (pronounced *BOW-skay*) is a diminishing plant community found along the floodplains of major rivers in the southwest. The most extensive bosque in New Mexico stretches more than 200 miles along the middle Rio Grande from near Santa Fe to the southern state line. The name comes from the Spanish word for woodlands, but stately cottonwood trees characterize a tall forest canopy in the bosque in Albuquerque.

A hike through Rio Grande Valley State Park offers an intimate glimpse of the unique plant community. The park is in the heart of the city, but for most of this 8.5-mile walk hikers will be unaware of the surrounding urban area. Two pedestrian bridges over the river allow a lollipop loop hike. Explorers can start at the Albuquerque Open Space Visitor Center and wander upstream along the river. A "ditch road" parallels the river just west of the

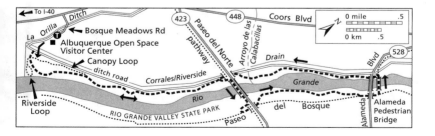

bosque, and an interlaced network of informal trails thread through the park between the road and the river. Trails come and go, but if you lose the path, join the ditch road until another trail drops back into the bosque.

Reach the Albuquerque Open Space Visitor Center from the Coors Boulevard exit 155 off I-40 by heading north on Coors for 4.5 miles. Turn right on Bosque Meadows Road and follow this road 0.2 mile to the visitor center parking area.

Walk to the west side of the parking area where a sign on a gap in the fence points toward the bosque access. Through the fence, meet the road along La Orilla Ditch and turn left. Follow this road 0.3 mile, then angle left to cross the Corrales/Riverside Drain on a small bridge. Bear right to cross over the ditch road and follow the signs pointing to the bosque access and the Riverside Loop. Turn left onto the Riverside Loop and continue east toward the Rio Grande. At mile 0.5, turn left onto the Canopy Loop. From here, head upstream (north) on the loop trail or any of the other trails between the Corrales Drain and the Rio Grande. The Canopy Loop heads back toward the drain and meets a major trail at mile 0.9. This pleasant path stays under a canopy of cottonwoods as it heads north. Follow this path, the ditch road, any of the informal trails, or best, a combination of all three to the north.

Huge cottonwoods line one of the informal trails in the Rio Grande Valley State Park.

As the trail network approaches Paseo del Norte, angle toward the ditch road. At the intersection of the ditch road and the highway, pick up the pedestrian path that parallels the highway. Turn right and use the pathway to cross the Rio Grande. Although Paseo del Norte is a busy road, it is separated from the path by stout railings. Once on the east bank of the river, drop to the paved pathway along the eastside drain, turn left and pass under Paseo del Norte through a tunnel.

North of Paseo del Norte, continue either on the paved Paseo del Bosque or angle left back into the heart of the bosque. Walk about a mile north to Alameda Boulevard. Pass under the road through a tunnel and turn right onto the Alameda pedestrian bridge. Cross the bridge to the west bank of the river. It's time to head south toward the visitor center, so take one of the paths under Alameda and start the meandering route south. The bosque paths get sandy as they approach the Arroyo Calabacillas. Cross the arroyo at mile 5.6 and in a few minutes pass through one of the tunnels under Paseo del Norte. Although the route is now retracing the first part of the hike, it is easy to pick a different route on the return leg. At the La Orilla Ditch, turn right and return to the visitor center.

68 | MANZANO PEAK

Distance: 11 miles, day hike or backpack
Difficulty: difficult
Elevation range: 8,000 to 10,098 feet
Elevation gain: 2,350 feet
Best time of year: April to November
Water: carry water
Maps: USGS Manzano Peak; USFS Manzano Wilderness
Managed by: Cibola National Forest, Manzano Wilderness,
   Mountainair Ranger District
Features: long-range views, solitude

The Manzano Mountains are a southern extension of the Sandia Mountains that dominate Albuquerque's skyline. Both ranges have similar rugged west faces and sloping eastern flanks. The loop hike in Ox and Kayser canyons is an excellent route to the summit of Manzano Peak, the highest point of the range. Like most other trails in the Manzanos, these trails are well marked and well maintained, and walking them is pure pleasure. Views from the crest reach to the isolated mountain ranges beyond the Rio Grande to the west and stretch for 100 miles across the plains to the east.

The east side of the Manzanos was transformed in 2007 and 2008 by three wildfires that burned more than 25,000 acres. Dozens of homes were lost when the fires spread from the mountains to the foothills. Although most of the trails in the Manzano Wilderness were unaffected, the access routes to the trailheads were burned over. Only short stretches of the access trails are through burned forests, and most of the trails remain as attractive as ever.

To reach the trailhead, take I-40 east from Albuquerque to exit 175 at Tijeras. Bear right onto NM 337 south, immediately continuing straight across a T intersection. Travel on NM 337 for 30 miles and turn right onto NM 55 at another T intersection, then continue 12 miles to the village of Manzano. Bear right onto NM 131, which is signed for Manzano Mountains State Park, located 2.5 miles from the village. At the park entrance, turn right onto FR 253 heading for Red Canyon Campground. Enter the burned area and in 2.5 miles, bear left onto FR 422, an all-weather gravel road. In 2.2 miles, reach a sign for the Ox Canyon Trail 190. A short, rough road to the right leads to a small parking area.

The trailhead lies within the burned area, but it doesn't take long to enter unburned forest. From the trailhead, follow the signs as Trail 190 skirts the toe of a ridge to enter Ox Canyon, then meets an old route coming up from the right. The trail turns left, heading upcanyon, and at mile 0.2 intersects the Box Spring Canyon Trail 99. Bear left to stay in Ox Canyon and begin a moderate climb through tall Douglas firs. Two short switchbacks lead past small talus slides made of banded metamorphic rock.

As the trail swings left to cross the head of Ox Canyon at mile 1.5, watch for views downcanyon out onto the plains to the east. The trail now turns in broad switchbacks as it climbs to the crest, meeting the Crest Trail 170 at mile 3.2.

Much of the approach to the Ox Canyon Trailhead was burned by the Trigo Fire.

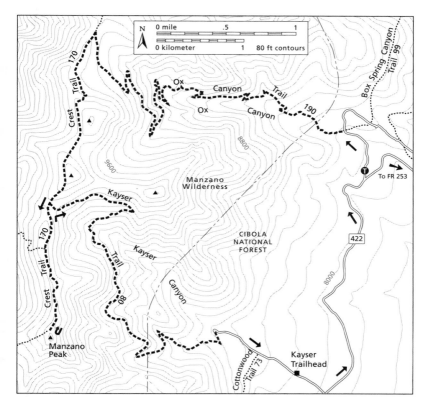

Turn left onto the Crest Trail and continue climbing. The trail soon turns away from the ridgeline but continues to climb, gaining the top of the ridge at mile 3.6. Watch for cairns that mark the trail where it becomes obscure as it passes through small meadows. At mile 4.5, intersect the Kayser Trail 80 coming in from the east. Continue straight on the Crest Trail heading toward Manzano Peak. Cross a narrow ridge above Kayser Canyon, then watch for a sign pointing the way to the peak. At the sign, bear away from the main trail to reach the summit at mile 5.2. From the top, views to the west and north include the Manzanos, the Rio Grande Valley, and the towns of Belen and Los Lunas.

From the peak, backtrack down to and along the Crest Trail, continuing north toward the Kayser Trail. At the junction with the Kayser Trail, turn right, heading downhill across a meadow to a cairn at the edge of the forest below. From here, the trail is easy to follow through the fir forest as it drops along a ridge and skirts the head of the deep Kayser Canyon at mile 6.8. Turn down widely spaced switchbacks as the trail descends across three drainages, reaching the end of the trail on a four-wheel-drive road at mile 8.6.

Turn right and walk down the road, passing the Cottonwood Trail 73 at mile 8.9 and the Kayser Trailhead in another 0.4 mile. At mile 9.5, reach FR 422 and turn left. Walk on FR 422 north for 1.5 miles to return to the Ox Canyon Trailhead.

69 | MANZANO CREST TRAIL

Distance: 12 miles one-way, day hike or backpack
Difficulty: moderate
Elevation range: 7,500 to 9,400 feet
Elevation gain: 1,800 feet
Best time of year: April to November
Water: Upper Fourth of July Spring, carry water
Maps: USGS Capilla Peak and Bosque Peak;
  USFS Manzano Wilderness
Managed by: Cibola National Forest, Manzano Wilderness,
  Mountainair Ranger District
Features: long hike along mountain crest, views, solitude

One-day loop hikes along the Manzano Crest are difficult to put together, so this long walk along the ridgeline makes setting up the lengthy required shuttle worthwhile. Walking north from Capilla Peak to the Albuquerque Trailhead is a delightful one-way trip that stays on or near the crest of the Manzanos for 9 miles. Views are outstanding for much of the trip, and hikers will likely have the trail to themselves along the little-used middle portions of the route. This hike is especially rewarding in October when the bigtooth maples are blazing red and migrating raptors are frequently sighted following the ridgeline. Fossils of ancient sea life are common in the limestone that comprises the crest of the range. Few campsites are located along this route, and water is available only near the end—conditions that mandate careful planning for an overnight stay.

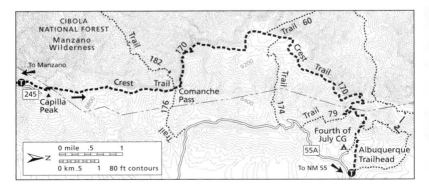

To the east lie extensive areas burned by the Trigo and Big Spring fires, but the crest of the range was untouched by the flames. To set up a shuttle for this hike, from Albuquerque take I-40, NM 337, and NM 55A to Tajique. At the southern end of Tajique, turn right onto FR 55, which is signed for Fourth of July Campground. Go 6.5 miles to the Albuquerque Trail, which is a half mile from the campground. Leave a vehicle at the parking area and backtrack to Tajique and turn right onto NM 55. Go south about 9 miles to the town of Manzano and turn right onto FR 245, which is signed for Capilla Peak. It is 9 miles to the trailhead near Capilla Peak Campground. The last 4 miles are steep and rough; a high-clearance vehicle is recommended, but low-slung cars frequently make the trip. Park at the sign for the Crest Trail.

Most of the trails in the Manzano Wilderness were untouched by the fires of 2007 and 2008.

Begin hiking downhill on the Crest Trail 170, entering a Douglas fir forest at the head of Cañon del Ojo del Indio. Descend steeply into the canyon on several switchbacks. After passing near the normally dry Ojo del Indio, begin a short climb through shadeless oak scrub. Pass over two low saddles before reaching the top of Comanche Ridge at mile 1.9. There are continual views into Comanche Canyon to the west as the trail passes another saddle and skirts to the west of a knoll before dropping to reach Comanche Pass at mile 3.1.

At a four-way intersection atop Comanche Pass, continue on the Crest Trail past the Comanche Trail 182 to the left and the Canyon Trail 176 to the right. Begin a long climb by passing through a fenced gate, then bearing left. To the left are views of Capilla Peak and the trail just traveled. At mile 4.1, the trail begins to climb steeply, at first on switchbacks, then cutting across the shoulder of the ridge. As the trail passes a knoll to the west and begins to level, hikers soon gain the ridge and again enjoy views in all directions. Along the crest, watch for abundant fossilized shells in the limestone.

As it approaches the east slope of Bosque Peak, the trail becomes indistinct and hikers must sight from cairn to cairn to stay on the correct route. The trail passes along the east slope of Bosque Peak to intersect the faint Encino Trail 18 to the left and, a bit farther on, the Bosque Trail 174 to the right. Continue north on the Crest Trail across a huge rocky meadow where it is important to follow the cairns marking the trail and not be misled by cattle trails that crisscross the area. Begin to descend from Bosque Peak, crossing more meadows and oak scrub along the way. At mile 8.2, reach a saddle that offers views of Albuquerque to the north.

From the saddle, the trail climbs the ridgeline before skirting a low peak to the left. As the trail swings left, Fourth of July Canyon is to the right and the twin Guadalupe and Mosca peaks are straight ahead. Continue dropping to the north, switchbacking down the east side of a ridge at mile 9.2. At mile 9.4, leave the Crest Trail and turn right onto Cerro Blanco Trail 79. Begin a long, moderate descent through a shady maple and oak forest on the slopes of Fourth of July Canyon. At mile 10, turn left onto the Fourth of July Trail 173 and round the head of several small drainages before reaching the bottom of Fourth of July Canyon. Pass the intersection with the Albuquerque Trail 78 at mile 10.5, then drop past Upper Fourth of July Spring. In a quarter mile, bear left onto the trail marked for the Albuquerque Trailhead. From the junction it is about a mile to the trailhead.

70 FOURTH OF JULY/ALBUQUERQUE LOOP

Distance: 4.3 miles, day hike
Difficulty: easy
Elevation range: 7,500 to 8,300 feet
Elevation gain: 800 feet
Best time of year: September to November
Water: Upper Fourth of July Spring, carry water
Maps: USGS Bosque Peak and Tajique
Managed by: Cibola National Forest,
   Mountainair Ranger District
Features: spectacular fall colors

The short loop through Fourth of July Canyon and Cañon de la Gallina is a New Mexico classic. The dominance of bigtooth maple and Gambel oak in these drainages creates brilliant fall colors found in few other locations in the state. The bright red maples outdo the better-known aspen for adding splashes of color to the mountains. Beneath a canopy of flame-colored foliage, this easy autumn stroll is not to be missed. The colors reach their peak in late September and early October.

To reach the trailhead from I-40 at Tijeras, take NM 337 and then NM 55 about 35 miles to Tajique. At the southern end of Tajique, turn right onto FR 55, which is signed for Fourth of July Campground. Go 6.5 miles to a short gravel road leading to the trailhead for the Albuquerque Trail 78 and turn right to reach the trailhead.

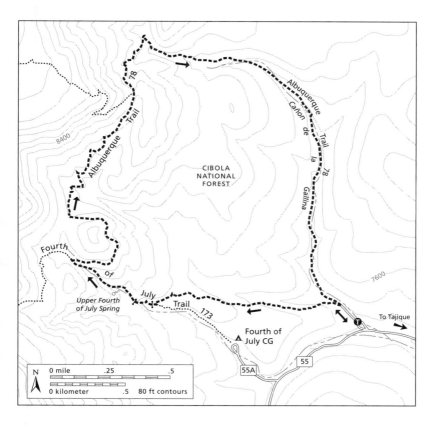

Start hiking up the Cañon de la Gallina on a wide trail in the pine forest. In a few hundred feet, turn left and head toward the Fourth of July Trail. Meet the Fourth of July Trail 173 in 1 mile. Trail 173 follows an old road up the canyon bottom. Pass through two gates as the trail climbs on gentle grades. About 1.5 miles from the start, climb more steeply through a rocky, narrow stretch of canyon, passing Upper Fourth of July Spring. Seep spring monkey flowers and horsetails grow in profusion, but keep a watchful eye open for poison ivy, which is common in this canyon. Just past the spring, meet the Albuquerque Trail 78. Take a sharp right onto this trail and begin a steeper climb around a hill and into another small drainage.

At mile 2, leave the drainage bottom and climb a dry drainage to a small saddle. Drop into the head of Cañon de la Gallina, for now enjoying the maples from a distance. The trail descends to the canyon bottom and into a fine stand of maples. At mile 3.4, pass a small spring, and soon the trail widens to an old road that leads back to the trailhead.

Bigtooth maple leaves in October (Photo by Jessica Martin)

71 | COPPER CANYON/SOUTH BALDY LOOP

Distance: 10.4 miles, day hike or backpack
Difficulty: strenuous
Elevation range: 6,800 to 10,400 feet
Elevation gain: 3,600 feet
Best time of year: April to November
Water: lower Water Canyon
Maps: USGS Magdalena and South Baldy
Managed by: Cibola National Forest,
  Magdalena Ranger District
Features: remote canyons, ridge-top views

The Magdalena Mountains are a small jewel of a mountain range rising out of the deserts of central New Mexico. Their highest point, South Baldy, rises to 10,783 feet. The steep mountain face and grassy summits make possible dramatic views in all directions. The best way to take in the sights is to walk to the Magdalena Crest Trail 8 via the Copper Canyon Trail. This long, challenging loop leads into the heart of the Magdalena Range, climbing the steep mountain face to the crest through one canyon and descending from the crest along another. The ascent up Copper Canyon is gentle at first, but steepens as it approaches the ridgeline; Water Canyon provides a gradual drop from the high country. Campsites and water are plentiful along the middle stretch of Copper Canyon but are limited in Water Canyon.

This loop begins and ends near the Water Canyon Campground. From Socorro, take US 60 west. Drive about 16 miles to FR 235, marked with a large sign for Water Canyon Campground, and turn left. At the end of the pavement in 5 miles, turn right on the gravel FR 406. Pass the campground entrance in 0.2 mile and continue straight on the now dirt FR 406. Park at the dead end in 0.8 mile. Note that no water is available at the campground.

From the trailhead, cross Copper Canyon and follow the sign that points the way to the Copper Canyon Trail 10. Begin walking uphill on an old road on an easement through private property. The trail skirts a large meadow, passing an old ranch house, and then passing under a canopy of large piñon and alligator juniper. Enjoy the assortment of old blazes that marks the trail. As the canyon narrows about 0.8 mile from the start, pass a fork in the road angling sharply to the right. From this point, water is intermittently found in the canyon bottom as the trail enters ponderosa pine and mixed conifer forest.

After crossing the stream at mile 1.4, the trail gently climbs to the slopes above the canyon bottom. At mile 3.1, pass the ruins of a prospector's cabin. Water can be found in the stream near the cabin throughout the year. Just up the canyon, come to the junction of two branches of the trail leading to the crest. Take the left fork, which may be signed for Magdalena Crest Trail 8 and FR 235.

The last mile to the crest is considerably steeper than the trail below. As the switchbacks grow tighter near the ridgeline, enjoy sweeping views downcanyon. Reach a meadow just below the crest and follow the faint trail over the top to the junction with the Crest Trail 8 at mile 3.9.

Turn left (south) onto Trail 8, crossing a grassy slope before reentering the woods. At the next small meadow, the trail turns a switchback over the ridge

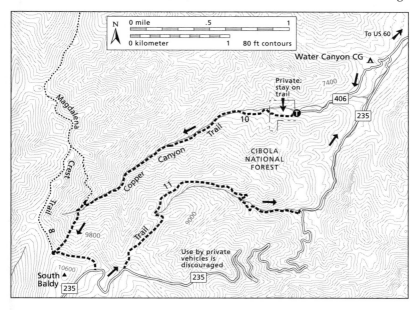

and descends into deep forest on the east side. After a brief descent, the trail climbs again to reach a spur ridge just below the summit of South Baldy at mile 4.2. Drop to FR 235, turn left, and begin a 0.5-mile stretch on the road to meet Trail 11. At a sign on a broad saddle, turn left onto Trail 11 and begin the long descent back to the trailhead.

At the bottom of the first steep pitch is a lovely pine-covered saddle that makes a good, though waterless, campsite. Beyond the saddle, the trail drops steadily along a long spur ridge, with views through the trees back to the grassy slopes of the crest. After crossing the ridge, the trail winds through several drainages. The southern exposure creates an extraordinary juxtaposition of plants: on a 20-foot stretch of trail, hikers can pass yucca, scrub oak, white fir, and alligator juniper.

At mile 7, the trail switchbacks down to the bottom of Water Canyon. The trail is now less steep as it follows the canyon floor. Reach FR 235 at mile 7.8. Turn left onto the road and continue down Water Canyon another 1.8 miles to the junction with FR 406. Turn left and walk FR 406 back to the trailhead.

Old blaze on an alligator juniper along the Copper Canyon Trail

Waterfall in Potato Canyon (Photo by Bob Julyan)

72 | POTATO CANYON

Distance: 6 miles out-and-back, day hike
Difficulty: easy
Elevation range: 6,750 to 7,450 feet
Elevation gain: 800 feet
Best time of year: April to November
Water: intermittent flow in Potato Canyon, carry water
Maps: USGS Mount Withington; USFS Apache Kid and
 Withington wildernesses
Managed by: Cibola National Forest, Withington
 Wilderness, Magdalena Ranger District
Features: isolated mountain range, wild country, scenic
 waterfall

The northern half of the long San Mateo Mountains holds one of New Mexico's least-used wilderness areas, the Withington. Because this wilderness area is so far from the normal tourist routes, just driving to it can be an adventure. This range is for experienced hikers who can follow ill-defined trails. Help is far away, so prepare carefully for any trip to the area. Potato Canyon, named for a rounded rock spire on a bordering ridge, holds the most accessible trail in the range. A walk on the brittle shales of the lower canyon is pleasantly shaded by a canopy of Arizona walnut and ends at a pretty waterfall.

To reach the trailhead from Magdalena, 27 miles west of Socorro on US 60, take NM 107 south. This dirt road is passable to all vehicles when dry. Go about 17 miles to the intersection with FR 52 and bear right. Take this rough

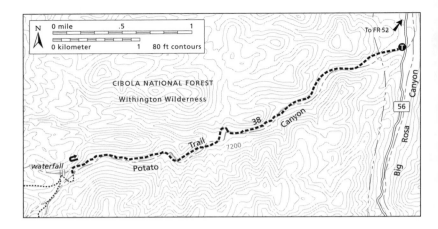

road for 3.5 miles to FR 56 and bear left. A high-clearance vehicle will make the 3-mile journey to the trailhead a bit easier.

Begin the trip by walking into the mouth of Potato Canyon where it joins the much larger Big Rosa Canyon. The old road soon narrows to a trail at the Withington Wilderness boundary at mile 0.25. Follow the trail, which is marked with old blazes, up the canyon bottom. The grade is gentle except for a few spots where it skirts rock piles in the stream channel. At mile 1.6 enter a wooded flat before the canyon suddenly narrows between long cliffs. At mile 2.8, the trail climbs steeply up and over a rock ledge, but to see the waterfall, continue up the stream channel. After enjoying the cool shade and tumbling water, return to the trailhead by the same route.

73 | SAN LORENZO CANYON

Distance: 1 to 8 miles, day hike
Difficulty: easy
Elevation range: 5,250 to 5,400 feet
Elevation gain: 100 feet
Best time of year: year-round
Water: carry water
Maps: USGS Lemitar and San Lorenzo Spring
Managed by: Bureau of Land Management, Socorro Field Office
Features: narrow canyons, endless exploration possibilities

Hidden in the foothills of Polvadera Mountain outside Socorro, San Lorenzo Canyon is the central feature of a network of sandstone cliffs and convoluted

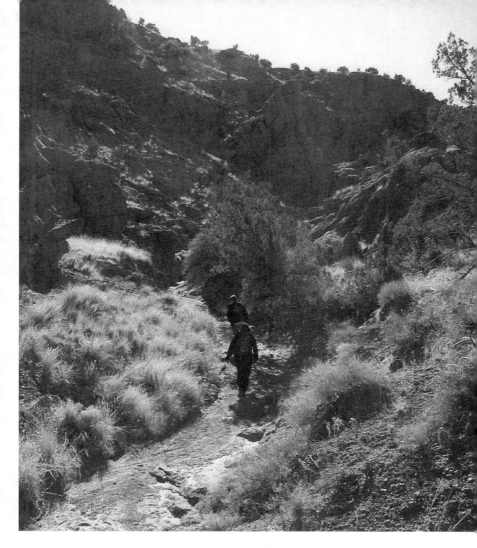

Exploring the side canyons is the main attraction at San Lorenzo Canyon.

rills. Tilted layers of rock tower above the broad floor of the main canyon, but the claustrophobic side canyons are the main attraction. In the mile-long canyon, hikers will find more than a dozen inviting entrances into the cliffs that are large enough to enter on foot. Some side canyons are mere slices in the rock carved by countless gully washers; a few have a broad, sandy bottom broken by ledges; and others splinter off into narrow, intertwined fingers. A few of the larger cracks twist and climb to the rim above.

To reach the trailhead, take exit 156 off I-25 at Lemitar. Pick up the frontage road immediately on the west side of the interstate. Turn right and take

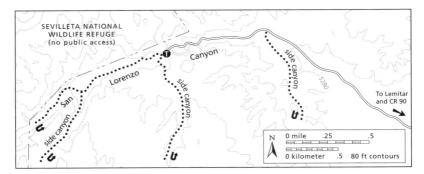

the frontage road north for 4.5 miles. At a T intersection, turn left onto the dirt CR 90. This all-weather road is passable to all vehicles in dry weather. After 2 miles, turn right at the sign for San Lorenzo Canyon. The canyon entrance is located another 2 miles up this road, which follows a wide arroyo bottom.

To explore the canyon, hikers can park near the canyon entrance or drive another mile to a jumble of boulders that blocks wheeled access. Hiking upcanyon from this point offers an easy route to view the soaring cliffs and colorful rocks of the area. The canyon meets the boundary of the Sevilleta National Wildlife Refuge in about a half mile. Public entry to the refuge is prohibited, so turn around here.

Wander back downcanyon to poke up inviting side canyons. The side canyon a few yards south of the vehicle turnaround is a wonderful alcove of rock that offers a route to the rim and excellent viewpoints both up and down the main canyon. Side drainages to the north are often dotted with shimmering cottonwoods and bushy white oaks. Exploring four or five side canyons can easily make a delightful day in the rocks.

74 CHUPADERA PEAK

Distance: 9.5 miles, day hike
Difficulty: moderate
Elevation range: 4,520 to 6,273 feet
Elevation gain: 1,800 feet
Best time of year: mid-September to early May
Water: carry water
Map: USGS Indian Wells Wilderness
Managed by: Bosque del Apache National Wildlife Refuge
Features: winter hiking, long-range views

The Bosque del Apache Wildlife Refuge is known for its winter concentrations of snow geese and sandhill cranes, but the refuge stretches from the Rio

Grande to the desert summits to the west. The trip to Chupadera Peak shows the splendor of the desert sections of the refuge and offers an opportunity for a delightful winter hike in the sunshine. The trip to the peak crosses a broad creosote plain before entering a richly colored desert grassland where the 6,273-foot peak serves as the backdrop. The carefully designed trail leads to the summit where hikers are rewarded with a spectacular view of the Rio Grande rift.

To reach the trailhead, take exit 139 off I-25 at San Antonio. Head east 1 mile to the village, then turn right onto NM 1. In 6.5 miles, cross a railroad track. Watch for the first dirt road on the right, which is located about 0.4 mile beyond the railroad crossing. Turn right onto the dirt road, pass under the railroad, and reach the trailhead about 0.4 mile from the pavement.

A craggy chute leads to the the ridge below Chupadera Peak.

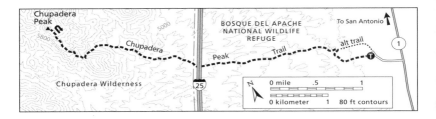

Begin hiking on the well-marked trail heading west through tall sagebrush and mesquite. The trail heads up a gravelly arroyo, and at mile 0.4 turns right to climb to a low ridge. Meet an alternate trail from the parking area coming in from the right. Turn left to begin a long, gradual climb up the ridge. The destination, Chupadera Peak, remains in view the entire route. The trail winds through creosote bushes and almost-stately prickly pear cacti. At mile 2.2, duck through a culvert under I-25 and enter the Chupadera Wilderness. Here the vegetation turns to attractive desert grassland dotted with huge prickly pear and soaptree yucca. Continue up an arroyo pointing toward the peak until mile 3.2. Here the trail leaves the arroyo and enters an amphitheater of rock. The trail passes through a small canyon to the left and climbs through the chocolate rhyolite. Steep switchbacks lead to a ridge at mile 3.8. Ascend the ridgeline, with grand views to the south and west. This last segment gains about 600 feet in a mile as the trail works its way to the peak.

Pass through a fence just short of the summit, and wind through the grasses to reach the top. The view encompasses the Organ Mountains, the Sacramento Range, and the massive hulk of the San Mateo Mountains. After enjoying the view, return to the trailhead by the same route.

75 | VICKS PEAK

Distance: 12 miles, backpack
Difficulty: strenuous
Elevation range: 7,400 to 10,250 feet
Elevation gain: 3,100 feet
Best time of year: April to November
Water: Nave and San Mateo springs
Maps: USGS Vicks Peak and Blue Mountain;
    USFS Withington and Apache Kid wildernesses
Managed by: Cibola National Forest,
    Apache Kid Wilderness, Magdalena Ranger District
Features: wild country, great views, solitude

The Apache Kid Wilderness is located in the southern half of the San Mateo Mountains. Named for a renegade Apache reportedly buried there, the wilderness has almost 100 miles of primitive trails but very few access points. The lower half of the wilderness is reached easily from Springtime Campground, and hikers with ample time can take trips of more than 50 miles into the central range. The Apache Kid Wilderness can get hot in summer, but the usually light snowfalls in the range make it an ideal spot for a spring or late fall trip.

The journey to the summit of Vicks Peak is an excellent introduction to the range. It is a long and strenuous hike to the summit, too much for most hikers to make in one day. Start with plenty of water and plan to replenish the supply at San Mateo and Nave springs. Waterless campsites are located on the flat saddle at the site of Myers Cabin near the base of Vicks Peak. Plan to reach Myers Cabin the first day, then visit the peak the next morning before returning to the trailhead.

To reach Springtime Campground from Socorro, leave I-25 at exit 115, which is about 45 miles south of town. Get on NM 1 and continue south, parallel to the interstate, about 10 miles to FR 225. Turn right and follow FR 225 13.5 miles to the Springtime Campground entrance. Turn right, enter the campground, and park at the trailhead for Trail 43.

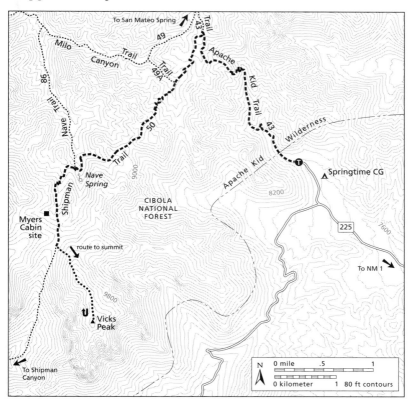

The results of a recent lightning strike on a ponderosa pine

Begin hiking on the well-maintained Apache Kid Trail 43. Under ponderosa pines, the first section of trail makes a moderate climb that can be hot from late spring through the summer. The trail ascends a small drainage for 1.2 miles before bearing west and beginning a steep climb on switchbacks. At mile 2.1, reach an intersection on a saddle at the foot of a rocky knob. With the most difficult portions of the hike behind, take a long rest before turning left onto the Shipman Trail 50. (Water is found at San Mateo Spring, past the junction, 0.5 mile north on Trail 43.) Trail 50 is not as easy to follow as Trail 43, but numerous markers help keep hikers on the correct route.

Trail 50 stays atop a broad ridge before dropping into the head of Milo Canyon, reaching the bottom at mile 2.7. Pass the junction with Trail 49A, a branch of the Milo Trail 49, to the right. Continue straight, switchbacking up to another saddle at mile 3.3. Traversing conifer forest, the trail again drops, this time to reach Nave Spring at mile 4.3, where a small but dependable flow of water is located just down from the trail. After the spring, climb steeply to the intersection with the Nave Trail 86, then cross another saddle. Again drop into a small drainage before climbing to a broad saddle at mile 5.2. This is the site of Myers Cabin, and campsites are easily located in the open forest.

From the saddle, a faint, unmaintained path climbs the ridge to the southeast. Leave Trail 50 and angle up through the forest by the easiest route. At mile 5.7, the forest opens up near the base of an unnamed peak. Continue over the peak, then follow the ridge to the southeast to the wooded summit of Vicks Peak. The spectacular view from Vicks reaches far: east to the Capitan Range and south to the Elephant Butte and Caballo reservoirs along the Rio Grande. Return by the same route.

76 EL CAMINO REAL

Distance: 3 miles, day hike
Difficulty: easy
Elevation range: 4,750 to 5,200 feet
Elevation gain: 50 feet
Best time of year: September to May
Water: carry water
Map: USGS Prisor Hill
Managed by: El Camino Real de Tierra Adentro
   National Historic Trail
Features: historic segment of 300-year-old road

El Camino Real de Tierra Adentro served as the major route from Mexico City to the settlements in New Mexico in the seventeenth and eighteenth centuries. Pioneered by colonizer Juan Oñate in 1598, the Royal Road to the Interior carried trade caravans with wagonloads of supplies that were the lifeblood of the early European towns in New Mexico. The waterless 90-mile segment, known as the Jornada del Muerto ("journey of the dead man"), was the roughest passage on the 1,500-mile journey. It was named for the sad fate of German Bernard Gruber, who during his escape from imprisonment by the Inquisition near Santa Fe, died on the lonely plain in 1670.

Modern hikers can get a taste of this difficult journey by hiking one of the few short section of the trail currently open to public use. The trail follows a section of the old road and ends on the Yoast Escarpment at an overlook of the Paraje del Aleman, the trailside camping spot named for the German Gruber.

Reach the trailhead by taking exit 79 off I-25 at Truth or Consequences. Follow Business I-25 south into town for about 2 miles to the intersection with NM 51. Turn left on NM 51 and continue east for 17 miles to the rail

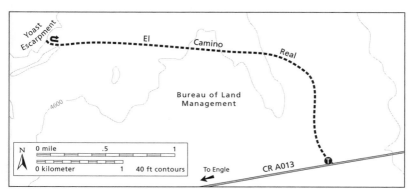

From the ground, traces of El Camino Real are often faint.

stop at Engle, passing Elephant Butte reservoir en route. At Engle, turn right onto CR A013, a paved road for the next 13 miles. After the pavement ends, continue on gravel; the trailhead is 17.5 miles south of Engle on CR A013.

Begin by following the wide dirt track near the BLM information kiosk. The track skirts around the south side of a low hill and meets with El Camino Real at mile 0.6. The subtle, multiple ruts of the old road head north through a desolate creosote plain, angling away from the county road. The ground is hard-packed desert pavement, a conglomerate of sun-baked rocks and sand as firm as any asphalt highway. Although distant mountains surround the plain, the local terrain is flat and featureless. The exception is a low, elongated mound about a mile ahead. The road slowly approaches the mound. It is easy to imagine the day-to-day drudgery of the long trip from Mexico along this section of the road.

After passing the mound, come to the edge of a low escarpment and the current end of the open portion of trail. The view north continues across level ground, but in the distance, a green patch marks the site of the Paraje del Aleman. Imagine the contrasting feelings of the early travelers along the route: water lies ahead, but it seems so distant. Although more of the route will be opened to hiking in the future, for now this is the turnaround point of the trip.

11 | Broad and Valles Canyons

Distance: 9 miles, day hike
Difficulty: easy
Elevation range: 4,750 to 5,200 feet
Elevation gain: 900 feet
Best time of year: September to May
Water: carry water
Maps: USGS Sierra Alta and Souse Springs
Managed by: Bureau of Land Management,
   Las Cruces Field Office
Features: Chihuahuan Desert vegetation,
   narrow slickrock canyons, petroglyphs

At Broad Canyon the foothills are softly stroked with creosote bush and the rolling slopes are slashed with cliffs of tan volcanic rocks tilted this way and that. For those who enjoy something a bit different, it is a place of solitude and wild exploring. Both Valles and Broad canyons are narrow defiles filled with rocky delights: swirling water-cut channels carved into the soft tuff, huge rounded boulders tumbled by flash floods, and tight, unexpected bends in the canyon floors. Much of the walking route to the canyon passes through private land on an easement, and hikers should stay on the described route.

Travel north on I-25 from Las Cruces about 15 miles to exit 19. Turn left onto NM 157 and go west for 2 miles to NM 185. Turn right and go another 12 miles. Between mileposts 25 and 26, turn left onto CR E006. This road has a few rough spots but when dry is passable to all vehicles. In about 7 miles

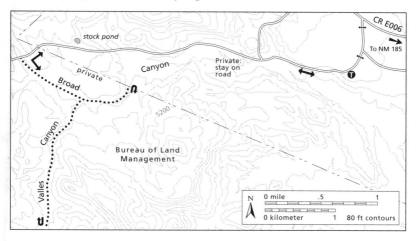

The route up Broad Canyon shows a contrast between the white rocks of the canyon bottom and the red cliffs.

near two rusting water tanks, bear left at a fork, and pass through a gate. In 0.2 mile, come to another fork. This time take the right fork, passing through another gate, and park in another 0.2 mile, just before the road pitches down the canyon wall.

Begin walking down the shelf road into Broad Canyon, which at this point is indeed a wide gash through the grassland hills. At the bottom of the hill, cross a deep gully and pick up the road on the other side. The road continues along the canyon bottom at the base of a rocky slope covered with stout prickly pear cacti. At mile 1.7, the road turns away from the canyon and climbs over a low saddle, passing a large stock pond halfway up. Over the saddle, descend to again meet Broad Canyon. Now turn left, leaving the road, and follow the slickrock of the canyon bottom. This is the meat of the hike, walking on scoured tuff in the deepening canyon. Boulder hop down-canyon about 0.7 mile, passing the entrance to Valles Canyon on the way. Boulder hopping and climbing down slickrock ledges, pass a soaring wall of red tuff before coming to a fence that marks private property. Hikers must turn around here, but they can pause to enjoy the shade of a cluster of large oaks before backtracking upstream. Stay to the left (west) side of the canyon and watch for a petroglyph panel at the entrance to Valles Canyon. Turn left into this twisting, narrow watercourse that is full of surprises. Hikers can follow Valles Canyon for a mile before backtracking to Broad Canyon, turning left and walking back to the road. Once at the road, turn right and return to your vehicle by the same route.

78 | INDIAN HOLLOW

Distance: 4.5-mile loop, day hike or backpack
Difficulty: moderate
Elevation range: 5,100 to 6,700 feet
Elevation gain: 1,600 feet
Best time of year: year-round
Water: at campground, intermittent flow in Indian Hollow
Maps: USGS Organ and Organ Peak
Managed by: Bureau of Land Management, Aguirre Springs
  Recreation Area, Las Cruces Field Office
Features: sheer granite cliffs, large alligator junipers,
  secluded canyon

The granite crags of the Organ Mountains are one of the most spectacular features of southern New Mexico. The east face of the range jumps abruptly from the desert floor near Las Cruces, and the ragged towers of vertically jointed granite are said to resemble the tubes of a pipe organ. Much of the Organs are under the jurisdiction of the White Sands Missile Range and are

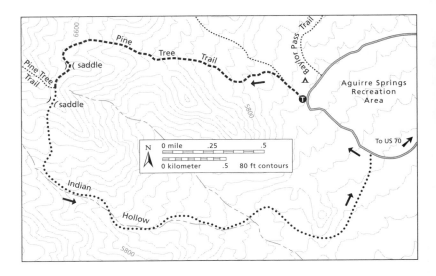

off-limits to visitors. The best access to the range is at the Aguirre Springs Recreation Area, and the primitive route into Indian Hollow is the most interesting hike. Indian Hollow, although near the developed campground, is rugged country with confusing terrain. Few visitors make the trek into the canyon.

To reach the trailhead from the junction of I-25 and US 70 in Las Cruces, go east on US 70 toward San Augustin Pass. About 14 miles from the in-

terstate, turn right onto the road to Aguirre Springs Recreation Area. Continue about 6 miles to the Pine Tree Trailhead and park. Note that a small fee is charged for day use in the recreation area.

Begin climbing the Pine Tree Trail in a huge amphitheater of granite with towering cliffs in three directions. This north-facing slope supports a surprisingly lush plant community dominated by huge alligator junipers. At 0.25 mile from the start, the Pine Tree Trail splits into two branches. Take the left fork and continue climbing, with views of Baylor Pass to the right. Just short

Alligator juniper bark

of mile 1, reach a saddle and cross over to the opposite side of the ridge with views of conical Sugarloaf Peak straight ahead. Continue climbing to a second saddle at mile 1.5 where a short spur left leads to a viewpoint.

Within 200 feet of the saddle, a second, fainter trail angles off to the left. Take this lesser-used trail, which leads to Indian Hollow. Follow the light tread south, watching for rock cairns that mark the way. Continue climbing, steeply at times, skirting around the head of a side canyon. After about 0.5 mile on this faint trail, reach a spur ridge with steep canyons on either side. Drop off the east face of the ridge and descend into Indian Hollow, carefully picking a route down to the canyon bottom. Use caution on the steep slope. A trickle of water is usually found in this section of Indian Hollow, and shady and level ground makes it an interesting place for an overnight stay. Hikers can explore up two canyons heading south, but be on the watch for the boundary of the White Sands Missile Range about 0.5 mile away—do not enter without getting prior permission.

To return to the trailhead, walk north down Indian Hollow. Trails come and go along the way, but the streambed is easy to follow. After 1.25 miles, watch closely for rock cairns that mark a trail to the left that leads out of the canyon to the main road. The trail crosses several drainages before crossing a low saddle just to the south of a distinctive knob on the ridge. The trail here is faint; head generally west to reach the main road. At the road, turn left and walk uphill to return to the parking area in about 0.75 mile.

79 BAYLOR PASS

Distance: 5 miles one-way, day hike
Difficulty: moderate
Elevation range: 4,900 to 6,380 feet
Elevation gain: 1,200 feet
Best time of year: year-round
Water: at main campground only, carry water
Maps: USGS Organ and Organ Peak
Managed by: Bureau of Land Management, Aguirre Springs and Organ Mountains recreation areas, Las Cruces Field Office
Features: historic pass, scenic views, easy shuttle

The National Recreation Trail over Baylor Pass roughly follows the route taken by the Confederate cavalry while engaging the Union infantry in 1862 during the Civil War. Near Las Cruces, Colonel John Baylor was attacked by Union troops under Major Isaac Lynde. Baylor's inferior force nonetheless held its ground against the Union, and apparently, the sight of blood was enough to send Lynde packing out of nearby Fort Fillmore, a supply base he considered indefensible. Legend has it that, as the Union soldiers destroyed the supplies at Fort Fillmore in preparation for their retreat, they were loath to pour out a store of good medicinal whisky, instead using it to fill their canteens. As they retreated toward San Augustin Pass, the July sun and whisky soon dehydrated the marchers. Baylor easily caught Lynde's stragglers, who readily surrendered for a drink of water. Then Baylor and several hundred mounted troops dashed across the pass that would bear his name, and surprised Lynde's main Union force at San Augustin Spring, where Lynde accepted Baylor's demand for unconditional surrender.

This hike is best done with a shuttle. Drive east on US 70 from the intersection with I-25 in Las Cruces. In about 11 miles, turn right onto Baylor Pass Road. In 0.8 mile, continue straight over a cattle guard onto a gravel road. A mile beyond, leave a vehicle at the well-marked trailhead on the left side of the road. Return to US 70, turn right, and continue 2 miles over San Augustin Pass to the road to Aguirre Springs Recreation Area. Turn right and continue about 6 miles to the Baylor Pass Trailhead. A small fee is charged for day use.

Most of the elevation gain to the pass is accomplished in the first mile as the trail winds through juniper-piñon woodland. In about a mile, pass directly beneath the lofty Rabbit Ears, twin peaks of craggy granite. Cross over a spur ridge to parallel a drainage leading to Baylor Pass. In spring, hikers will be jolted by a stiff headwind at this point. Reach the pass about 2 miles from the start and enjoy the long-distance views to the east of the city of Las Cruces, jagged volcanic peaks, and the Black Range on the far horizon.

The ragged summits of the Organ Mountains as seen from Baylor Pass

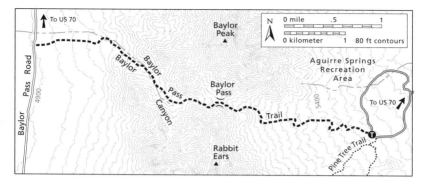

From Baylor Pass, the trail switchbacks down through scrub oak, white-thorn acacia, and manzanita, a striking contrast to the plants on the east side of the mountain. In the round bowl of upper Baylor Canyon, the trail is cut into decomposed granite, which makes for slippery footing. Well into the bowl at 3.3 miles, pass a waterless primitive camp shaded by a single tree.

The trail heads toward the mouth of the canyon. Just before arriving there, at a point where a short spur trail leads left to a viewpoint, the trail abruptly turns right and descends. Drop quickly over several switchbacks before crossing the canyon bottom and reaching the alluvial fan. On the open desert, drop through the last mile to the western end of the Baylor Pass Trail.

80 | Dripping Springs Natural Area

Distance: 5-mile loop, day hike
Difficulty: easy
Elevation range: 5,420 to 6,275 feet
Elevation gain: 900 feet
Best time of year: year-round
Water: carry water
Map: USGS Organ Peak
Managed by: Bureau of Land Management, Las Cruces Field Office
Features: historic structures, wildlife

The tourist industry has been a staple in the desert southwest for more than 100 years. Evidence of this is abundant in Ice Canyon at the base of the Organ Mountains. In the 1870s, Confederate Civil War veteran Eugene Van Patten established a mountain camp resort at Dripping Springs, attracting visitors from all over the country. In 1917, Van Patten sold his property to

Nathan Boyd, who established another southwest staple in the canyon: a sanatorium. Boyd expanded the facilities in the canyon and improved the road from Las Cruces to the foot of the mountains.

The Dripping Springs Natural Area holds the historic structures of the two resorts as well as a variety of interesting natural features. The water at the springs attracts abundant bird- and wildlife; the rocky canyons hold strange rock formations and waterfalls. A small trail network allows visitors to see all the features of the area on foot.

To reach the natural area from the intersection of I-25 and University Avenue (exit 1) in Las Cruces, head east on University. At the city limits, the road becomes Dripping Springs Road. Continue east, climbing into the foothills. The pavement ends at 6 miles from the interstate. Continue on the smooth gravel road past the junction with Baylor Canyon Road, and reach another paved section of road. Enter the Dripping Springs Natural Area and reach the visitor center about 10 miles from the interstate. A nominal fee is required for day use.

Begin hiking at the east end of the parking area at the clearly marked trailhead. Walk toward the mountains on the former road to the resorts, now a wide gravel path. Enjoy the desert birdlife along the Ice Canyon arroyo as the trail climbs gradually toward the mountain front. At the junction with the Crawford Trail, head right and enter a broad desert grassland. The looming

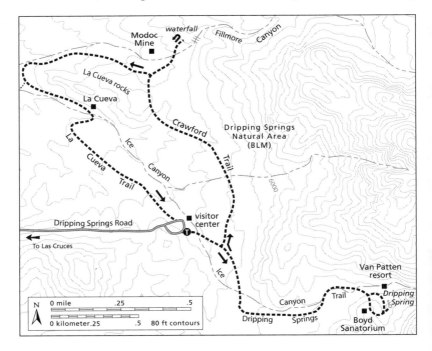

The narrows in Fillmore Canyon

crags of the Organs are more impressive as you approach the base of the towers. After 1.2 miles, pass the livery stables of the Van Patten resort and at a trail junction, bear left toward the Patten place. Explore the resort area and old hotel, then take the path leading from the hotel to Dripping Spring. Next, climb to the Boyd Sanatorium buildings. A rock stairway leads from the dining hall to a short trail that gains a rock ledge overlooking the Boyd place and a small, water-filled reservoir. Beyond the reservoir is the Fort Bliss Military Reservation, where entry is not permitted.

Turn around and head back to the Boyd dining hall. Head back downhill and turn left to loop back to the main trail. Retrace your steps about a mile to the Crawford Trail and turn right. Follow this route along the base of the Organ spires about a mile to reach Fillmore Canyon. Turn right onto this trail and visit the Modoc Mine. The trail continues up the canyon bottom for another 200 feet and ends at a desert waterfall. Once again, access upcanyon is prohibited by the military reservation.

Backtrack to the junction of the Fillmore and Crawford trails. Turn right and walk around the back side of La Cueva rocks. At mile 4.2, turn left onto the La Cueva Trail and in a few minutes visit La Cueva and learn the tragic

The Boyd Sanatorium at Dripping Springs

tale of the hermit who lived there. From the cave, drop downhill to a granite slab just above the bottom of Ice Canyon. Walk down the slab to the arroyo and turn left to continue on the trail up the canyon. The trail soon climbs out of the canyon, swings west, and then heads to the visitor center about a half mile away.

Opposite: *Blooming yucca at White Sands National Monument*

SOUTHEASTERN MOUNTAINS

81 | ALKALI FLAT TRAIL

Distance: 5 miles, day hike
Difficulty: moderate
Elevation range: 3,900 to 4,000 feet
Elevation gain: 100 feet
Best time of year: year-round, but better October
    through April
Water: carry water
Map: USGS Heart of the Sands
Managed by: National Park Service,
    White Sands National Monument
Features: world's largest gypsum dune field,
    endless exploring, animal tracks

A hike at White Sands is a unique experience. This huge sand pile is composed of gypsum, not the more common quartz. Gypsum sand is soft-grained and smooth, giving these dunes a different, pleasant feel to bare feet. The fine sand also makes for easy animal tracking. The gypsum weathers out of the ancient seabed rocks of surrounding mountains. It is dissolved and transported by runoff, accumulating in Lake Lucero in the western part of the monument. The gypsum precipitates out of the evaporating lake water and is deposited on the lake bottom. In this desert environment, the lake is completely dry most of the year. Strong, westerly winds then push the gypsum eastward into large dunes.

White sand is an intense solar reflector and hiking on the dunes requires some special preparation. To prevent sunburn, always use a heavy coat of sunscreen. Dark glasses are also essential to prevent damage to the eyes, but also simply to make the journey more pleasant. No water is available in the

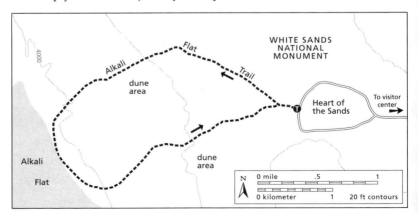

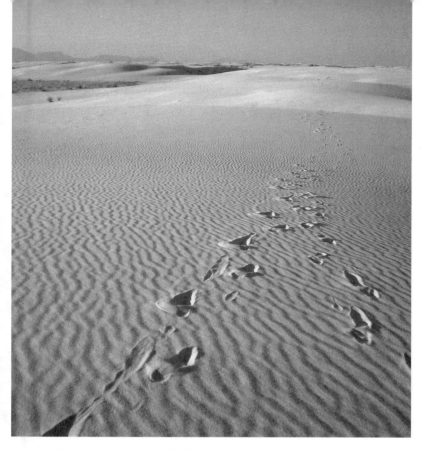

Tracks of dune explorers at White Sands National Monument (Photo by Jessica Martin)

dunes, so take an adequate supply. All-terrain sandals or running shoes are the best footwear for dune hiking.

Three trails are maintained by the Park Service, but hiking is possible just about anywhere in the dune field. Hikers should pick a location that strikes their fancy or follow the Alkali Flat Trail as described. Note that hikers on this trail are required to register at the trailhead and in all cases to return by sunset. Before setting out cross-country, stop and orient yourself with respect to the San Andres Mountains to the west, and the lofty Sacramento Mountains, as well as low-flying jets from Holloman Air Force Base, to the east. These are useful features by which to navigate. Use these landmarks as bearings out on the dunes. Given calm winds, hikers can easily follow their tracks back to the road.

Camping at White Sands is permitted only at the lightly used backcountry campsites located off a 1-mile trail that starts 6 miles from the visitor center. A permit is required for a nominal fee and is available at the visitor center.

Note that test firing at the adjacent White Sands Missile Range occasionally requires the park to close the backcountry to camping.

To reach the trailhead from Alamogordo, take US 54/70 south and continue west on US 70 when US 54 bears left. The entrance to White Sands National Monument is about 15 miles southwest of town. Continue about 7 miles on the park road to the Heart of the Sands and the well-marked trailhead.

Begin hiking west on the Alkali Flat Trail. The trail is marked with numerous orange and white posts. Find the first post, then spot the next trail marker before moving on. Continue in this manner, walking from post to post, through the dune field. The trail traverses the dunes themselves and often crosses vegetated interdunal basins. For much of the trip out to the flat, the San Andres Mountains lie straight ahead. Walking is slow in the soft sand, and distances are difficult to judge. Pass the return leg of the trail on the left at mile 0.3. At mile 2.3, the trail reaches the edge of Alkali Flat, the lakebed where gypsum sand is formed. The trail continues out a short distance onto the flats, which can be an unpleasant place when the wind blows. From the flats, the route swings south for the return. Now with the Sacramento Mountains ahead, follow the posts back to the trailhead.

82 | DOG CANYON

Distance: 9.5 miles, day hike or backpack
Difficulty: strenuous
Elevation range: 4,400 to 7,400 feet
Elevation gain: 3,300 feet
Best time of year: September to May
Water: at the visitor center, and in Dog Canyon at mile 2
Maps: USGS Alamogordo South and Sacramento Peak
Managed by: Oliver Lee Memorial State Park; Lincoln
    National Forest, Sacramento Ranger District
Features: historic route, running water, spectacular scenery

Holding permanent running water and a steep route over the rampart of the southern Sacramento Mountains, Dog Canyon has been tramped by Mescalero Apaches, Mexican and American soldiers, and Texas ranchers. It is said that this route to the high country was a particular favorite of Apache war parties because of the ease with which they could ambush pursuers at the "eyebrow" section, a narrow ledge below 800-foot walls of limestone. In 1880, the Ninth Cavalry lost several men along this section when Apaches rolled large boulders down on them from above.

The Dog Canyon Trail follows the historic route from the Tularosa Valley to Joplin Ridge. It is a steep, arduous climb with no shade or water for the first 2.5 miles; avoid Dog Canyon in midsummer. The scenery is grand every step of the way, displaying the harsh beauty of the Chihuahuan Desert. Limestone cliffs deposited on the ocean floor about 250 million years ago soar more than 3,000 feet above. Below them lies the Tularosa Valley, a huge fault-block basin with no drainage outlet.

To reach the trailhead from Alamogordo, take US 54 south from its junction with US 70 in south Alamogordo. Drive 8 miles to Dog Canyon Road, which is signed for Oliver Lee Memorial State Park. Turn left, drive 4 miles, and stop at the entrance to pay a small fee. Continue on the main road and park at the visitor center and trailhead.

The trail immediately begins climbing through desert vegetation, including yucca, agave, ocotillo, sotol, and mesquite. The first section of trail climbs away from Dog Canyon on a steep, rocky trail. Views open along the way to include the white sand dunes on the floor of the Tularosa Valley, and in the morning sun, the striking colors of the Organ and San Andres mountains on the other side of the basin. After a jog to the south, at mile 0.6 the trail finishes the intense climb on a broad bench that offers a bit of level walking.

The trail again approaches Dog Canyon. At mile 2, a side trail to Fairchild Spring angles off to the left. The climb intensifies, rising 400 feet over the next 0.5 mile to reach a lovely grassy flat. This flat has oaks, alligator junipers, cholla cacti, the unusual, fragrant ash tree, and huge boulders tumbled from the cliffs that soar above. Ideal campsites can be found near the larger trees.

From the flat, descend into Dog Canyon to reach the stream for the first time. Water is available here, dropping from the mesas above through a series of waterfalls. Shady cottonwoods offer relief from the sun, and the ruins of a line cabin are streamside. To prevent further damage to this sensitive area, camping is no longer permitted along the stream.

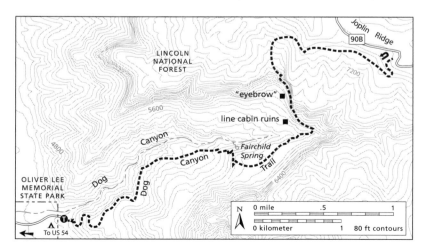

Dog Canyon slices through hundreds of limestone beds that form nearly vertical walls. (Photo by Jessica Martin)

The trail continues from behind the line cabin to ascend the steepest section of the canyon, the "eyebrow," at mile 3.2. After a switchback to the left, the trail crosses a narrow ledge high above the canyon floor. Great views downcanyon open up, but hikers should keep their eyes on the trail. Climbing continually, the trail skirts around to a gap in the cliffs. Now paralleling a drainage to the left, the trail continues its steep climb to the flanks of Joplin Ridge about 4 miles from the start. Making a more moderate ascent, the trail swings east to meet the rough FR 90B descending from FR 90. Return to the trailhead by the same route.

83 | THREE RIVERS PETROGLYPH SITE

Distance: 3 miles, day hike
Difficulty: easy
Elevation range: 5,000 to 5,200 feet
Elevation gain: 200 feet
Best time of year: year-round
Water: at campground
Map: USGS Golindrina Draw
Managed by: Bureau of Land Management,
     Las Cruces Field Office
Features: outstanding petroglyphs

Jornada-style petroglyphs are located at hundreds of sites across the desert regions of southern New Mexico. Related to the famous black-and-white

Mimbres pottery style, these drawings are characterized by animal motifs, flat-headed human or godlike portraits, and complex geometric designs. A short hike along a lava cliff at the Three Rivers Petroglyph Site leads past an astounding array of hundreds of examples of this rock art. Bighorn sheep, horned lizards, fish, birds, spirals, and intertwining lines are pecked into the basalt. In a state where ancient rock art is a common feature, this is by far one of the most spectacular collections. The site and a nearby campground are carefully managed by the Bureau of Land Management, and a small fee is collected for visiting the area.

To reach the trailhead, take US 54, 30 miles north of Alamogordo or 28 miles south of Carrizozo, to CR B30. Head east, following the signs for the Three Rivers Petroglyph Site and Three Rivers Campground. In 4.5 miles, turn left at the entrance to the petroglyph site.

From the trailhead, follow the trail up to a low ridge, staying on the well-worn path as it climbs the basalt. At the black rocks, watch for the plentiful petroglyphs engraved on just about any flat surface. Each branch of the trail leads to more pecked artwork, so plan on taking as many side trails as

Geometric patterns are a common theme of the rock art at Three Rivers Petroglyph Site.

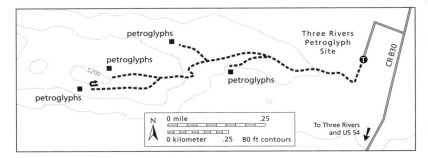

possible. The trail continues past the main group of rock art to a round knoll to the north and offers dramatic views of the Sierra Blanca to the east. This makes a good turnaround point. On the return, hikers are certain to discover ancient pictures they missed on the way up.

84 | Big Bonito Loop

Distance: 9.25 miles, day hike or backpack
Difficulty: difficult
Elevation range: 7,800 to 10,100 feet
Elevation gain: 2,300 feet
Best time of year: late April to November
Water: Bonito Creek, Bonito Seep
Maps: USGS Nogal Peak; USFS White Mountain Wilderness
Managed by: Lincoln National Forest, White Mountain
     Wilderness, Smokey Bear Ranger District
Features: quiet canyons, open grassland peaks, scenic views

The White Mountain Wilderness is one of the most attractive backcountry areas in New Mexico. The mountains are the highest in southern New Mexico, with rounded, gentle hills along the crest that give the range its characteristic beauty. Montane grasslands, an unusual vegetation type found in only a few areas of the state, cover much of the crest, providing the chance to walk an open ridgeline with extensive views of the range itself and of the valley and canyons below. The geology also creates a well-watered range with many springs just below the crest. Campsites are plentiful in the grasslands.

To reach the trailhead from Ruidoso on US 70, go 12 miles north on NM 48 and turn left onto NM 37. After 1.3 miles, turn left onto FR 107, which is signed for Bonito Lake. Continue on this narrow paved road past the lake and past the turnoff for the South Fork Campground, where the pavement ends on FR 107. At 7.5 miles from NM 37, continue slowly through Bonito Riding Stables and reach the trailhead in another half mile.

Trail 36, the Big Bonito Trail, immediately enters the wilderness as it crosses Argentina Canyon and begins to parallel Bonito Creek, heading upstream. Bee balm, yarrow, mountain parsley, and Richardson's geranium bloom here throughout the summer. The trail crosses the stream many times as it climbs steadily up the canyon floor. Pass the collapsed remains of the shaft and headframe of the Silver Spoon Mine at mile 0.8.

At mile 1.1, intersect the Little Bonito Trail 37. Bear left to stay on the Big Bonito Trail as the canyon turns abruptly south, offering a view of the not-too-distant crest. At mile 1.7, reach the junction with the Aspen Canyon Trail 35. The route returns to this junction later in the hike. Bear left onto the Aspen Canyon Trail and begin climbing in earnest. Beware of abundant stinging nettle close to the trail. Soon leave the forest behind and enter the grasslands, climbing several switchbacks. On the ascent, the views open to include Nogal Peak to the north and the Capitan Range to the east.

At a minor saddle near mile 3, turn right and continue climbing through a grassy bowl, gaining 500 feet to the next ridge. During the rainy season, the tread may disappear beneath a luxurious growth of alpine grass. Here the climb moderates, ascending the ridge to meet the Crest Trail 25 at mile 3.7 on a saddle between Elk Point to the east and White Horse Hill to the west.

From this high saddle, turn right and west onto the Crest Trail, skirting around the northern base of White Horse Hill. Drop quickly through several long switchbacks to Bonito Seep at mile 4.8. At the trail junction, leave the Crest Trail and head right to pick up the south end of the Big Bonito Trail and drop into a grassy canyon that parallels the flow of water coming from Bonito Seep.

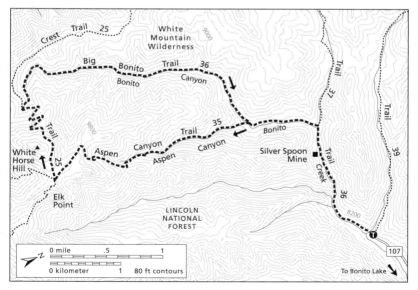

The scoured bed of Big Bonito Creek along the Big Bonito Trail

Beyond the grassy bowl near the crest, the trail loses altitude. Bonito Canyon is shady and cool much of the way, often thick with Gambel oaks. The trail continues north for 1.5 miles before swinging to the east to meet the Aspen Canyon Trail again at mile 7. At the junction, bear left and backtrack to the trailhead, passing the Little Bonito Trail 37 along the way.

85 | ARGENTINA PEAK

Distance: 6.5 miles, day hike or backpack
Difficulty: moderate
Elevation range: 7,800 to 9,198 feet
Elevation gain: 1,400 feet
Best time of year: late April to November
Water: Spring Cabin Spring, Argentina Spring
Maps: USGS Nogal Peak; USFS White Mountain Wilderness
Managed by: Lincoln National Forest, White Mountain Wilderness, Smokey Bear Ranger District
Features: running water, old mines, extensive views

Argentina Peak is one of the easiest destinations along the crest of the White Mountains, and the views from the trail are no less spectacular than those from other, higher locations. Cool and shady canyons lead up to and down from the grasslands along the crest, and water is consistently available at several springs along the way. Campsites are limited along this route, but a few scenic spots are located along the crest and at Spring Cabin.

To reach the trailhead from Ruidoso on US 70, go 12 miles north on NM 48 and turn left onto NM 37. After 1.3 miles, turn left onto FR 107, which is signed for Bonito Lake. Continue on this narrow paved road past the lake and past the turnoff for the South Fork Campground. Continue straight on FR 107 where the pavement ends. At 7.5 miles from NM 37, continue slowly through Bonito Riding Stables and reach the trailhead in another half mile.

Begin hiking on the Big Bonito Trail 36, immediately crossing the wilderness boundary. Signs of the huge flood in July 2008 are everywhere as you pass up the canyon. Cross and recross the stream several times before reaching the remains of the shaft and headframe of the Silver Spoon Mine at mile 0.8. As you continue upcanyon, note the numerous insect-killed Douglas firs that have fallen near the trail, and if the wind is blowing hard, be watchful for standing dead firs that might fall with a strong gust. At mile 1.1, come to the junction with the Little Bonito Trail 37. Bear right and continue climbing on Trail 37 above the stream. The grade is modest as the trail ascends, but noticeably increases as the trail passes through a fence and follows a ridge at mile 1.8.

Signs of elk are abundant as the trail crosses a drainage and enters a meadow at mile 2.1. Several routes lead to the Crest Trail from this point; the right-hand route will meet the Cut Across Trail 38, a shortcut to Argentina Canyon, in 0.2 mile, but all routes strike the crest in a grassy saddle at mile 2.5.

At the crest is a five-way intersection. Trail 29 leads west to Spring Cabin and its spring for those who need water or a quiet campsite. To continue to

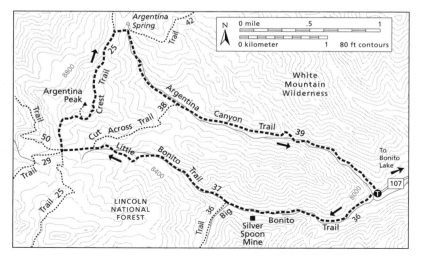

The head of Argentina Canyon

Argentina Peak, turn right onto the Crest Trail 25, climbing steeply out of the saddle. Cross a small meadow that offers nice views to the south and west. The trail skirts the eastern base of Argentina Peak, which is far easier to summit than it appears and is worth making a short diversion from the trail. To reach the top, leave the Crest Trail near the base of a large, dark rock that projects from the ridge and follow a steep route that leads to the back of the peak. After enjoying the summit, rejoin the Crest Trail a few yards to the north of the peak. As the Crest Trail drops from the north side of Argentina Peak and returns to the crest, the views become increasingly grand. For the next 0.4 mile, skirt the head of Argentina Canyon.

Intersect the Argentina Canyon Trail 39 above Argentina Spring at mile 3.5. Turn right onto Trail 39 and drop to the bottom of the drainage. At the rock trough of the spring, bear right again in 0.2 mile at the intersection with the Clear Water Trail 42, which climbs steeply out of the drainage. Descend steeply, parallel to the small stream on a rutted trail that crosses the bottom of the drainage several times. Pass through old, falling aspen stands as signs of flooding in the canyon are increasingly apparent. Again intersect the Cut Across Trail at mile 4.2 and continue downhill on Trail 39. About 2.5 miles from the crest, cross the wilderness boundary and reach the trailhead.

86 | LAST CHANCE CANYON

Distance: 8 miles, day hike or backpack
Difficulty: moderate
Elevation range: 4,550 to 5,200 feet
Elevation gain: 1,200 feet
Best time of year: September to May
Water: White Oak Spring and along Last Chance Canyon
Maps: USGS Red Bluff Draw and Queen
Managed by: Lincoln National Forest,
        Guadalupe Ranger District
Features: large springs, high canyon walls, solitude

The story of how this canyon got its name is told so often that it just might contain a kernel of truth. Around 1881, a group of ranchers pursued Apache raiders into the Guadalupe Mountains and soon became lost amid the twisted canyons draining the southeast flank of the range. After their canteens were empty, they rode from rim to rim, searching for water without finding a spring. With their horses almost spent, they spotted the limestone walls of yet another canyon—it was their last chance. According to the legend, the abundant springs they found there saved their lives, and they named the spot Last Chance Canyon.

Just down the road from popular Sitting Bull Falls, Last Chance Canyon offers the last chance to escape the crowds at the falls and enter a lonesome limestone wilderness, one of my favorite spots in all of New Mexico. A couple of miles up the canyon is a spring and travertine wall similar to the ones in Sitting Bull Canyon, but less visited. With abundant water and myriad side canyons to explore, Last Chance is an excellent place for an overnight stay. Be warned, however, that ill-advised management decisions

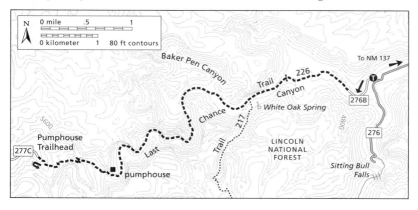

Limestone stairs in Last Chance Canyon

have permitted cattle grazing in the canyon bottom that has destroyed segments of the riparian zone and detracted from the overall experience of a trip into this idyllic setting.

The mouth of Last Chance Canyon is located near the Sitting Bull Falls Recreation Area off NM 137. Twelve miles north of Carlsbad, turn west onto NM 137 and continue on this paved road about 24 miles to FR 276, the road to Sitting Bull Falls. Turn right and drive about 6.5 miles to FR 276B on the right. Turn and park at the pullout at the start of FR 276B.

From the trailhead, continue along the rough FR 276B for 0.4 mile to the end of the road and start of Trail 226. Travel up the south side of the wide canyon bottom with towering limestone walls clothed in Torrey yuccas, sotol, bear grass, and prickly pear cactus. Traverse a low ridge at mile 0.9 before descending into the canyon bottom, shaded by some large hackberry trees, crossing the stream, and passing through a gate at mile 1.1.

As the canyon walls squeeze in against the canyon bottom, the trail crosses limestone ledges. Small ponds of clear water stand in the canyon bottom, flowing from White Oak Spring in the side canyon entering from the south. Listen for the incongruous trill of a belted kingfisher searching for minnows in a desert canyon. Soon pass a massive gray and orange wall of travertine deposited at the mouth of White Oak Canyon. The travertine cliff has many intricate faces and includes an unusual natural bridge on its western end.

Beyond White Oak Spring, follow a flat as Last Chance Canyon widens. At mile 2.1, cross to the south side of the canyon bottom as the trail swings south along a bend in the canyon. At the mouth of Baker Pen Canyon, which enters from the right, find several shady campsites. At mile 2.7, near gray stair-step limestone ledges, the trail crosses the stream channel and climbs to a bench above. Climb steeply through several switchbacks to cross a spur ridge. For the next stretch, use caution as the trail is barely scratched into the slopes high above the canyon floor.

At mile 3, drop down to the stream and walk up the rock ledges near the pools of clear water. Most of the pools are only a few inches deep, but several are wonderful holes more than six feet deep. Although the trail follows the north bank of the stream, it is easier and more interesting to follow the canyon bottom upstream. Continue in the streambed around a couple of bends until reaching the ruins of a tin pumphouse with rusting machinery. The trail passes a large spring, then crosses the stream bottom. In a minute, reach the junction of Last Chance with a side canyon entering from the right. From here hikers can follow rock cairns to reach the Pumphouse Trailhead in 1 mile, or return to the starting point by the same route.

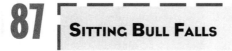

87 | Sitting Bull Falls

Distance: 7.5 miles, day hike
Difficulty: moderate
Elevation range: 4,660 to 5,725 feet
Elevation gain: 1,100 feet
Best time of year: year-round
Water: Sitting Bull Falls, Sitting Bull Spring
Map: USGS Queen
Managed by: Lincoln National Forest,
    Guadalupe Ranger District
Features: running water, unusual waterfall

Sitting Bull, a Dakota Sioux from the northern Great Plains, probably never set foot in New Mexico. But a much-repeated legend claims that cowboys chased a group of Indians that included the old chief into Sitting Bull Canyon

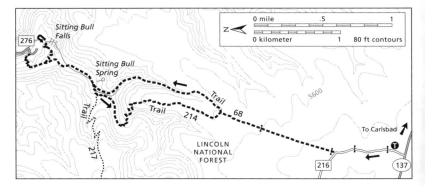

and thereby discovered the falls. Unfortunately for the story, Sitting Bull was in Canada in 1881, the year of the reputed discovery.

An equally improbable explanation tells of early Eddy County resident Bill Jones spinning tales of the old days in the Guadalupes. His description of the falls was met with derisive comments from his brothers, who called it "pure bull." "Well, Sitting Bull," suggested one brother, "if those falls are really there, we'll name them after you!"

One can drive to the base of Sitting Bull Falls in the recreation area (a fee is required), but dropping in from the mesa above makes the trip a memorable one. This longer semi-loop hike begins on NM 137 and drops into Sitting Bull Canyon, passing along the way the spring that ultimately trickles through matted green and red plants to create this unusual waterfall.

To reach the trailhead, turn west on NM 137 from US 285, 12 miles north of Carlsbad. In about 24 miles, continue straight when the road to Sitting Bull Falls goes right. Climb the escarpment and enter the Lincoln National Forest, passing the U.S. Forest Service's Guadalupe Work Center about 11 miles from the falls road intersection. Basic supplies and gas are available at Queen, just beyond the work center. Continue about 1 mile to a sign for Trail 68 on the right side of the road.

Approach Trail 68 by walking through a gate on a primitive road. After 0.4 mile, pass through another gate. In a few hundred yards the road, here marked FR 216, bears left. Bear right through a gate on what is now identified as Trail 68. At mile 1.5, reach Trail 214, the return leg of this trip. Take the right fork. Soon the trail parallels a deep draw on the left. A low rock wall marks where the trail turns left to enter the draw, which soon deepens into a full-fledged canyon. Enjoy the views of the canyon below and of the plains in the distance as you descend, but watch for loose rocks.

About 2 miles from the start, reach the bottom of the canyon and cross to the west side. The trail now meanders across the canyon bottom. As the trail swings west, pass Sitting Bull Spring on the right. From here on down,

Opposite: *Sitting Bull Falls*

clear running water flows along the stream bottom. Descend a bit more into the bottom of a large canyon, and then bear right at the junction with Trail 214. Continue downstream, arriving at another trail junction 3 miles from the start. First, bear right and take the short spur trail to see the top of the falls, then return to the junction and continue down the cliff on the trail marked for FR 276. At the bottom of the hill, reach a parking lot, cross to the east side, and pick up the trail leading to the bottom of the falls. Enjoy the falls from below.

Begin the return trip by retracing your steps to the lower junction with Trail 214. Turn right onto this trail and follow Sitting Bull Canyon for about 0.3 mile, passing the junction with Trail 217 along the way. Ascend a series of pleasant switchbacks to rejoin Trail 68 about 1.5 miles from where you left it. Turn right and backtrack to the parking area.

88 | DEVILS DEN CANYON

Distance: 5 miles, day hike
Difficulty: moderate
Elevation range: 6,550 to 7,300 feet
Elevation gain: 800 feet
Best time of year: March to May, September to December
Water: Devils Den Spring
Map: USGS El Paso Gap
Managed by: Lincoln National Forest,
 Guadalupe Ranger District
Features: remote, spectacular canyon

In a dry land with only a thin veneer of unfriendly vegetation, the devil gets blamed for everything. The Southwest has more devil's canyons, stairways, thrones, peaks, and ridges than one can count. Devils Den Canyon is a rugged gorge slashed through the western rim of the Guadalupes, ending in a spectacular pour-off along the mountain front. In the surrounding hills, a large herd of mule deer supports a small population of mountain lions. Watch for large cat prints in the soft sand.

The trailhead is a long way from the nearest town, but water and supplies are available along NM 137. Lincoln National Forest has a water tap for campers and hikers at its Guadalupe Work Center located about 35 miles from US 285 on NM 137. Basic supplies and gas are available at Queen, just beyond the work center. Primitive camping is permitted along NM 137 and FR 540, including a large wooded area suitable for group camping at the trailhead.

The trailhead for the Devils Den Canyon Trail is at the end of the gravel portion of FR 540 southwest of Carlsbad. To get to the trailhead, take NM 137 west from US 285 about 12 miles north of Carlsbad. In 24 miles, pass the road to Sitting Bull Falls. Pass the Queen store on the right in 38 miles. Go 3.5 miles past the store, and turn left onto FR 540. In 0.5 mile, bear right, and continue about 12 miles to the end of the all-weather gravel road at its junction with FR 201. This road has many spectacular viewpoints, so enjoy the drive.

From the end of the gravel section of FR 540, walk south on the dirt continuation of FR 540, also known as the Guadalupe Ridge Trail. A sign at the intersection with FR 3008 at mile 0.3 points right to the Camp Wilderness Ridge Trail. Bear right onto FR 3008 and for the next 0.25 mile, head up a rocky hill. Stay on the main track as side branches come and go. Pass a shallow stock pond at mile 0.6, then continue across a narrow ridge with the Big Canyon watershed on the left and the Devils Den Canyon on the right. A recent wildfire has opened up the view to both sides. At mile 1.2, in the middle of an easy climb, turn right onto an old road signed for Trail 200. In 100 feet, another sign marks the start of the Devils Den Trail 200. Head down the trail, soon bearing right onto a long-abandoned road that gradually drops downhill on the rocky and rutted surface. Pass through a recent burned area as views of the canyon open up ahead.

At mile 1.7, the abandoned road ends at the ruins of a cabin above Devils Den Spring. Pick up the trail to the left of the cabin and follow rock cairns down steep limestone switchbacks to the bottom of a side canyon just below the spring. The trail continues to the mouth of the side canyon, then swings

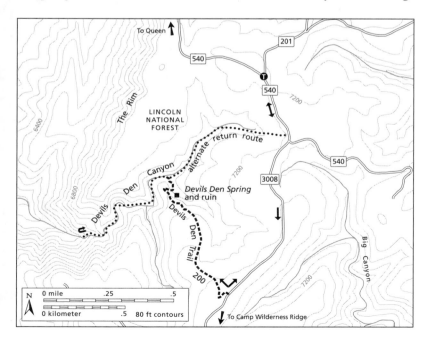

Limestone forms the trail surface in Devils Den Canyon.

west into Devils Den Canyon. Starting above the canyon floor, the trail soon drops to the rocky streambed. From here, walking along the canyon floor is much more interesting than taking the trail.

After passing a side canyon entering from the left, walk through a horseshoe bend. On the other side, flat ground and shady junipers invite camping for a day. Head down the canyon floor over stair-step limestone ledges and between high cliffs. The canyon comes to an abrupt end at the 600-foot pour-off, where views are outstanding.

From the pour-off, turn around and return to the trailhead by the same route. If you don't mind off-trail scrambling, you can return via an alternate route by first returning to the canyon confluence at the foot of the switch-backs at Devils Den Spring. From there, scramble up the left fork, ascending more limestone stairways to return to FR 540. About a quarter mile from the confluence, take the right fork, which in another half mile brings you to FR 540 near its junction with FR 3008. Turn left and retrace your steps about a quarter mile to the trailhead.

89 | YUCCA CANYON

Distance: 5 miles, day hike or backpack
Difficulty: moderate
Elevation range: 4,550 to 6,000 feet
Elevation gain: 1,600 feet
Best time of year: September through May
Water: carry water
Map: USGS Grapevine Draw
Managed by: National Park Service,
   Carlsbad Caverns National Park
Features: rugged canyon, long-range views, solitude

Although spectacular, Carlsbad Caverns can leave visitors eager for an escape from the crowds. One solution is to hike one of the park's backcountry

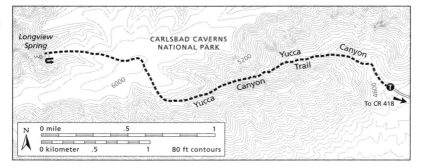

trails, such as the Yucca Canyon Trail. Few make the trip to this distant corner of the park, and hikers will most likely have about 10 square miles of desert mountains to themselves. Permits are not required for day hiking in the backcountry, but hikers planning an overnight stay need to stop at the Carlsbad Caverns Visitor Center for a free permit. Note that a user fee is charged to enter the park.

The Guadalupe Mountains are one of the world's largest biologically created structures. The entire range—and indeed a much more extensive, mostly buried, limestone structure more than 300 miles long—is a fossil reef formed at the margin of a shallow arm of a sea during the Permian period, about 250 million years ago. The reef is made from the secretions of calcareous algae and the remains of sponges, bryozoans, brachiopods, and other shelled invertebrates. Over millions of years, these plants and animals grew on the remains of their ancestors, building a pile of lime almost 2,000 feet thick.

A walk up Yucca Canyon is also a climb through the reef. Though at first glance the limestone layers appear to be homogenous, a close examination along the trail's transect of the canyon shows that each layer—ranging in thickness from a few inches to a couple hundred feet—has its own characteristics. Specific fossils are common in one layer but not the next. The texture of the limestone also changes from massive to thinly laminated layers. Some layers are tinted red and include more sand than lime, an indication of a period when the reef was exposed above sea level.

Horned lizard

A huge pile of limestone: the Guadalupe Mountains

To reach the trailhead, head south on US 62/180 from the city of Carlsbad to Whites City. In another 5 miles, turn right onto paved Washington Ranch Road (CR 418), signed for Slaughter Canyon Cave. Follow the signs for the cave about 10 miles to a fence at the national park boundary. Turn left onto a rocky double-track heading west, parallel to the fence. This road is rough and requires a high-clearance vehicle. Continue about 2 miles to the trailhead.

From the parking area the trail immediately drops, crosses the streambed, and turns up Yucca Canyon. The limestone of the Capitan Reef is visible in every direction, forming canyon walls more than 1,500 feet high. The trail climbs steadily on the south wall of the canyon, high above the bottom. At mile 0.7, again cross the canyon bottom. The trail frequently switches between the north and south walls, and the climb is considerably steeper. The narrowing canyon supports alligator juniper and Texas madrone, which provide occasional shelter from the sun. A series of switchbacks leads high above the canyon floor, then the trail drops back to stream level. Atop the ridge at mile 1.5, the view to the south is never-ending and includes the southern portion of the Guadalupe Mountains in Texas and the rolling hills of the Pecos Valley.

Once on top of the ridge, the trail is more difficult to follow. Look for the faint tread heading north and for small cairns along the path. The trail leads through piñon pine and juniper on the mesa top. By heading southwest on the ridge for about a half-mile, hikers will find a delightful selection of isolated viewpoints to the north and south. By now it should be obvious how the nearby Longview Spring got its name: the view into West Slaughter Canyon is spectacular. After taking in the views, return to the trailhead by the same route.

90 RATTLESNAKE CANYON

Distance: 6 miles, day hike or backpack
Difficulty: moderate
Elevation range: 4,100 to 4,600 feet
Elevation gain: 900 feet
Best time of year: September to May
Water: carry water
Map: USGS Serpentine Bends
Managed by: National Park Service,
   Carlsbad Caverns National Park
Features: quiet desert canyon, Chihuahuan Desert
   vegetation

The overwhelming majority of the Chihuahuan Desert lies south of the international border in Mexico, but arms of the desert reach up the Rio Grande and Pecos River valleys to embrace a portion of New Mexico. While monotypic stands of creosote bush cover the vast majority of this desert's area, it is the thick-leaved succulents that are its defining species. Soaptree yucca is the

Fossils of sea life are commonly found in the limestone of the
Guadalupe Mountains. (Photo by Jessica Martin)

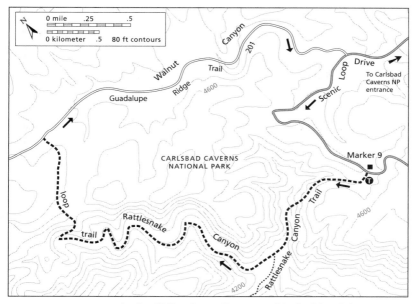

most common yucca in the Chihuahuan Desert and is the New Mexico state flower. Dense clusters of three- to four-foot-long leaves sprout like spikes from the top of the trunk. Even more spectacular is the Spanish dagger, a yucca species that can grow up to forty feet tall. The most distinctive of the Chihuahuan Desert plants is the lechuguilla, a low-growing succulent found only in this region. The thick, sharp-pointed lechuguilla leaves grow about twelve inches tall, giving the plant its apt nickname, "shin dagger."

Rattlesnake Canyon is a short but intensely scenic trip into this world of unusual plants. The loop traverses open desert slopes and follows serpentine canyons that continually offer surprises to hikers. The moderately difficult trip can be done as a day hike, or as an overnighter that includes the opportunity for more extensive backcountry exploration. Note that campfires are not allowed in the backcountry, and a free permit is required for all overnight use.

The trailhead is located along the Scenic Loop Drive in Carlsbad Caverns National Park, reached by driving about 16 miles south of the city of Carlsbad on US 62/180 and turning west at Whites City into the park. From the visitor center, head back toward the park entrance for a few hundred feet and turn left onto the one-way, gravel loop road. Continue about 4 miles to Marker 9 on the Scenic Loop Drive and park.

Begin hiking heading west (left) and follow rock cairns to drop into a small drainage. The trail swings north through thick stands of creosote bush as it climbs slightly before skirting the south wall of a larger drainage. Limestone blocks along the trail hold entire cities of sea life fossil remains.

Just over 0.5 mile from the start, reach a trail junction on the sandy floor of Rattlesnake Canyon. Hikers can take a spur trip on the Rattlesnake Canyon Trail by turning left and walking 2 miles to the park boundary, returning to the main trail by the same route. To continue on the described loop trip, turn right at the trail junction, traveling in the direction of Guadalupe Ridge to the north.

Follow the trail up Rattlesnake Canyon by watching for rock cairns that mark the way. As the trail weaves through four sweeping bends of the wash, towering beds of limestone form the sometimes sheer, sometimes sloping canyon walls. At the apex of the fourth bend, after about 1.5 miles in the canyon bottom, the trail leaves the wash to climb the slope to the right (north). Climb steeply over a low ridge, then drop into Walnut Canyon. The trail makes a gentler climb to meet the Guadalupe Ridge Trail 201 at mile 2.8. Turn right and follow this wide trail as it heads east and again drops into Walnut Canyon. The trail stays near the canyon bottom for 1.5 miles and ends at the Scenic Loop Drive. Turn right and walk with caution along the road 1 mile back to the trailhead.

Opposite: *Towers of volcanic rock loom over the Middle Fork of the Gila River.*

GILA RIVER REGION

91 | DATIL WELL

Distance: 3.5-mile loop
Difficulty: easy
Elevation range: 7,425 to 7,675 feet
Elevation gain: 300 feet
Best time of year: March to November
Water: carry water
Map: USGS Datil
Managed by: Bureau of Land Management,
  Socorro Field Office
Features: historic features, views of Plains of San Augustin

New Mexico is crisscrossed with historic trails from each of the major periods of its long history. Representative of the intense ranching era of the early twentieth century is the Magdalena Stock Driveway. Whenever a railroad pushed deeper into the interior of the state with a new branch line, cattlemen and sheep brokers instantly had new markets. Stock driveways developed so the ranchers could herd their stock to the railhead. When the Atchison, Topeka, & Santa Fe Railway was extended to the tiny settlement of Magdalena in the northern San Mateo Mountains, the town became the shipping point for ranches on thousands of square miles in the northern Gila River watershed. Dozens of lesser trails were consolidated in 1918 with establishment of the Magdalena Stock Driveway. The driveway was routed to have water available every 10 miles between Springerville, Arizona, and

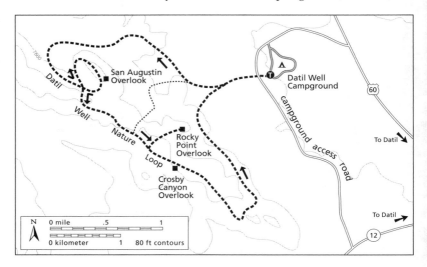

Magdalena. As many as 150,000 sheep and 21,000 cattle made the journey over the trail in a single year. Datil Well was one of the water sources established to promote the use of the trail.

A BLM campground marks the site of Datil Well, and a highly scenic loop trail provides a detailed glimpse of the terrain encountered by the stock being driven to market. The campground makes a pleasant stop for any travel in west-central New Mexico, and the trail is a wonderful addition to any tour of this region.

Reach the Datil Well Campground by heading west from Socorro on US 60. In 27 miles, pass through the town of Magdalena and continue another 36 miles to Datil. Bear right at the intersection with NM 12 and find the campground in another mile.

The trail, marked as the Datil Well Nature Loop, begins near campsite 6 on the campground

In June, hikers at Datil Well are surrounded by the metallic sounds of cicadas.

loop. Soon after starting on the trail, walk across a dirt road and continue west. In 0.1 mile, bear right where the return leg of the trail enters from the left; in a few hundred feet, bear right again at the junction with a second trail return leg. In piñon-juniper woodland, cross a footbridge and circle around the base of a hill before climbing up the west side of the knoll. In June, this area is abuzz with the metallic sounds of thousands of cicadas searching for mates. Watch for lime-green patches of lichen growing on the soil.

At mile 1.2, reach a short trail loop to the San Augustin Overlook. Turn left and take the loop to enjoy the view of the great plain to the east. In the afternoon, the view includes the radio telescopes at the nearby Very Large Array. Back on the main trail, descend to the ridge and head east. In a few minutes, pass another trail junction. Continue on the main trail to take the spur to the Rocky Point Overlook. The view from this grand overlook, an area of volcanic tuff coated with brightly colored lichens, encompasses the San Mateo and Magdalena mountains to the east. After returning to the main trail, pass the Crosby Canyon Overlook at mile 2.2 and enjoy views to the south.

The trail continues to follow the ridgeline before descending to the north at mile 2.7. Cross two footbridges before reaching the trail back to the campground. Turn right to return to the trailhead.

92 | PUEBLO CREEK

Distance: 8 miles, day hike or backpack
Difficulty: easy
Elevation range: 5,600 to 6,200 feet
Elevation gain: 800 feet
Best time of year: March to November
Water: Pueblo Creek
Map: USGS Saliz Pass
Managed by: Gila National Forest,
    Blue Range Wilderness, Reserve Ranger District
Features: minerals, isolated mountain scenery

The little-used Blue Range Wilderness abuts the Arizona–New Mexico border, part of the larger Blue Range Primitive Area. The area receives only a few hundred visitors each year, helping make this hike lovely from spring to fall. The isolated canyon of Pueblo Creek cuts through the wilderness and is a natural corridor for plants and animals from Mexico to extend their range into southern New Mexico. The canyon bottom has a canopy of

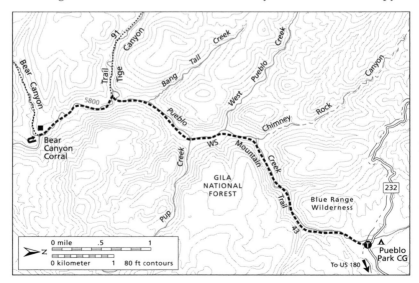

Pueblo Creek flows intermittently in its steep, rocky canyon.

broad-leafed trees that includes Arizona sycamore and Arizona alder and is home to Mexican jays, red-faced warblers, and painted redstarts. The WS Mountain Trail 43 follows the canyon about 9 miles to WS Lake, but the canyon itself is the main attraction. A rock outcrop on the east side of the canyon yields shiny bytownite crystals, a translucent mineral often cut into gems. The mineral can be found in scattered rocks along the second half of the described route.

From Silver City, take US 180 northwest for 62 miles to the town of Glenwood. From Glenwood, continue north on US 180 about 27 miles to the junction with FR 232. Turn left and drive this good gravel road 5.6 miles to Pueblo Park Campground. The trailhead is just across the road.

From the parking area, pass through a hikers gate, enter the Blue Range Wilderness, and begin hiking south on the WS Mountain Trail 43. The rugged trail is well marked with rock cairns. In the first quarter mile, the trail crosses the Pueblo Creek canyon bottom twice before climbing high above on the east canyon wall. Travel through mixed conifer forest, crossing over rugged side drainages. Drop back to the canyon bottom at mile 0.8 just below a pile of huge boulders that choke the channel.

The canyon broadens near Chimney Rock Creek, which enters from the west at mile 1.6. Water often flows in the Pueblo Creek bottom below this point. Continue down the benches under a tree canopy that alternates between broad-leaved trees including some massive Arizona walnut trees and ponderosa pine. Mesas of juniper and piñon pine rise higher above the canyon floor as small side streams enter from east and west, adding water to the canyon bottom. Fine campsites are located near the confluences with Pup Creek at mile 2.3 and Bang Tail Creek at mile 2.7.

The trail now frequently crosses the canyon bottom and shallow water flows almost constantly. At the junction with the Tige Canyon Trail 91 at mile 3.1, continue down the canyon under tall Arizona alders. Cliffs of volcanic breccias drop to the water in many locations. Reach Bear Canyon and a small corral at mile 4. Benches above the stream offer several campsites and Bear Canyon beckons explorers looking for more adventure. Return to the trailhead by the same route.

93 | WHITEWATER BALDY

Distance: 11 miles, day hike or backpack
Difficulty: difficult
Elevation range: 9,100 to 10,895 feet
Elevation gain: 1,900 feet
Best time of year: mid-May to November
Water: Bead Spring and Hummingbird Spring
Maps: USGS Grouse Mountain; USFS Gila Wilderness
Managed by: Gila National Forest, Gila Wilderness,
Glenwood Ranger District
Features: fine views, deep forest

The Crest Trail 182 is well used and easy to follow as it ascends a high ridge from the trailhead to Hummingbird Saddle and beyond to the summit of Mogollon Baldy, 12 miles away. A shorter trip leads to the summit of Whitewater Baldy; at 10,895 feet, it is the highest point in the Mogollon Range. Because water and campsites are readily available at Hummingbird Saddle, this hike is popular. The route leads through a deep Douglas fir forest and offers some wonderful views of the Gila River Region. The trail is exposed all along the ridge, so hikers should be prepared for severe weather. Plan to

Fall is a colorful time to hike to the summit of Whitewater Baldy.
(Photo by Jessica Martin)

be off the summit of Whitewater Baldy during storms, which are likely most summer afternoons. Note that some snow may linger until early June on the higher sections of this trail.

To reach the trailhead, drive about 4 miles north of Glenwood on US 180 and turn right onto NM 159. Take this winding road past the town of Mogollon, and continue about 18 miles from the highway to the Sandy Point Trailhead.

Begin hiking south on the Crest Trail 182 toward Hummingbird Saddle and Mogollon Baldy. The trail begins a moderate climb through Douglas fir forest, a shady walk even in summer. Although moderate, the climbing is constant for the first 1.5 miles. Watch for occasional views north toward Mineral Creek on the ascent. As the climb levels at mile 1.5, a short spur trail to the left leads to the lush Bead Spring. Resume the ascent as the trail swings to the east of Willow Mountain before gaining the ridge at a low saddle at mile 3.1. Continue along the rolling ridgeline, climbing to a knoll above Hummingbird Saddle at mile 4.3. From the knoll, the view west is down Whitewater Creek. Drop down to Hummingbird Saddle at mile 4.7, where water from the nearby spring and plenty of fine campsites are available.

A faint, unofficial trail leads south from the saddle to the summit of Whitewater Baldy straight ahead. Follow the trail along the shoulder of the crest, climbing steeply and slowly in the thin air. On the summit, head around to the south side where the view extends far south to the Gila River canyons. Return to the trailhead by the same route.

94 THE CATWALK AND BEYOND

Distance: 5.2 miles, day hike
Difficulty: moderate
Elevation range: 5,100 to 5,800 feet
Elevation gain: 1,200 feet
Best time of year: mid-March through November
Water: Whitewater Creek
Maps: USGS Holt Mountain and Mogollon;
USFS Gila Wilderness
Managed by: Gila National Forest,
Glenwood Ranger District
Features: deep, narrow canyon, historic pipeline, unique trail

The Catwalk National Recreation Trail is one of the most unusual hikes in the Southwest. The route follows that of a pipeline constructed to supply water to a mining mill and town located at the mouth of Whitewater Canyon. The town of Graham was founded in 1893, just after the discovery of rich

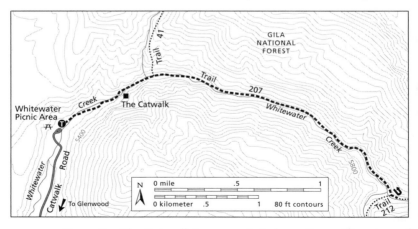

Opposite: *The Catwalk is suspended above the swift waters of Whitewater Creek.* (Photo by Jessica Martin)

ore within the canyon. Although water always flowed within the canyon, Whitewater Creek was often dry at the townsite. The solution was to run a 4-mile-long pipe to carry water from within the canyon. As one might guess from its name, the canyon is a narrow gorge of tumbling water. The pipeline (and hence the trail) was often forced to cling to the rock walls. In the narrowest section, the pipe was suspended above the stream supported by spikes driven into the rocks. The precarious pipeline was difficult to maintain, and miners were often forced to walk the line to fix leaks. Their balancing act gave the pipeline the name "catwalk."

The gold and silver mines were worked for twenty years, and finally closed down in 1913. In 1935, the pipeline route was converted into a walking trail by the Civilian Conservation Corps. The trail maintains the unique design of the pipeline, frequently traveling above the raging water on steel grates and following the serpentine turns of the canyon, which in places is only ten feet wide. Where the canyon widens, the route is scraped onto the cliffs high above the rapids.

From Silver City, take US 180 northwest for 62 miles to the town of Glenwood. Turn right at the signed intersection onto Catwalk Road and continue for 5 miles to the Whitewater Picnic Area. The road fords Whitewater Creek twice, the second time right at the picnic area. During spring runoff or after summer thunderstorms, these fords may be impassable. Call ahead to the Glenwood Ranger District (see "Sources of Additional Information" in back) to check on road conditions.

The trail begins on the left (north) side of the creek at the Gila National Forest's Whitewater Picnic Area. The first half mile of the trail is paved and universally accessible. The route cuts through the narrowest portion of the gorge on a series of stairs, bridges, skinny ledges, and metal grates. Because of narrow passages, hikers with backpacks will find this section of trail challenging. The roar of the water is constant. Sections of the eighteen-inch pipe scattered about, and bolts and concrete piers that once supported the pipeline are visible in many places.

About 1 mile from the start, the Catwalk Trail crosses a suspension bridge and ends on a narrow ledge. Just before the bridge, turn left at the sign marking Trail 207. The trail climbs for a short distance to intersect Trail 41 at mile 1.1. After returning to stream level, watch for sections of the pipeline that once carried water down the canyon. At mile 1.2, the route climbs and descends several steep hills on the north bank of the stream. Fishing is excellent along this stretch, particularly in the fall. Groves of tall pines offer ideal lunch spots near the water.

At mile 2.4, come to the intersection with Trail 212 where the South Fork enters Whitewater Creek. Bear right onto Trail 212, cross the stream, and look for the remains of a power-generating station at the confluence. Fine campsites are located under the large trees. Return to the trailhead by the same route.

95 FRISCO BOX

Distance: 9 miles, day hike or backpack
Difficulty: difficult
Elevation range: 6,300 to 8,300 feet
Elevation gain: 2,100 feet
Best time of year: year-round
Water: San Francisco River
Map: USGS Dillion Mountain
Managed by: Gila National Forest, Reserve Ranger District
Features: hot springs, narrow box canyon

Box canyons—gorges so steep and rugged that they become impassable—offer first-class adventures for hikers. The San Francisco River is a major stream draining the northern portion of the Gila River region, and its box canyon is a classic example. Most of the river valley is filled with wide, grassy meadows, but at the Frisco Box, the river flows through a ridge of

The upper reach of the Frisco Box

erosion-resistant granite. The water tumbles over the granite boulders, creating deep pools between sheer walls.

Hiking into the Frisco Box requires a good deal of wading and at times some swimming. High water in spring makes the river crossings difficult, and water temperatures can be surprisingly cold in October; it is best to hike the Box in summer. Backpackers should plan to camp in the meadows along the river before reaching the Box and should always keep a watchful eye on the level of the river. Summer storms in far-off mountains can send a flash flood down the canyon. Before starting off on this hike, check with the Reserve Ranger District (see "Sources of Additional Information" in back) for road and stream conditions.

Getting to the trailhead requires a long drive on a rough but passable gravel road. Access the trailhead via FR 35, which is located on US 180 about 6.5 miles east of Luna and 6.5 miles west of the intersection of US 180 and NM 12 near Reserve. Signs at the beginning of FR 35 point to the Frisco Warm Spring trailhead. Head north on FR 35 (a right turn coming from Reserve). The road is well-maintained but travel along it is slow. A

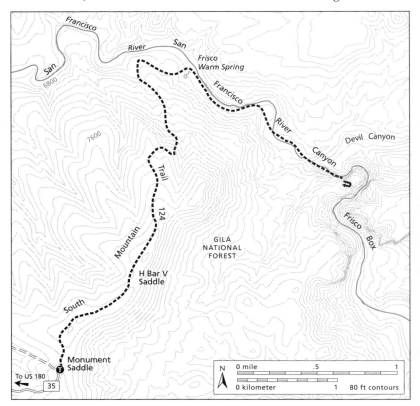

high clearance vehicle will make the 12.5 miles to the trailhead easier, but there are normally no obstacles to a low-slung car. The trailhead is located at Monument Saddle and often is not marked. Beyond the saddle, FR 35 passes through a gate and quickly degrades. Use a topographic map or a GPS to help identify the trailhead.

From the parking area at the saddle, locate the trail heading north. Lines of rock point the way, and in about 200 feet, a sign on a tree identifies the Frisco Divide Trail 124. The faint trail parallels the fence as it climbs from the saddle to the summit of South Mountain. Staying on the ridgeline, continue north, enjoying dramatic views into valleys to the east and west. Follow old blazes and rock cairns to stay on the trail. H Bar V Saddle is at mile 1, and a short climb leads to a second summit. Leave the fence line at mile 1.4 and descend steeply along the ridge. At mile 1.8, the trail turns to the right and begins the steep drop into the San Francisco River canyon. The trail loses about 1,200 feet over the next mile before bearing right onto a relatively level bench above the river. Two rolling hills lead to Frisco Warm Spring and the canyon bottom at mile 3.3.

Drop to the river, turn right, and head downstream. Camping spots are located in pine stands on either bank. An informal trail cuts off the meanders of the river. Continue about a mile downstream through several river crossings to where Devil Canyon enters from the left. The dramatic entrance to the Frisco Box is just ahead.

Hiking is more challenging in the Box. Pick a route with care, boulder hopping much of the way. It is often difficult to wade through pools, and swimming may be necessary. Continue downstream until boulders completely bar further exploration. Return to the trailhead by the same route.

96 | TURKEY CREEK HOT SPRINGS

Distance: 10 miles, day hike or backpack
Difficulty: moderate
Elevation range: 4,750 to 5,200 feet
Elevation gain: 800 feet
Best time of year: April to October
Water: Gila River, Turkey Creek
Map: USGS Canyon Hill
Managed by: Gila National Forest, Gila Wilderness,
  Wilderness Ranger District
Features: riparian vegetation in desert canyon, hot springs

Well-watered canyon bottoms offer some relief from the unremitting heat on the sun-blasted slopes of the Gila Wilderness. The presence of water creates a riparian environment that seems heaven-sent in the middle of

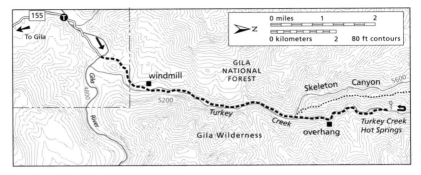

the desert. The canyon of Turkey Creek is particularly inviting, offering hikers a corridor to enter the southern Diablo Range in the Gila Wilderness. Fed by springs—some of them hot—the flow in the canyon supports a tall canopy of broad-leafed trees. Most attractive is the white-trunked Arizona sycamore, which spreads its branches to create deep shade and provide welcome relief from the intense southern sun. Other portions of the canopy are formed by net-leafed hackberry, cottonwood, and western soapberry.

Scattered throughout the Gila River region are about a dozen hot springs. Heated by radioactive decay deep within the earth, water rises to the surface through the region's extensive fault system. Hot springs are found where the heated water flows to the surface. The best of these springs is located along Turkey Creek, where water hits the surface at about 160 degrees Fahrenheit, but when mixed with creek water, cools to form delightful thermal pools. Separate soaking pools line the creek bottom for 0.25 mile, ranging in size from a private bath to a 200-foot-long pool nestled between two large rocks. Any of the pools makes a perfect reward for the sometimes difficult journey up the canyon.

As with other trips in the southwest mountains, weather plays an important role in determining the ideal hiking times. Summer temperatures can reach 100 degrees Fahrenheit. Runoff in the Gila River can block access to Turkey Creek in March and early April. Also, following summer rains, hikers must watch for flash floods in the narrow canyon bottom. The best time for a trip to the hot springs is late spring or mid- to late fall.

To reach the trailhead, drive northwest from Silver City on US 180. In 25 miles, reach the intersection with NM 211 and turn right toward the town of Gila. Continue 4 miles to the intersection with NM 153. Go straight ahead onto NM 153 as NM 211 bears left. In 4 miles, continue on the gravel FR 155. This rough road winds over a pass and drops steeply into Brushy Canyon before paralleling the Gila River. Park 9.5 miles from the end of the pavement at the end of the road. It is a good idea to check on road conditions with the Silver City Ranger District (see "Sources of Additional Information" in back) before heading out.

Dozens of pools filled with heated water line the bottom of the canyon of Turkey Creek.

Begin hiking behind the dirt berm at the end of the passable road. The roadway continues to a washout where a short trail segment skirts the obstacle and rejoins the road in a few hundred feet. (When in doubt, head upstream parallel to the river.) In 0.5 mile, make the first ford of the river and continue on a wide gravel bar on the north bank. Cross the knee-deep river two more times in the next mile, with stretches of sandy road in between.

The route is a bit confusing on the other side of the third Gila River crossing. The main road angles right to stay along the river, but the trail passes near the base of the cliff to the left (north). Several routes lead across the point of land to the dry bed of Turkey Creek near an abandoned ranch with a windmill. Just beyond the windmill, a sign points to the trail. Cross the now-flowing Turkey Creek and the trail becomes easy to follow. Hikers who miss the trail should follow the dry bed of Turkey Creek north and upstream until they rejoin the trail.

Continue up the canyon of Turkey Creek under sycamores and hackberries. The stream is intermittent for the first mile but soon flows constantly off to the right of the trail. About 3 miles from the start, the trail splits for 100 yards and the lower route along the canyon bottom eliminates the steep climb over a ridge. After the branches rejoin, watch for Skeleton Canyon coming in from the left. The trail heads up this dry canyon, climbing steeply; but to reach the hot springs, follow rock cairns that lead across Skeleton Canyon and continue hiking up the flowing Turkey Creek.

The unmaintained trail up Turkey Creek requires considerable routefinding and boulder hopping. After 0.5 mile of rough trail beyond Skeleton Canyon, pass a huge overhang on the east bank. In a few hundred yards, a deep pool forces the trail to go under a rockfall at mile 4. Hikers must drag their packs under a rock, then continue past some swimming holes. The route is no longer obvious, but a few trails continue upcanyon on the east bank. Green algae growing along the creek banks signal that the hot springs are just upstream. Pools, constructed of native rock, and swimming holes are found in the next 0.25 mile of canyon.

Above the springs, the canyon opens up with plenty of campsites in the oaks along the canyon floor. Slickrock terraces make this stretch attractive, and the camp spots are within a few minutes' walk of the springs. After exploring and enjoying the thermal pools, return to the trailhead by the same route.

97 MIDDLE FORK/LITTLE BEAR LOOP

Distance: 12-mile loop, backpack
Difficulty: moderate
Elevation range: 5,800 to 6,400 feet
Elevation gain: 800 feet
Best time of year: April to October
Water: Middle Fork Gila River
Maps: USGS Woodland Park, Burnt Corral Canyon, and Little Turkey Park; USFS Gila Wilderness
Managed by: Gila National Forest, Gila Wilderness, Wilderness Ranger District
Features: wild canyon scenery, hot springs

Aldo Leopold roamed the Gila National Forest in the early 1900s as a forest ranger, and the wild character of the landscape motivated him to develop the idea of preserving such areas as untouched by modern man. In 1924, 755,000 acres of the Gila was set aside as the world's first wilderness area. Although today the area is not as pristine as Leopold may have wished, the Gila has much to offer. While wild mountain scenery and abundant wildlife attract many visitors, many hikers find that the canyons of the Gila are its most appealing feature.

Of the three major headwaters of the Gila River, the Middle Fork has the best scenery and the best trout fishing. The Middle Fork Trail follows the river for more than 30 miles, offering the opportunity for a six- to seven-day trip. High rocky walls dominate the hike through the narrow canyon, and groves of lush riparian vegetation—sycamores, hackberries, and cotton-woods—provide relief from the open juniper woodlands that surround the gorge. Hot springs and good trout fishing in the spring and fall add to the appeal of the Middle Fork.

Hiking along the river is no easy feat. Frequent stream crossings, as many as six per mile, are tiring at low water and impossible during spring runoff and following heavy summer storms. The trail itself experiences frequent washouts and is often difficult to find. Hiking on sand and loose cobbles is apt to tire hikers faster than walking on a smooth trail. Plan on at least six hours of walking to complete this loop, and add more time to enjoy the many attractions of the canyon. Take advantage of numerous fine campsites found along the canyon floor. Before starting on a hike in the Middle Fork Canyon, contact the Wilderness Ranger District (see "Sources of Additional Information" in back) for current conditions. Hikers should carry a pair of running shoes or all-terrain sandals to wear on the stream crossings.

From the intersection of NM 90 and US 180 in Silver City, go east on US 180 1 mile to the junction with Pinos Altos Road/NM 15. Turn left and travel the winding and slow NM 15 through the Gila National Forest. In 22 miles, continue straight on NM 15 at the intersection with NM 35. Forty-two miles from Silver City, turn left just before reaching the Gila Visitor Center.

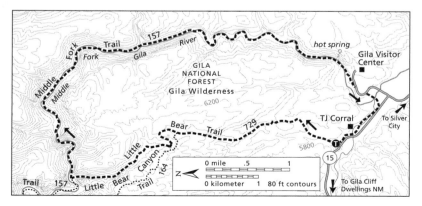

The Little Bear Trail leads through a shady canyon to the Middle Fork of the Gila River.

Continue toward Gila Cliff Dwellings National Monument 1 mile to the TJ Corral Trailhead and park there.

Begin hiking on the Little Bear Trail 729. The trail ascends a sloping mesa in open juniper woodland. It is a hot route in the middle of the day, so plan an early start and carry plenty of water. In 2.2 miles, pass the junction with the Woodland Trail 164 on the left. Continue straight to cross a small pass and begin to descend into Little Bear Canyon. At the canyon bottom, bear left and walk under tall pines—which provide welcome shade—in an interesting, narrow canyon. At mile 4.1, intersect the Middle Fork Trail 157. Campsites are located near here on the bench above the Middle Fork of the Gila River.

Continue on the described loop by turning right onto the Middle Fork Trail and walking downcanyon. The trail stays close to the river and soon makes the first of about thirty river crossings between here and the end of the trail. The trail alternates between crossing gravel bars, sand hills, and grassy meadows. As it passes through riparian areas over the next 2 miles, the trail is often difficult to follow. Hikers should find the easiest route and take their time making the knee-deep stream crossings. Soaring orange cliffs dominate the narrowest part of the canyon. Watch for raptors circling just above the rocks.

At mile 9.5, look for a small hot spring located on the left riverbank. The canyon broadens as it heads for its junction with the West Fork of the Gila. After crossing to the east bank, climb a short hill and reach the backcountry parking area at the Gila Visitor Center. Exit the parking lot and walk the entrance road out to NM 15. Turn right and walk the highway 1.2 miles to the TJ Corral Trailhead.

98 | WEST FORK OF THE GILA RIVER

Distance: 14 miles, day hike or backpack
Difficulty: moderate
Elevation range: 5,700 to 6,100 feet
Elevation gain: 500 feet
Best time of year: April to October
Water: West Fork of the Gila River
Maps: USGS Little Turkey Park and Woodland Park;
  USFS Gila Wilderness
Managed by: Gila National Forest, Gila Wilderness,
  Wilderness Ranger District
Features: fine views, fishing, historic ruins

The abundant wildlife, gentle climate, and presence of running water in the mountains of the Gila River headwaters have led to a long history of use by Native Americans and settlers of European descent. People of the Mogollon Culture built small villages in sheltering caves in the canyon walls overlooking flats along the rivers. Later, Apaches lived a nomadic lifestyle in the canyons and on the mesas, hunting, growing crops, and enjoying the region's many hot springs. Anglo hunters and ranchers followed in the 1880s.

The West Fork of the Gila River strings little snippets of this history together like beads on a necklace. Walking up the West Fork Trail, hikers first encounter the ruins of a cabin and the grave of one of its owners. The Grudging brothers ran cattle along the West Fork, and a dispute about stolen cows ended in the murder of Bill Grudging in 1893. A bit farther up the canyon, in a cave above their former agricultural fields, sits a small pueblo used by Mogollon farmers about 900 years ago. Nat Straw Canyon reminds visitors of the colorful hunter who roamed these mountains for forty years and whose stories were so outrageous that he

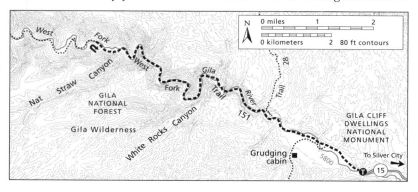

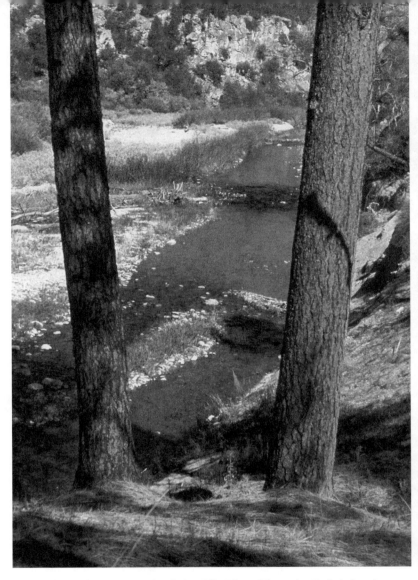

Pools along the West Fork of the Gila River (Photo by Bob Julyan)

earned recognition in a 1931 *Vanity Fair* piece called, "Golden Liars of the Golden West."

The trail along the West Fork of the Gila River runs 34 miles from FR 507 to Gila Cliff Dwellings National Monument and offers the opportunity for a long immersion in the backcountry. The lower miles of the trail receive the most use of any in the Gila Wilderness, but also offer the easiest access and the greatest concentration of historical features. Day hikers can wander up the trail to the Grudging Cabin or the cliff dwelling beyond. Those interested in a one- or two-night exploration of the canyon should set their sights on Nat Straw Canyon as a camp spot. The trip takes in the features of the lower canyon, including some great swimming and fishing holes, and leaves the crowds behind.

From the intersection of NM 90 and US 180 in Silver City, go east on US 180 1 mile to the junction with Pinos Altos Road/NM 15. Turn left and travel the winding and slow NM 15 through the Gila National Forest. In 22 miles, continue straight on NM 15 at the intersection with NM 35. Forty-two miles from Silver City, turn left just before reaching the Gila Visitor Center to stay on NM 15. Continue 2 miles to Gila Cliff Dwellings National Monument, and park. The trailhead is located at the west end of the parking area.

Begin hiking on the West Fork Trail 151, heading up the canyon of the West Fork under a thin canopy of pines. The first river crossing is at mile 1.2. Once across, hikers may take a short spur trail to the left that leads up a rise to the Grudging cabin and grave. Continuing up the canyon, the trail twists through picturesque meadows with orange cliffs for a backdrop. Sycamores, hackberries, and cottonwoods provide cooling shade along the river. Make several river crossings over the next 1.5 miles of pleasant, flat walking.

As the canyon narrows 2.3 miles from the start, the river winds between towering orange walls. Watch for a small cliff dwelling in a prominent cave on the left (southwest) wall of the canyon. After another mile of traveling up the winding canyon, pass the entrance to White Rocks Canyon to the left.

Around two sweeping turns in the river, the trail traverses a narrow stretch near mile 5. A few minutes' walk after a horseshoe bend at mile 5.8 leads to a broad stretch of meadows near Nat Straw Canyon. Excellent campsites are located from the confluence upstream along a mile of flat canyon bottom, with swimming holes, brown trout lies, and shady trees nearby. From this point, hikers can explore farther up the canyon or turn around and return by the same route.

99 | HILLSBORO PEAK

Distance: 10 miles round-trip, day hike or backpack
Difficulty: moderate
Elevation range: 7,100 to 10,000 feet
Elevation gain: 2,900 feet
Best time of year: April to October
Water: carry water
Maps: USGS Hillsboro Peak; USFS Aldo Leopold Wilderness
Managed by: Gila National Forest, Aldo Leopold
    Wilderness, Wilderness Ranger District
Features: fine views, solitude

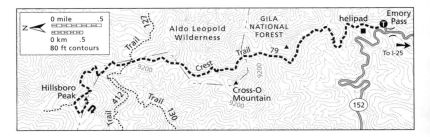

The huge Aldo Leopold Wilderness spans the crest of the Black Range from near Emory Pass to Diamond Peak 25 miles to the north. The wilderness boasts an extensive network of trails that sees few hikers. The trail to Hillsboro Peak follows the southern border of the wilderness and offers fine views into the wilder reaches of the Black Range. The views along the Crest Trail and from the peak itself make this hike a New Mexico classic.

Reach the trailhead on Emory Pass via NM 152, 31 miles west of I-25 and about 33 miles east of the town of Central. A sign at the pass directs hikers onto a short paved road that leads to the Emory Pass Vista and the Trail 79 starting point.

From the vista, pick up the Crest Trail 79 on the west side of the parking area. In 0.2 mile, the trail intersects a gravel road and leads past a helipad.

Circus beetle

A hiker approaches Hillsboro Peak.

Continue through an open gate onto a wide trail that descends along a fence. At the bottom of the hill, begin a moderate climb that remains steady most of the way to Hillsboro Peak. The trail is wonderfully designed to maintain a steady but never steep pitch as it passes through open conifer forest that offers frequent views to the north and east. During the summer rains, the trail is lined with many species of wildflower that reach the northern limit of their habitat in the Black Range.

The trail continues its gentle pitch up the west side of the ridge, then at a saddle switches to the east side of Cross-O Mountain. At mile 2.2, enter the Aldo Leopold Wilderness and soon catch the first look of Hillsboro Peak. At mile 3, reach a small saddle before resuming the climb, again on the west side of the ridge.

On a narrow ridge at mile 3.5, continue straight at a four-way intersection, passing the Hillsboro Peak Bypass Trail 412 on the left. The trail swings to the north side of the peak, where snow may be found near the summit through late April. Just below the peak at mile 4.8, bear left to stay on the

Crest Trail, passing a trail that leads to a spring. The large, flat area of the summit of Hillsboro Peak offers many good campsites, and the views from near the fire lookout tower are especially fine in all directions. Return to the trailhead by the same route.

100 | PERCHA BOX

Distance: 4.2 miles out-and-back, day hike
Difficulty: easy
Elevation range: 5,000 to 5,450 feet
Elevation gain: 600 feet
Best time of year: September to May
Water: carry water
Map: USGS Hillsboro
Managed by: Bureau of Land Management,
    Las Cruces Field Office
Features: running water, narrow canyon

Running water and narrow canyons are an attraction anywhere, but when both are found in desert hills, the combination makes a destination worthy of a day's exploring. The Percha Box offers hikers a chance to enjoy a desert stream that supports a lush riparian zone. Located in the former Hillsboro Mining District, a gravel road leads through desert grassland to the Box.

From the Hillsboro exit 63 off I-25, head west on NM 152. In about 14 miles, between mileposts 53 and 52, watch for a gravel pullout on the left (south) side of the road and park at this location.

From the gravel pullout, pass through a gate and head south on the rough jeep road into Ready Pay Gulch. Descend past roads leading to old mining claims and cross the dry streambed at mile 0.5. Continue on the road as it climbs up the opposite side of the gulch, passing a short, narrow section in

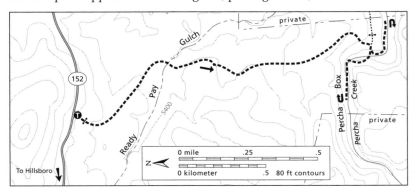

Willows line the desert pools in the Percha Box.

the canyon bottom on the left. The road winds through several thick stands of ocotillo as it continues along a low ridge. At mile 1.3 the road narrows and drops off the right side of the ridge with views into the Percha Box. Descend across limestone ledges and around a sharp bend to a fence line. A passage through the fence leads to a trail that quickly drops to reach the water at mile 1.6. Explore both up and down the canyon for about a quarter mile, but private land on both sides blocks further exploration. Upstream, the canyon passes through high cliffs; downstream, the riparian vegetation forms an attractive corridor. When you are finished exploring, head back up the switchbacks to the trailhead.

SOURCES OF ADDITIONAL INFORMATION

NATIONAL MONUMENTS, PARKS, AND PRESERVES

Bandelier National Monument
15 Entrance Road
Los Alamos, NM 87544
(505) 672-0343
www.nps.gov/band/

Carlsbad Caverns National Park
3225 National Parks Highway
Carlsbad, NM 88220
(575) 785-2232
www.nps.gov/cave/

Capulin Volcano National
 Monument
P.O. Box 40
Capulin, NM 88414
(575) 278-2201
www.nps.gov/cavo/

Chaco Culture National Historical
 Park
P.O. Box 220
Nageezi, NM 87037
(505) 786-7014
www.nps.gov/chcu/

El Camino Real de Tierra Adentro
National Trails Intermountain
 Region
National Park Service
P.O. Box 728
Santa Fe, NM 87504-0728
(505) 988-6098
www.nps.gov/elca/

El Malpais National Monument
123 East Roosevelt Avenue
Grants, NM 87020
(505) 783-4774
www.nps.gov/elma/

El Morro National Monument
HC 61 Box 43
Ramah, NM 87321
(505) 783-4226
www.nps.gov/elmo

Kasha-Katuwe Tent Rocks National
 Monument
Rio Puerco Field Office
Bureau of Land Management
435 Montaño Road
Albuquerque, NM 87107
(505) 761-8700
www.blm.gov/nm/st/en/prog
 /recreation/rio_puerco/kasha_
 katuwe_tent_rocks.html

Valles Caldera National Preserve
Valles Caldera Trust
P.O. Box 359
18161 Highway 4
Jemez Springs, NM 87025
(505) 661-3333; (866) 382-5537
www.vallescaldera.gov

White Sands National Monument
P.O. Box 1086
Holloman Air Force Base, NM
 88330
(575) 679-2599
www.nps.gov/whsa/

BUREAU OF LAND MANAGEMENT, NEW MEXICO

General website:
www.nm.blm.gov/

El Malpais National Conservation
Area
P.O. Box 846
Grants, NM 87020
(505) 287-7911
www.blm.gov/nm/st/en/prog
/recreation/rio_puerco
/el_malpais.html

Farmington Field Office
1235 La Plata Highway, Suite A
Farmington, NM 87401
(505) 599-8900
www.blm.gov/nm/st/en/fo
/Farmington_Field_Office.html

Las Cruces Field Office
1800 Marquess Street
Las Cruces, NM 88005
(575) 525-4300
www.blm.gov/nm/st/en/fo
/Las_Cruces_District_Office.html

Rio Puerco Field Office
435 Montaño Road NE
Albuquerque, NM 87107
(505) 761-8700
www.blm.gov/nm/st/en/fo
/Rio_Puerco_Field_Office.html

Taos Field Office
226 Cruz Alta Road
Taos, NM 87571
(575) 758-8851
www.blm.gov/nm/st/en/fo
/Taos_Field_Office.html

U.S. FOREST SERVICE, NEW MEXICO

General website:
www.fs.fed.us/recreation/states
/nm.shtml

Carson National Forest

Forest Supervisor
208 Cruz Alta Road
Taos, NM 87571
(575) 758-6200
www.fs.fed.us/r3/carson/

Camino Real Ranger District
P.O. Box 68
Peñasco, NM 87553
(575) 587-2255

Canjilon Ranger District
P.O. Box 488
Canjilon, NM 87515
(575) 684-2489

Questa Ranger District
P.O. Box 110
Questa, NM 87556
(575) 586-0520

Tres Piedras Ranger District
P.O. Box 38
Tres Piedras, NM 87577
(575) 758-8678

Cibola National Forest

Forest Supervisor
2113 Osuna Road NE, Suite A
Albuquerque, NM 87113-1001
(505) 346-2650
www.fs.fed.us/r3/cibola/

Magdalena Ranger District
P.O. Box 45
Magdalena, NM 87825
(575) 854-2281

Mount Taylor Ranger District
1800 Lobo Canyon Road
Grants, NM 87020
(505) 287-8833

Mountainair Ranger District
P.O. Box 69
Mountainair, NM 87036-0069
(505) 847-2990

Sandia Ranger District
11776 Highway 337
Tijeras, NM 87059
(505) 281-3304

Gila National Forest

Forest Supervisor
3005 East Camino del Bosque
Silver City, NM 88061
(575) 388-8201
www.fs.fed.us/r3/gila/

Glenwood Ranger District
P.O. Box 8
Glenwood, NM 88039
(575) 539-2481

Luna Work Center
P.O. Box 91
Luna, NM 87824
(575) 547-2612

Reserve Ranger District
P.O. Box 170
Reserve, NM 87830
(575) 533-6232

Silver City Ranger District
3005 East Camino del Bosque
Silver City, NM 88061
(575) 538-2771

Wilderness Ranger District
HC 68, Box 50
Mimbres, NM 88049
(575) 536-2250

Lincoln National Forest

Forest Supervisor
1101 New York Avenue
Alamogordo, NM 88310-6992
(575) 434-7200
www.fs.fed.us/r3/lincoln/

Guadalupe Ranger District
Federal Building, Room 159
Carlsbad, NM 88220
(575) 885-4181

Sacramento Ranger District
P.O. Box 288
Cloudcroft, NM 88317
(575) 682-2551

Smokey Bear Ranger District
901 Mechem Drive
Ruidoso, NM 88345
(575) 257-4095

Santa Fe National Forest

Forest Supervisor
P.O. Box 1689
Santa Fe, NM 87504
(505) 438-7840
www.fs.fed.us/r3/sfe/

Coyote Ranger District
P.O. Box 160
Coyote, NM 87012
(575) 638-5526

Cuba Ranger District
P.O. Box 130
Cuba, NM 87013
(575) 289-3264

Española Ranger District
1710 North Riverside Drive
Española, NM 87533
(505) 753-7331

Jemez Ranger District
P.O. Box 150
Jemez Springs, NM 87025
(575) 829-3535

Pecos Ranger District
P.O. Drawer 429
Pecos, NM 87552
(505) 757-6121

OTHER

Leave No Trace
P.O. Box 997
Boulder, CO 80306
1-800-332-4100
www.lnt.org

New Mexico Tourism Division
www.newmexico.org
/department/administration
/general_info.php

Northwest New Mexico Visitor
Center
1900 E Santa Fe Avenue
Grants, NM 87020
(505) 876-2783

INDEX

10K Trail, 191-192

Aguirre Springs Recreation Area, 219-223
Albuquerque, 186-197
Albuquerque Trail, 202-203
Alkali Flat Trail, 228-230
Apache Canyon Trail, 52-54
Apache Kid Trail, 214
Apache Kid Wilderness, 212-214
Argentina Canyon Trail, 238
Argentina Peak, 236-238
Aspen Canyon Trail, 235, 236
Atalaya Mountain Trail, 36-38
Atsinna Pueblo, 182

Bandelier National Monument, 113-122
Baylor Pass, 221-223
Bear Wallow Trail, 39, 41
Beattys Flats, 59-61
Big Arsenic Campground, 69, 70
Big Bonito Trail, 234-236, 237
Big Skylight Cave, 174
Big Tesuque Trail, 39-41
Big Tubes, 172-175
Bisti Section, Bisti{en}De-Na-Zin Wilderness, 159-160
Black Range, 274-276
Blue Dot Trail, 110-112
Blue Range Wilderness, 256-258
Borrego Trail, 41
Bosque del Apache National Wildlife Refuge, 210-212
Box Canyon Trail, 150-152
Boyd Sanatorium, 223-225
Broad Canyon, 217-219
Bull Canyon Trail, 84, 86
Bull-of-the-Woods Pasture, 75, 76, 79, 83

Caballo Mountain, 126-128
Capilla Peak, 201
Capulin Volcano Rim Trail, 100-102

Carlsbad Caverns National Park, 247-252
Catwalk National Recreation Trail, 260-262
Cave Creek, 54-56
Cebolla Mesa Trail, 68-69
Cerrillos Hills Historic Park, 184-186
Cerro Grande, 121-122
Cerro Grande Fire, 121-122, 123
Cerros del Abrigo Trail, 128-130
Chaco Culture National Historical Park, 163-170
Chain of Craters Wilderness, 177-179
Chavez Canyon, 146-148
Chupadera Peak Trail, 210-212
clothing, appropriate for hiking, 27
Columbine Canyon, 80-82
Columbine-Twining National Recreation Trail, 82-83
Columbine-Hondo Wilderness Study Area, 75-77, 80-83
Comanche Creek, 90-93
Continental Divide Trail, 156-158, 177-179
Copper Canyon Trail, 204-205
Cerro Picacho, 108-110
Crawford Trail, 225
Crest Trail (White Mountains), 235, 237-238
Crest Trail (Black Range), 275-276
Cruces Basin Wilderness, 153-155

Datil Well Nature Loop, 254-256
Deception Peak, 49-51
De-Na-Zin Section, Bisti{en}De-Na-Zin Wilderness, 161-163
Devils Den Canyon, 244-247
Dog Canyon Trail, 230-232
Dome Wilderness, 108-110
Dripping Springs Natural Area, 223-226

East Fork of the Jemez River, 133-136
East Fork Trail, 133-135, 135-136

East Pecos Baldy, 62
Elena Gallegos Open Space, 193-194
El Camino Real, 215-216
El Malpais National Monument and Conservation Area, 172-180

Falls Trail, 113-115
Fourth of July Trail, 202-203
Four Windows Cave, 174
Frijoles Canyon, 113-115, 115-117
Frisco Box, 263-265
Frisco Divide Trail, 264-265

Ghost Ranch, 148-152
Gila Cliff Dwellings National Monument, 272
Gila Wilderness, 258-259, 266-274
Glorieta Baldy, 53-54
Gold Hill, 75-77, 82-83
Gooseberry Springs Trail, 170-172
Guadalupe Mountains, 239-252
Guadalupe Ridge Trail, 252
Guaje Canyon Trail, 127
Guaje Ridge Trail, 123-125

Hamilton Mesa Trail, 59-60
Heart Lake, 83-85
Hillsboro Peak, 273-276
Horseshoe Lake, 88-89
Horseshoe Lake Trail, 88-89
Horsethief Meadow, 54-56
Hummingbird Saddle, 259

Indian Hollow, 219-221
Italianos Canyon Trail, 72

Jemez Falls, 136
Jemez Mountains, 108-144
Jornada del Muerto, 215-216

Kasha-Katuwe Tent Rocks National Monument, 106-108
Kayser Trail, 199-200
Kitchen Mesa Trail, 148-150

La Belle, 90-93
La Cueva Trail, 225-226

La Luz Trail, 188-190
La Vega, 44-46
Lake Peak, 50, 51
Lake Fork Trail, 84, 86
Lake Maloya Trail, 101
Last Chance Canyon, 239-241
Latir Mesa, 84-86
Latir Wilderness, 83-86
La Ventana, 180, 181
lightning safety, 19-20
Little Arsenic Campground, 69, 70
Little Bear Trail, 270
Little Bonito Trail, 235, 237
Little Horse Mesa, 97-101
Lobo Peak, 70-72
Lobo Peak Trail, 72
Long Canyon Trail, 76, 77
Longview Spring, 249
Lost Lake, 88, 89

Magdalena Mountains, 204-206
Magdalena Stock Driveway, 254-255
Manzanita Canyon Trail, 72
Manzano Crest Trail, 199, 200-202
Manzano Mountains, 197-203
Manzano Peak, 197-200
Manzano Wilderness, 197-202
McCrystal Place, 93-95
McCauley Hot Springs, 136
Mesa Montosa, 150, 152
Middle Fork of the Gila River, 269-271
Mogollon Range, 258-259
Mora Flats, 58-60
Mount Taylor, 170-172

Nambe Lake, 42-44, 50
Narrows Rim Trail, 179-180
North Crest Trail (Sandia Mountains), 191-192
North Ponil Creek, 95-97

Ojitos Canyon Trail, 143-144
Ojitos Wilderness Area, 104-106
Oliver Lee Memorial State Park, 231
Opportunity Trail, 100-101
Organ Mountains, 219-226
Ox Canyon Trail, 198

Pecos Wilderness, 42-43, 46, 49, 54-56, 57-58, 61-62, 64-65
Pecos Baldy Lake, 61-62
Peñasco Blanco, 168-170
Peñas Negras Trail, 138
Percha Box, 276-277
Petroglyph National Monument Trails, 186-188
Pine Tree Trail, 220
Pino Canyon Trail, 193-195
Ponderosa Ridge Trail, 100
Potato Canyon, 207-208
Pueblo Alto Loop, 163-166
Pueblo Bonito, 164
Pueblo Creek, 256-258
Puerto Nambe, 49

Rattlesnake Canyon, 250-252
Ravens Ridge, 50-51
Red Dot Trail, 110, 113
Rim Vista Trail, 141-142
Rio Chama Wilderness, 143-144
Rio Grande, 68-69, 112, 115
Rio Grande Bosque, 195-197
Rio Grande Valley State Park, 195-196
Rio Nambe Trail, 46
Rio Valdez Trail, 60
Rociada Trail, 60

Sacramento Mountains, 230-232
San Lorenzo Canyon, 208-210
San Luis Mesa, 156-158
San Mateo Mountains, 207-208, 212-214
San Pedro Parks Wilderness, 137-138
Sandia Mountains, 188-195
Sandia Wilderness, 188-195
Sandia Peak Tramway, 188-190
Sangre de Cristo Mountains, 36-97
Sawmill Park, 86-87
Sawmill Park Trail, 87
Shipman Trail, 214
Sitting Bull Falls, 241-244
South Boundary Trail, 66-67
South Crest Trail (Sandia Mountains), 191-193
South Mesa Loop, 166-168
Spirit Lake, 47-49

Stewart Lake, 57-58
St. Peters Dome Trail, 109-110
Sugarite State Park, 99-101
sun, protection from, 23

Tent Rock Canyon Trails, 106-108
Three Rivers Petroglyph Site, 232-234
Trampas Lakes, 64-65
Tsin Kletzin, 166-167
Turkey Creek Hot Springs, 265-268

Upper Alamo Trail, 119
Upper Camp Trail, 152

Vacas Trail, 138
Valle Grande Trail, 131-132
Valle Vidal, 90-97
Valles Caldera National Preserve, 128-132
Valles Canyon, 217-219
Van Patten resort, 224-225
Vicks Peak, 212-214

Water Canyon Trail, 204-206
water, carrying adequate for hiking, 21, 28
West Fork of the Gila River, 271-273
Wheeler Peak, 78-79
Wheeler Peak Trail, 75, 79
Wheeler Peak Wilderness, 78-79, 86-87, 88-90
White Mountain Wilderness, 234-238
White Rock Canyon, 110-113
White Sands National Monument, 228-230
Whitewater Baldy, 258-260
Whitewater Canyon, 260-262
wildfire safety, 20
wildlife, potential dangers from, 23-26
Williams Lake, 73-75
Window Rock, 139-140
Winsor Trail, 41, 42, 45, 49
Withington Wilderness, 207-208
WS Mountain Trail, 257-258

Yapashi Pueblo, 118-120
Yucca Canyon, 247-249
Zuni-Acoma Trail, 175-177

ABOUT THE AUTHOR

Under the influence of the writings of Edward Abbey, Craig Martin moved to the Southwest from his native Philadelphia in 1980, earning a living as a house framer. His first experience with a Pulaski was in 1981 as a ranger at Saguaro National Park, working a trail in the Rincon Mountains. After several years teaching middle school science, he and his family moved to Los Alamos, New Mexico, where he launched a career as a freelance writer. Over the next decade plus, Martin wrote twenty books, more than one hundred magazine articles, and for five years contributed a weekly trail column to the *Santa Fe New Mexican*.

In May 2000, the Cerro Grande Fire ripped through Los Alamos and melted Martin's diverse career threads into a single fiber. As project manager for the Volunteer Task Force, Martin helped coordinate the rebuilding of the trails around Los Alamos. Over the next three years, he supervised dozens of trail projects that involved more than 3,000 volunteers. For his work on the trail system, as well as his organization of the planting of 28,000 pine seedlings in the burned area and the hand seeding of 43 acres, Martin was awarded a 2001 National Volunteer of the Year Award from the Points of Light Foundation. In 2002, Martin received the Chief's Award from the U.S. Forest Service.

Martin currently serves as Open Space and Trails Specialist for his hometown. He lives on the edge of the Santa Fe National Forest with his wife, June.

THE MOUNTAINEERS, founded in 1906, is a nonprofit outdoor activity and conservation club, whose mission is "to explore, study, preserve, and enjoy the natural beauty of the outdoors.... " Based in Seattle, Washington, the club is now one of the largest such organizations in the United States, with seven branches throughout Washington State.

The Mountaineers sponsors both classes and year-round outdoor activities in the Pacific Northwest, which include hiking, mountain climbing, ski-touring, snowshoeing, bicycling, camping, canoeing and kayaking, nature study, sailing, and adventure travel. The club's conservation division supports environmental causes through educational activities, sponsoring legislation, and presenting informational programs.

All club activities are led by skilled, experienced volunteers, who are dedicated to promoting safe and responsible enjoyment and preservation of the outdoors.

If you would like to participate in these organized outdoor activities or the club's programs, consider a membership in The Mountaineers. For information and an application, write or call The Mountaineers, Club Headquarters, 7700 Sand Point Way NE, Seattle, WA 98115; 206-521-6001. You can also visit the club's website at www.mountaineers.org or contact The Mountaineers via email at clubmail@mountaineers.org.

The Mountaineers Books, an active, nonprofit publishing program of the club, produces guidebooks, instructional texts, historical works, natural history guides, and works on environmental conservation. All books produced by The Mountaineers Books fulfill the club's mission. Visit www.mountaineersbooks.org to find details about all our titles and the latest author events, as well as videos, web clips, links, and more!

The Mountaineers Books
1001 SW Klickitat Way, Suite 201
Seattle, WA 98134
800-553-4453
mbooks@mountaineersbooks.org

The Mountaineers Books is proud to be a corporate sponsor of The Leave No Trace Center for Outdoor Ethics, whose mission is to promote and inspire responsible outdoor recreation through education, research, and partnerships. The Leave No Trace program is focused specifically on human-powered (nonmotorized) recreation.

Leave No Trace strives to educate visitors about the nature of their recreational impacts, as well as offer techniques to prevent and minimize such impacts. Leave No Trace is best understood as an educational and ethical program, not as a set of rules and regulations.

For more information, visit www.lnt.org, or call 800-332-4100.

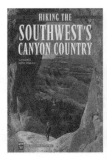